Acknowledgements

To all who have contributed to the development of this piano method, thank you for your kindness and generosity throughout the process.

Specifically, I am extremely grateful to the following: To God for giving me the wonderful gift of music. To my parents Daniel and Norma Gonzalez, for making the development of the gift possible. To my wife Karen, for her graphics work and support throughout this project. To our son David, for his creative insight. To my first piano teacher Mrs. John Pruitt, for her dedication to teaching piano. To Dr. Cleveland L. Page, for the inspiration to write this book. To Al Mendenhall, for his artwork contribution and kind words of encouragement. And to my students for sharing with me in the creative process of the book.

Thank you for the part you have played in making this project possible.

Soli Deo Gloria

Dr. Ruben Gonzalez

Preface

The goal of the Piano Companion® series is to prepare the piano student to play the music of the masters as soon as possible. This lesson book is offered as an introductory course to be used by students of all ages with the assistance of a qualified piano teacher or for self-directed study. Students with previous piano instruction may use this course as a refresher. All students should combine their studies with the online lessons at PianoCompanion.com.

The first five lessons in this book introduce the basic concepts of the hands, the keyboard, and reading music. Lessons six through seventeen guide the student through all major and minor keys with the introduction of musical concepts, hand positions, technical exercises, recital pieces, and theory exercises. Each lesson ends with a review of the musical concepts presented in the lesson.

The pace at which the student progresses depends on the time and effort invested by the student, and will be greatly influenced by the level of support offered by family and friends. Above all, the student should keep in mind that music is an expression of the soul to be enjoyed by all. So, enjoy the music!

Dr. Ruben Gonzalez
Coming alongside to help you make music!™

Contents

Lesson One

The Hands

Lesson One: The Hands

Sitting Position

- Position the bench far enough from the piano so you can stand between the piano and the bench.
- Sit tall on the forward portion of the bench closest to the piano.
- Place both feet flat on the floor.
- Adjust the bench height so that your elbows are level with the keyboard.

If your feet do not reach the floor, you may need to invest in a piano pedal extender.

Hands, Fingers, and Wrists

The hands and fingers are in a curved shape.

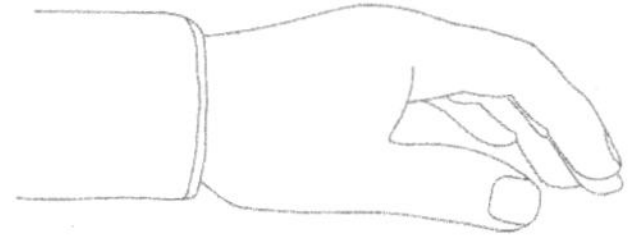

The fingers are numbered from one to five.

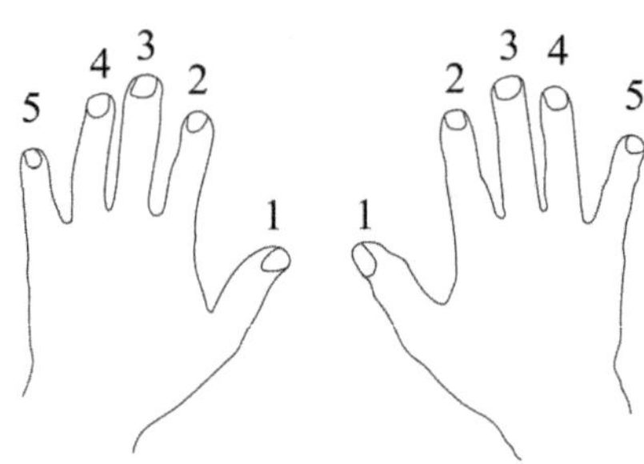

The wrists should remain flexible.

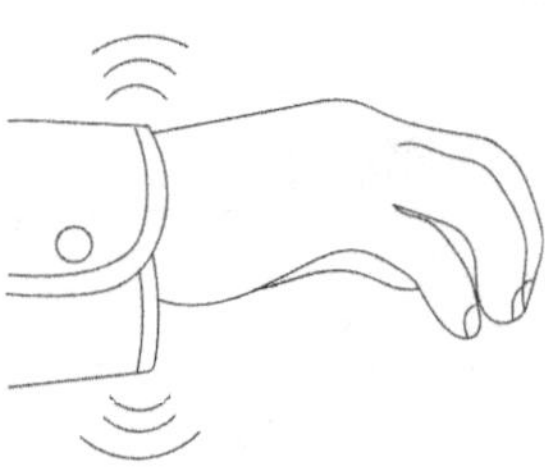

At The Piano

This is an example of how to sit at the piano with a good hand position.

Activity

Hand Position

Which hand position is correct?
(Draw a circle around the correct hand position and an "X" through the incorrect ones.)

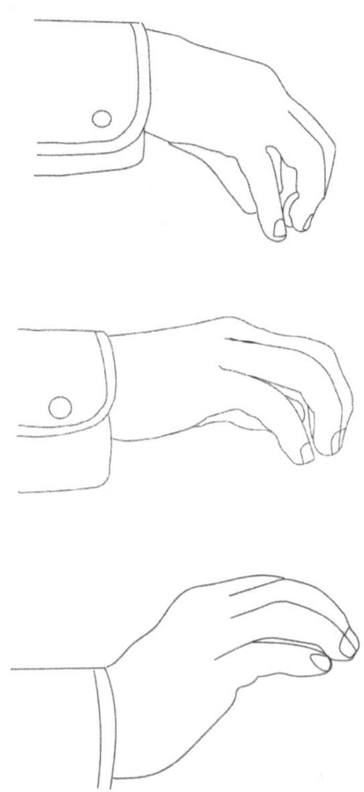

Finger Position

Which finger position is correct?
(Draw a circle around the correct finger position and an "X" through the incorrect one.)

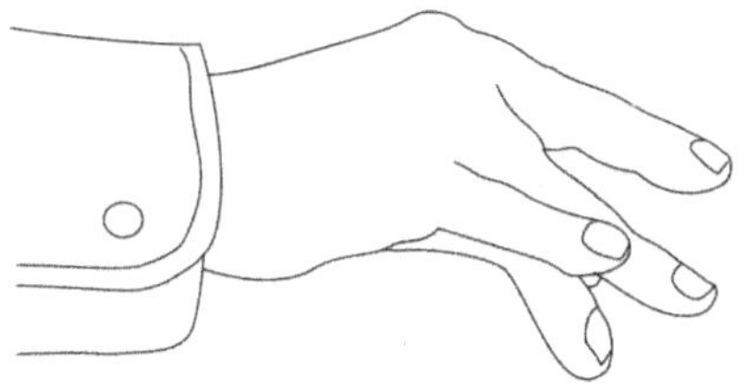

Lesson One: The Hands

Approaching The Piano

Playing the piano begins before you make a sound. Walking up to the piano, sitting, and bringing your hands to the keyboard are all part of approaching the piano. The graphic below demonstrates the final step of bringing your hands up to the keyboard.

Approaching the piano properly prepares the performer and the listener for the music to follow.

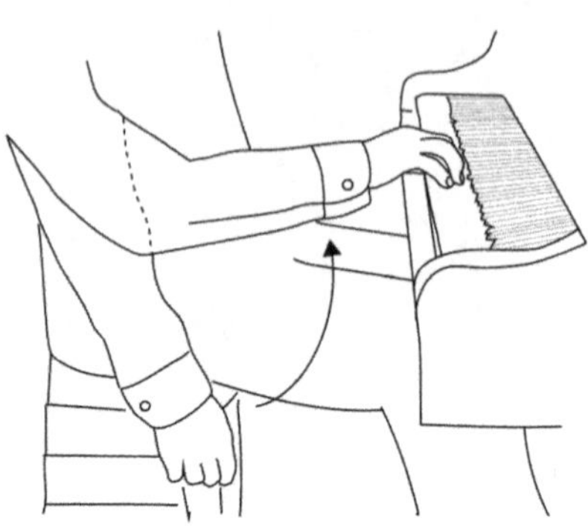

Making A Sound

A sound is made by pressing a key with a finger.

Two ways:

1) Finger Strength—While holding your hand over the keys, press a key.

2) Arm Weight—Press a key by using your arm weight through your fingers.

Activity

1. Practice approaching the piano.

   Walk up to your piano, stand between the piano and the bench, sit tall, place your hands on your lap or to your side, and feel your shoulders relax. Now begin the movement from your wrists and bring your hands to the keyboard. Repeat until you feel comfortable and relaxed with this motion.

2. Practice pressing the keys. *(Hands alone and then together.)*

   A. Using finger strength—Place the fingers over the keys, and while the arm is suspended in midair let the fingers move the keys.

   B. Using arm weight—Place the fingers over the keys and let the weight of the arm move the keys.

My First Finger Exercises!

Left Hand

Close the cover to the keyboard.
Place your left hand on the cover.
Tap the fingers shown below and call out the number as you tap.

L.H. 1 1 2 2 3 3 4 4 5 5 5 4 3 2 1

R.H. is for the right hand and L.H. is for the left hand.

Right Hand

Close the cover to the keyboard.
Place your right hand on the cover.
Tap the fingers shown below and call out the number as you tap.

R.H. 1 1 2 2 3 3 4 4 5 5 5 4 3 2 1

Both Hands

Close the cover to the keyboard.
Place your right and left hands on the cover.
Tap the fingers shown below and call out the number as you tap.

R.H. 1 1 2 2 3 3 4 4 5 5 5 4 3 2 1

L.H. 1 1 2 2 3 3 4 4 5 5 5 4 3 2 1

Trace your left hand in the space below and number the fingers.

Trace your right hand in the space below and number the fingers.

Review

1. Describe the proper sitting position at the piano.

2. What shape should the hand and fingers be in?

3. Number the fingers on the hands below.

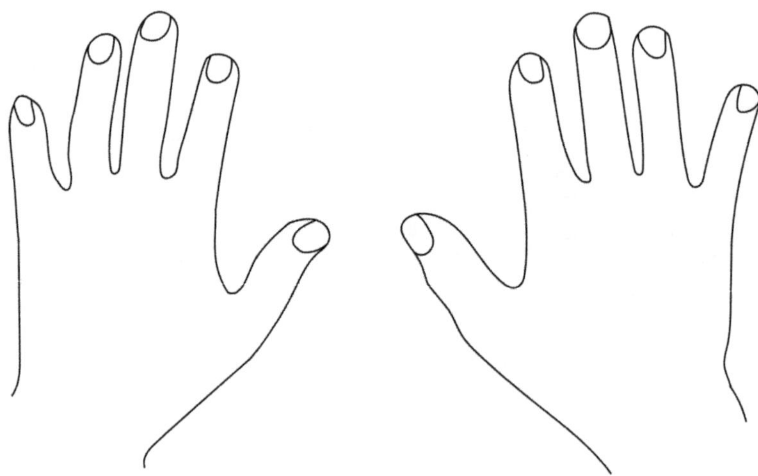

4. How is a sound made on the piano?

Lesson Two

The Keyboard (Part One)

Lesson Two: The Keyboard (Part One)

Keys

The piano has black keys and white keys.

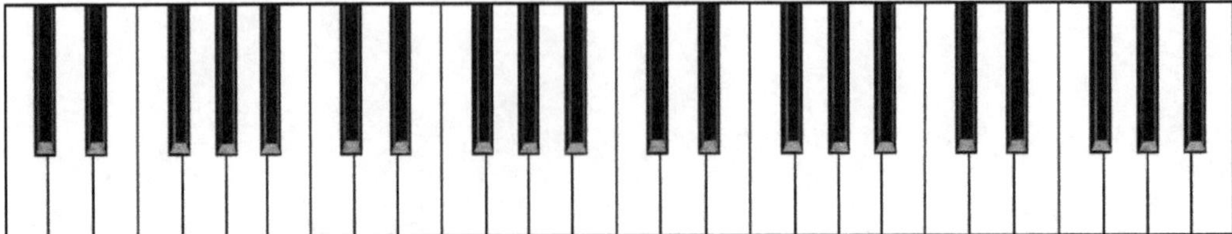

The black keys are arranged in groups of two and three.

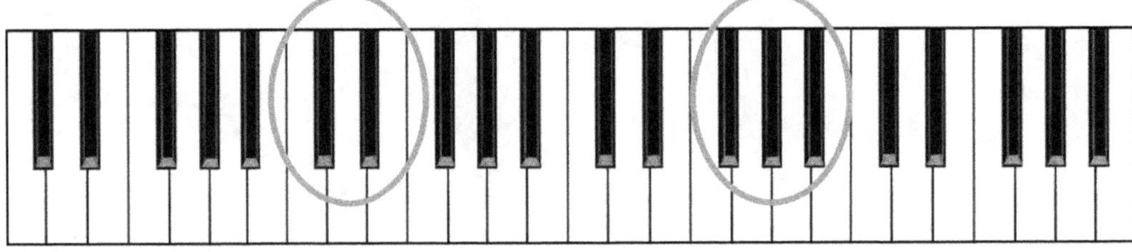

A standard piano has a total of 88 keys.

Sounds

Keys on the right side of the keyboard produce higher sounds than those on the left.

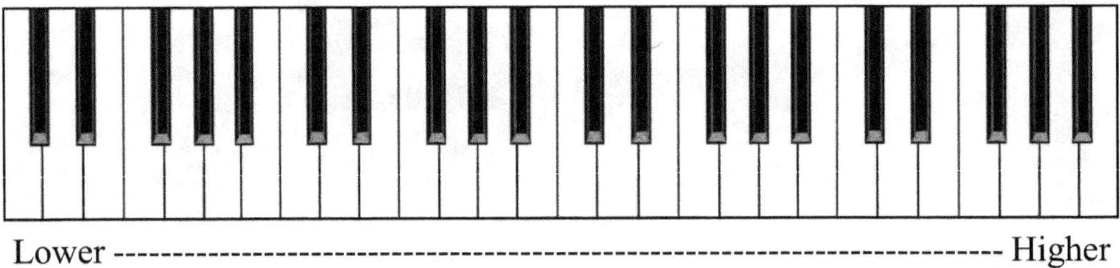

Lower --- Higher

Keys on the left side of the keyboard produce lower sounds than those on the right.

Keys in the middle of the keyboard produce medium-low to medium-high sounds.

Activity

Label the groups of two black keys with a red triangle.

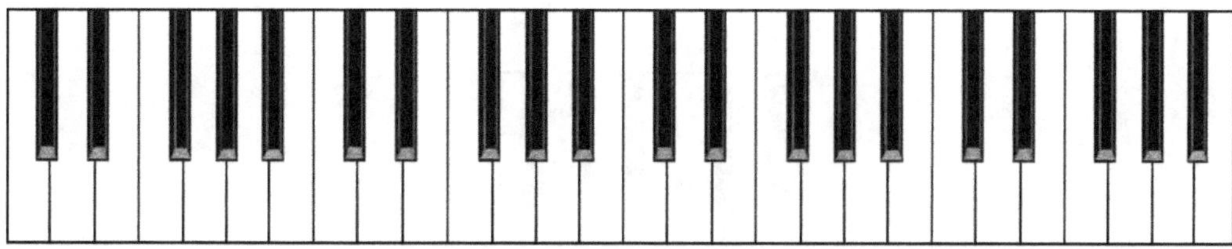

Label the groups of three black keys with a blue square.

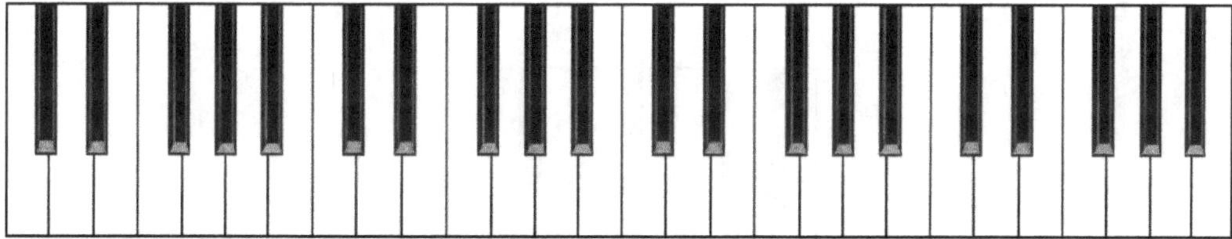

Draw a circle around the area of the keyboard where higher sounds are produced.

Draw a rectangle around the area of the keyboard where lower sounds are produced.

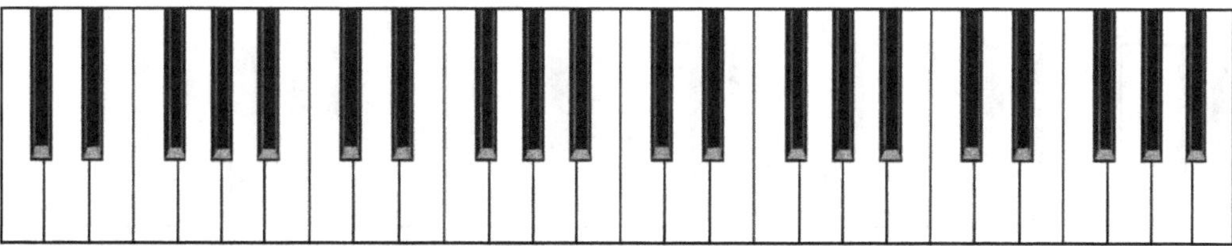

Making Sounds

Using your second and third fingers, play all the groups of two black keys you can find on the keyboard. *(Use your right hand first, then your left.)*

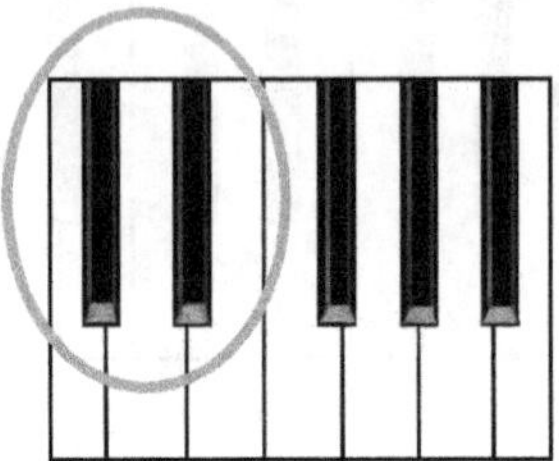

Using your second, third, and fourth fingers, play all the groups of three black keys you can find on the keyboard. *(Use your right hand first, then your left.)*

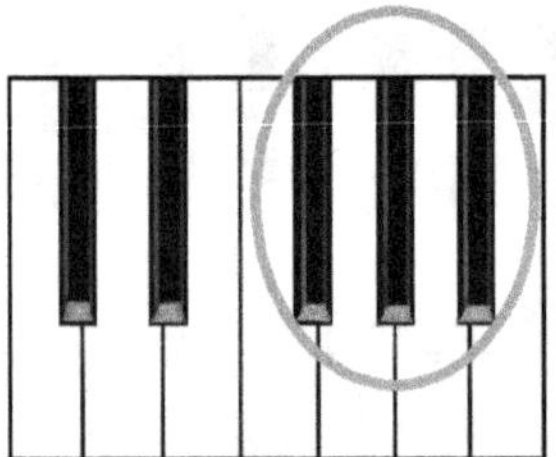

Play the circled keys in the area of the keyboard as indicated. Use the fingering described above. *(Use your right hand first, then your left.)*

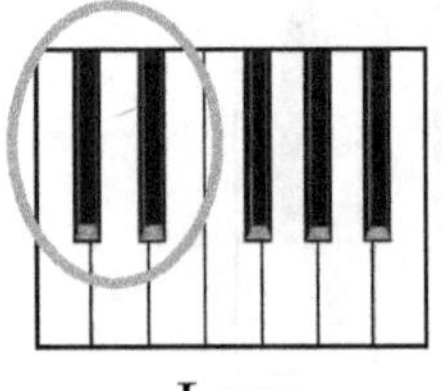

Low

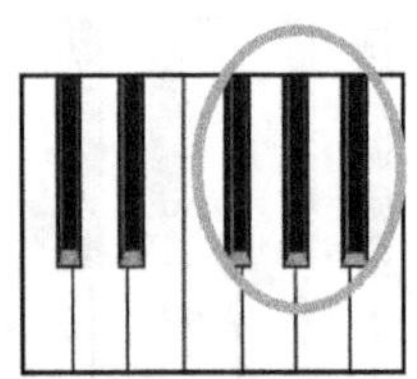

High

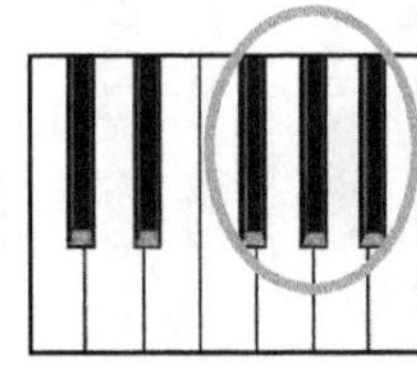

Low

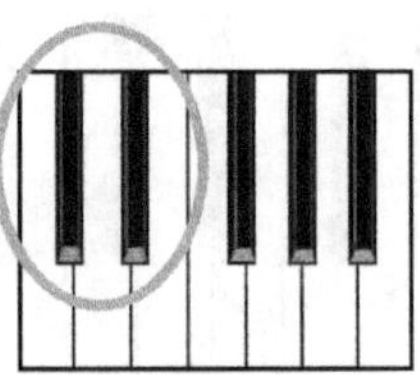

High

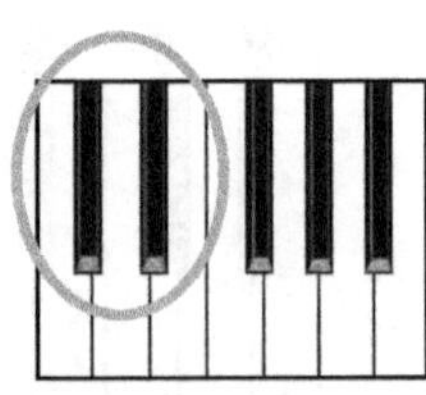

Low

My First Piece

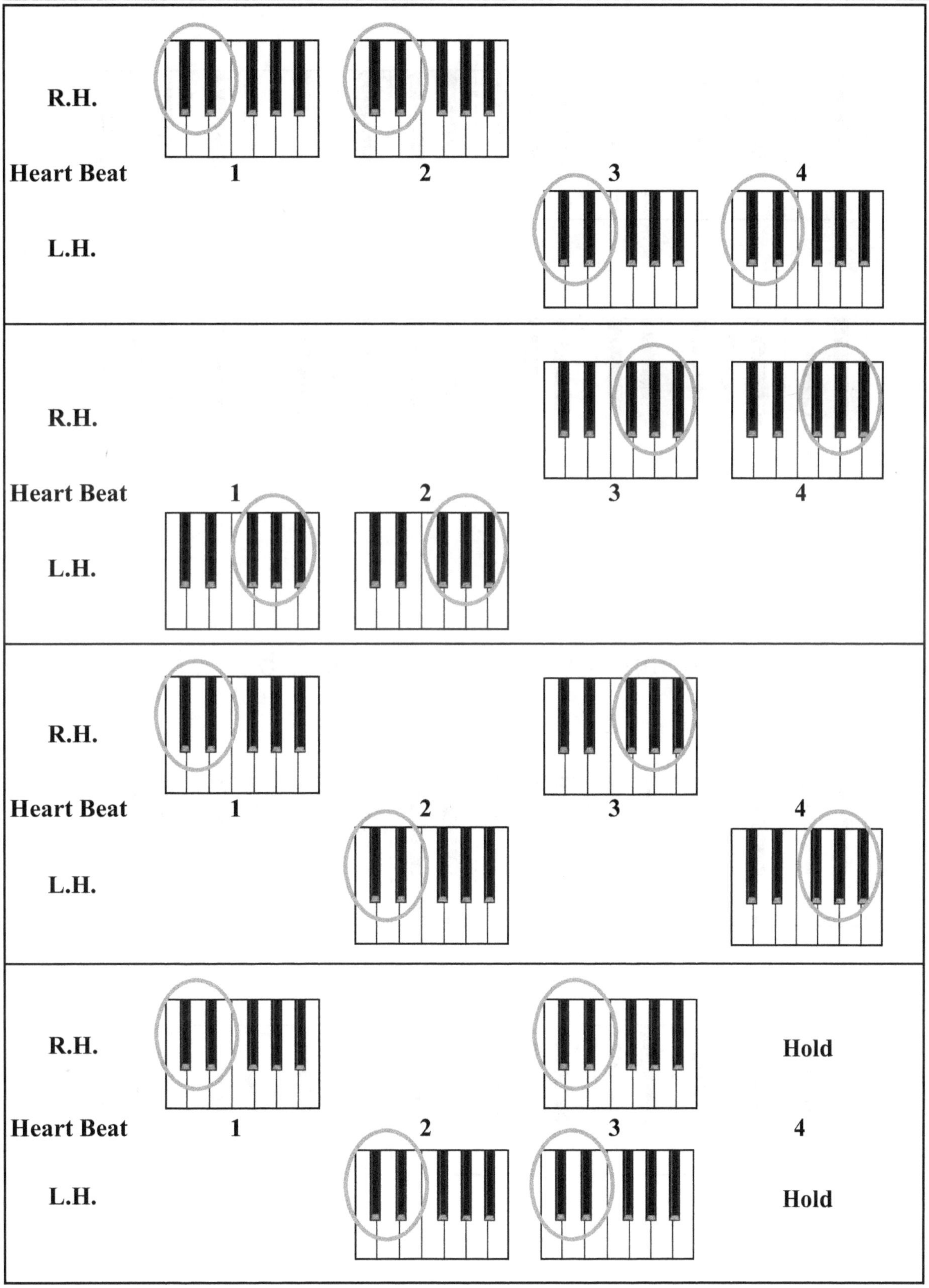

R.H.				
Heart Beat	1	2	3	4
L.H.				

R.H.				
Heart Beat	1	2	3	4
L.H.				

R.H.				
Heart Beat	1	2	3	4
L.H.				

R.H.				Hold
Heart Beat	1	2	3	4
L.H.				Hold

Instructions:
To begin this piece, place the second and third fingers of each hand over a group two black keys in the area of the keyboard that feels most comfortable for each hand.

Play each group of circled black keys with the hand indicated at the beginning of each row.

Each group of black keys is played once per every heart beat. Each row has four heart beats.

The last group of black keys for each hand is played with both hands at the same time and held for two heart beats.

Draw a circle around every group of two black keys.

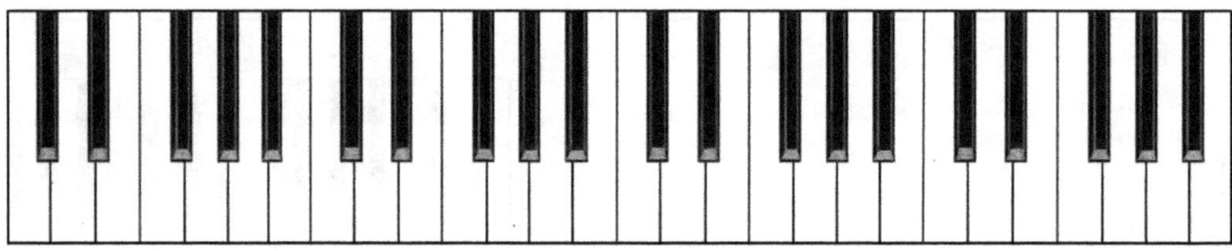

Draw a circle around every group of three black keys.

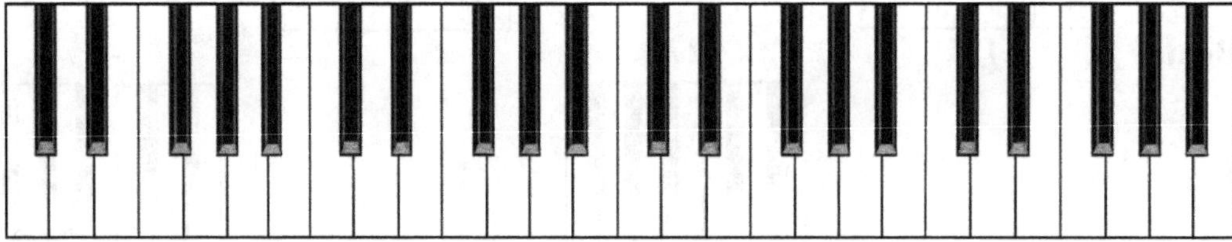

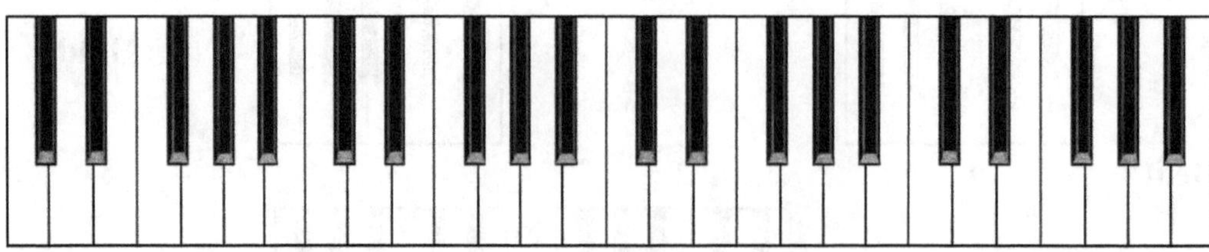

Identify the kind of sound produced by the keys in the circle.
(High, Low, Medium-High, or Medium-Low)

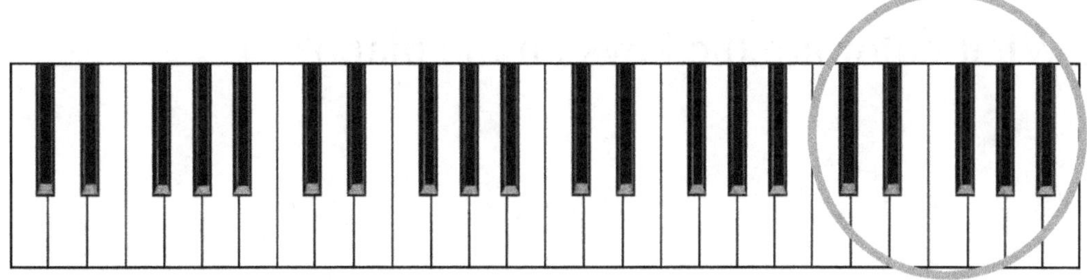

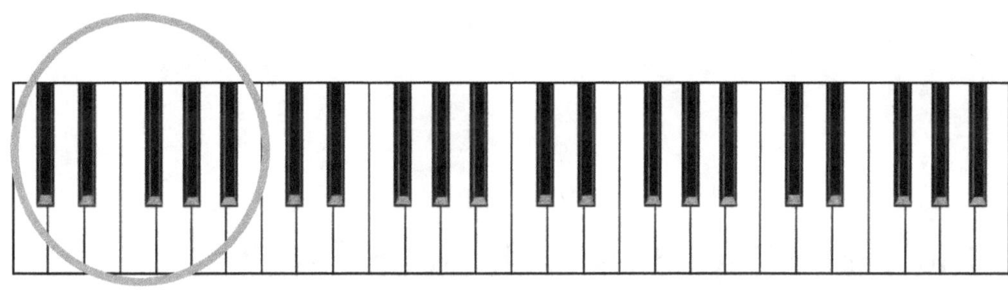

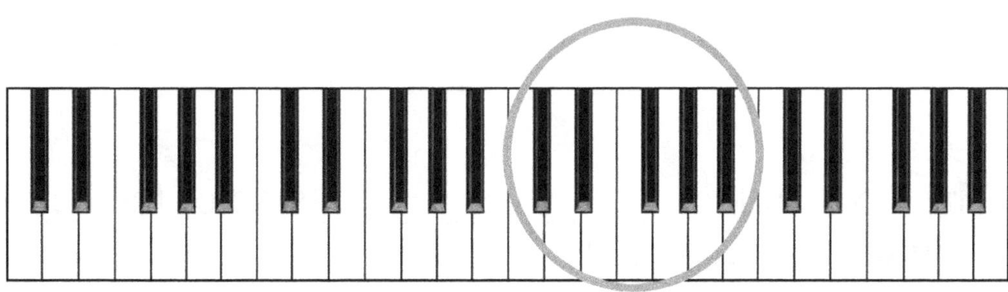

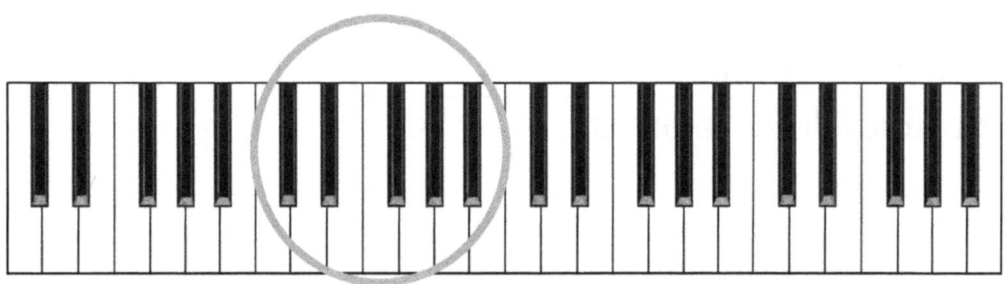

Review

1. What color are the keys on the piano?

2. How many <u>unique</u> groups of black keys does the piano have?

3. How many keys does each group have?

4. The keys on the _______________ side of the keyboard produce higher sounds.

5. The keys on the _______________ side of the keyboard produce lower sounds.

Lesson Three

The Keyboard (Part Two)

Lesson Three: The Keyboard (Part Two)

ABCs

The white keys on the piano are named using the first seven letters of the alphabet.

A B C D E F G

The names of the white keys are best learned by their relationship to the black keys as illustrated below.

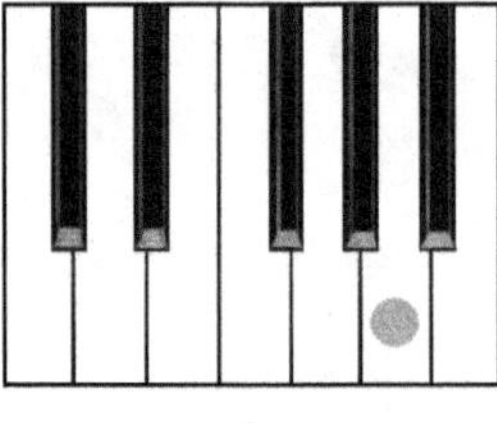

A
The key between the second and third black keys in the group of three.

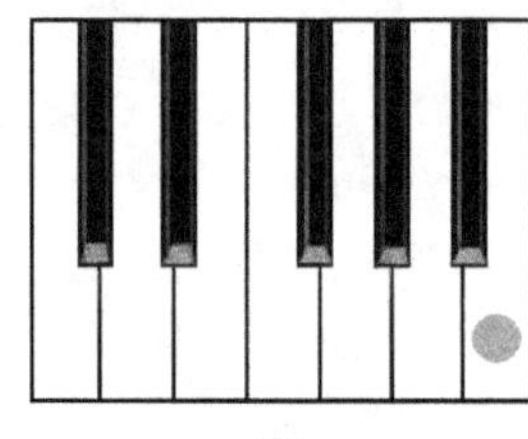

B
The key to the right of the group of three black keys.

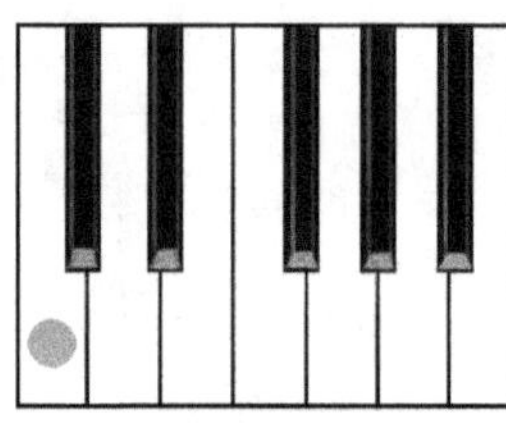

C
The key to the left of the group of two black keys.

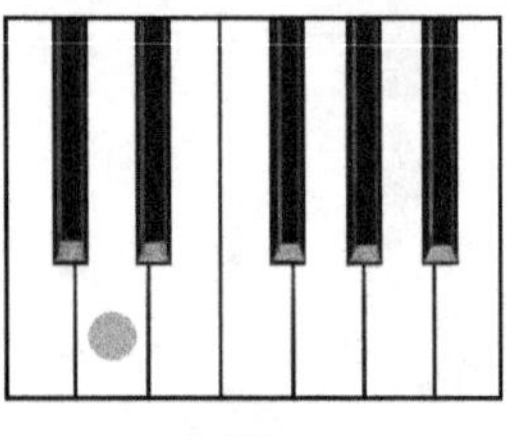

D
The key between the group of two black keys.

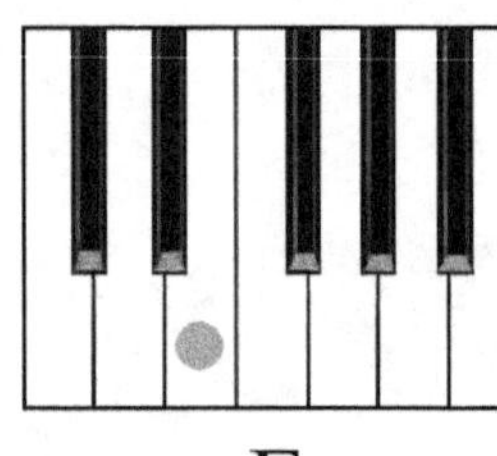

E
The key to the right of the group of two black keys.

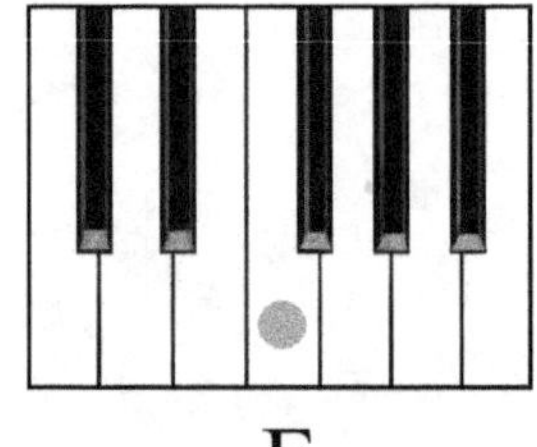

F
The key to the left of the group of three black keys.

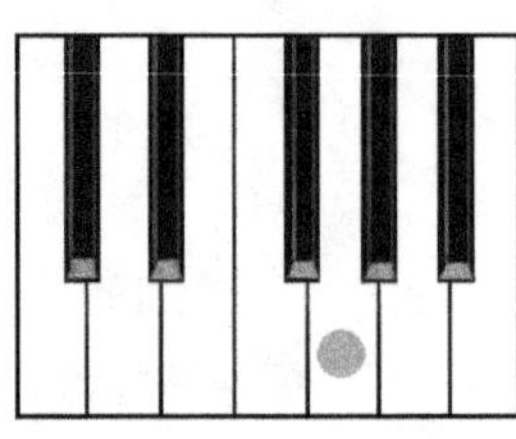

G
The key between the first and second black keys in the group of three.

Activity

For each keyboard, label every key that is named on the left.
(For example: On the first keyboard place an "A" on every key with that name.)

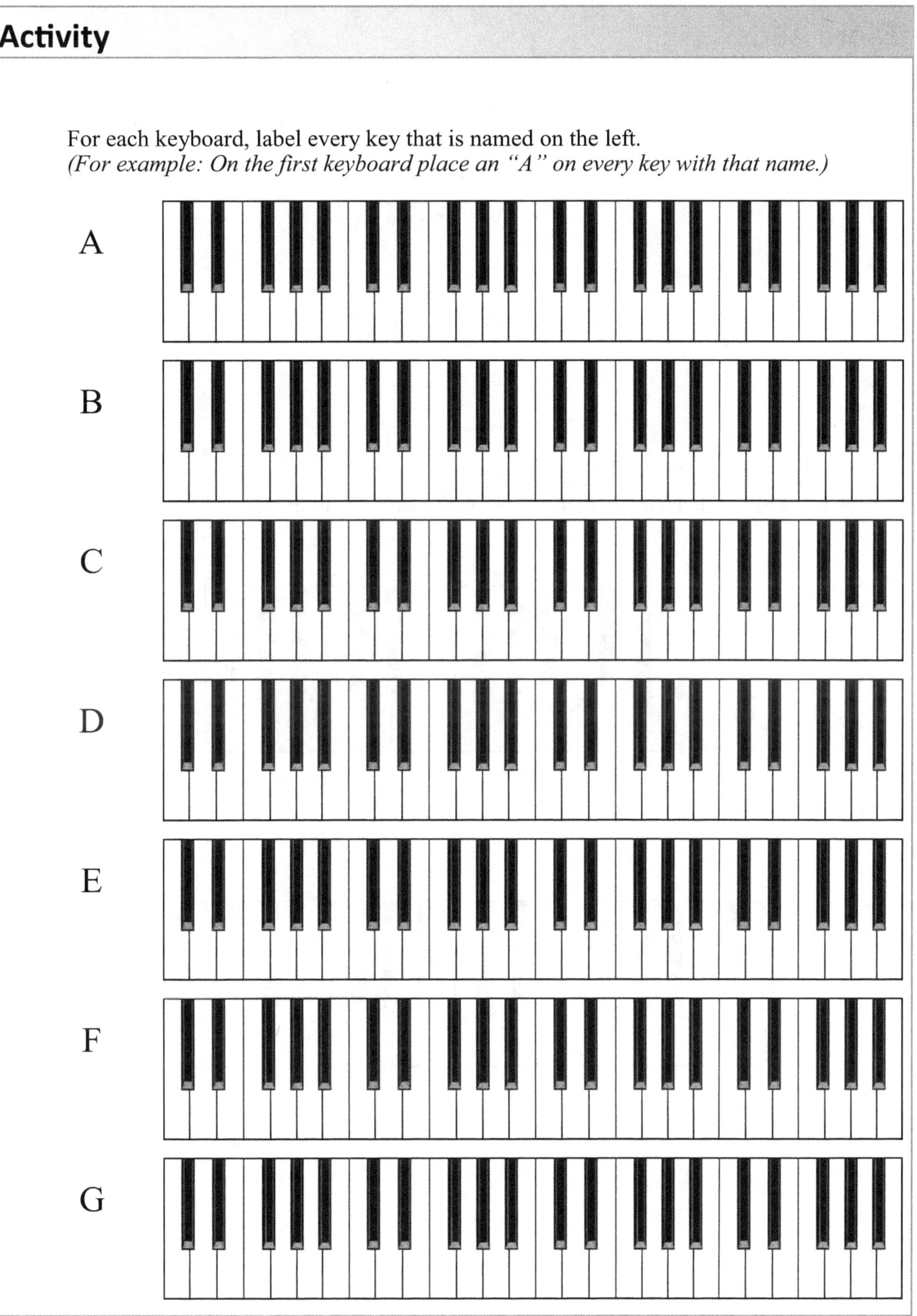

Lesson Three: The Keyboard (Part Two)

More ABCs

The black keys are also named using the first seven letters of the alphabet along with either a sharp (♯) or flat (♭) symbol.

C♯ D♯ F♯ G♯ A♯

D♭ E♭ G♭ A♭ B♭

The black keys are named in relation to a white key next to them.

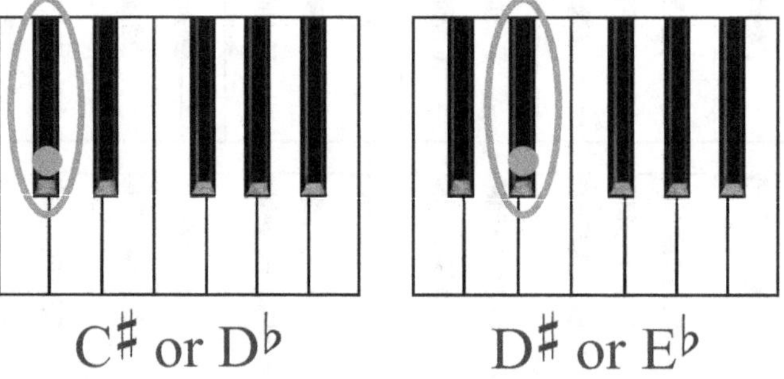

C♯ or D♭ D♯ or E♭

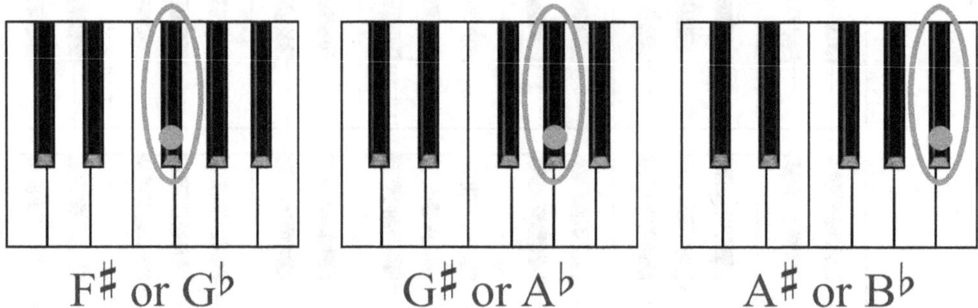

F♯ or G♭ G♯ or A♭ A♯ or B♭

Activity

On each keyboard, draw a circle around every key that is named on the left.
(For example: On the first keyboard draw a circle around each C♯ or D♭.)

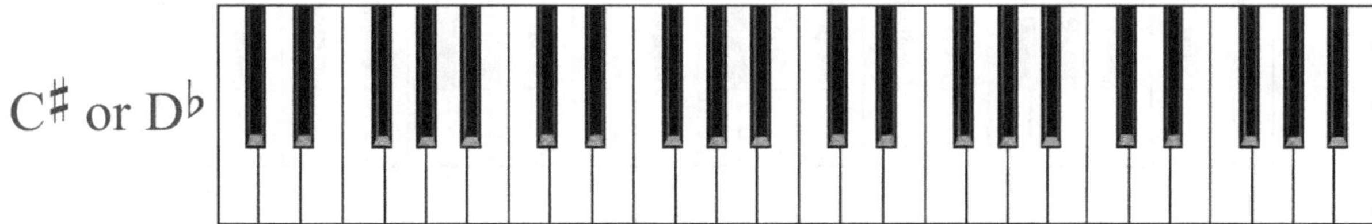

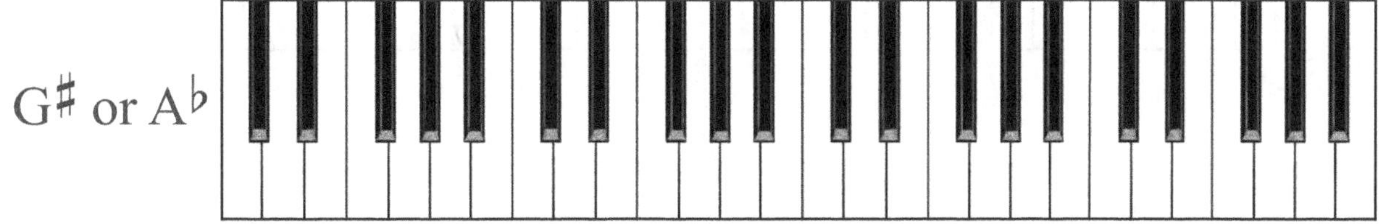

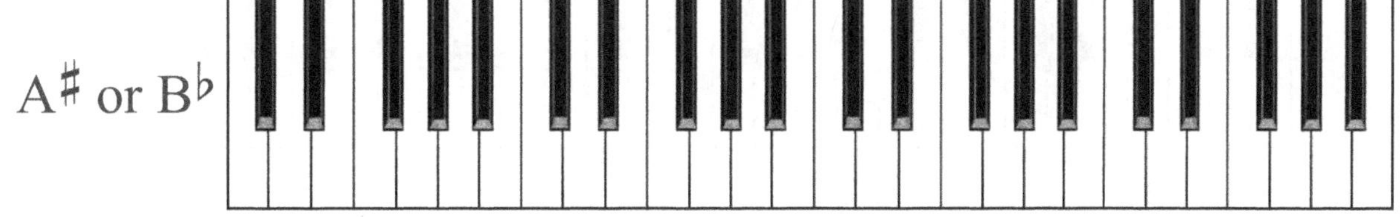

Lesson Three: The Keyboard (Part Two)

Spell the word on each keyboard by labeling the keys with the matching letter.

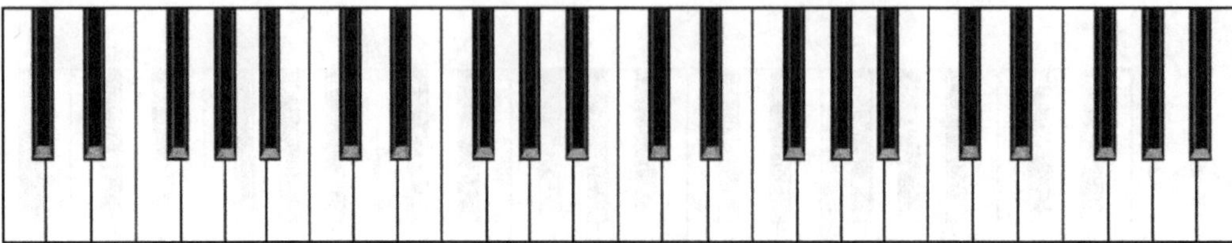

FACE

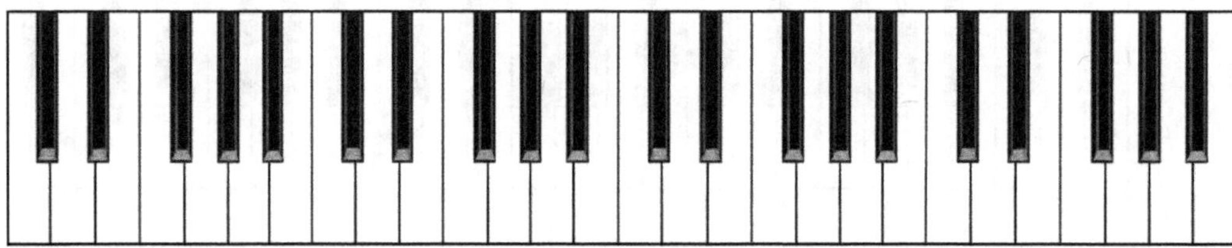

GABE

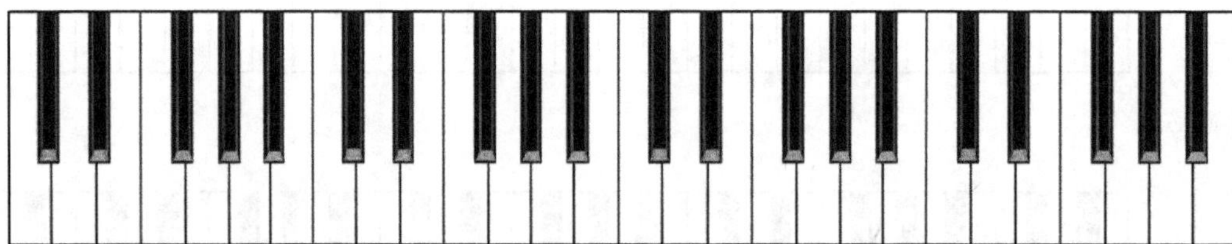

CAB

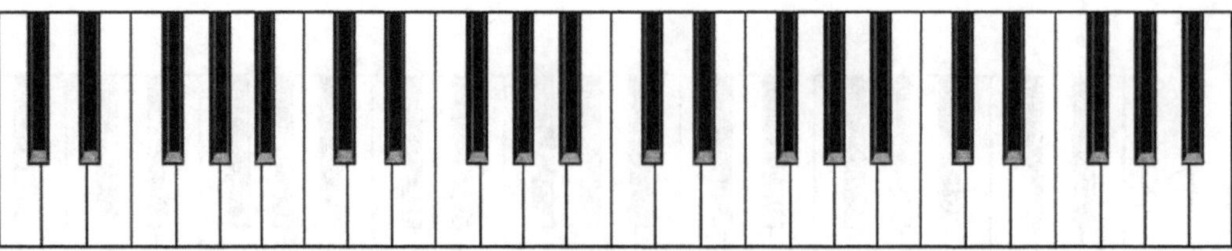

DEAF

What do the highlighted keys spell? Write the word in the box below each keyboard.

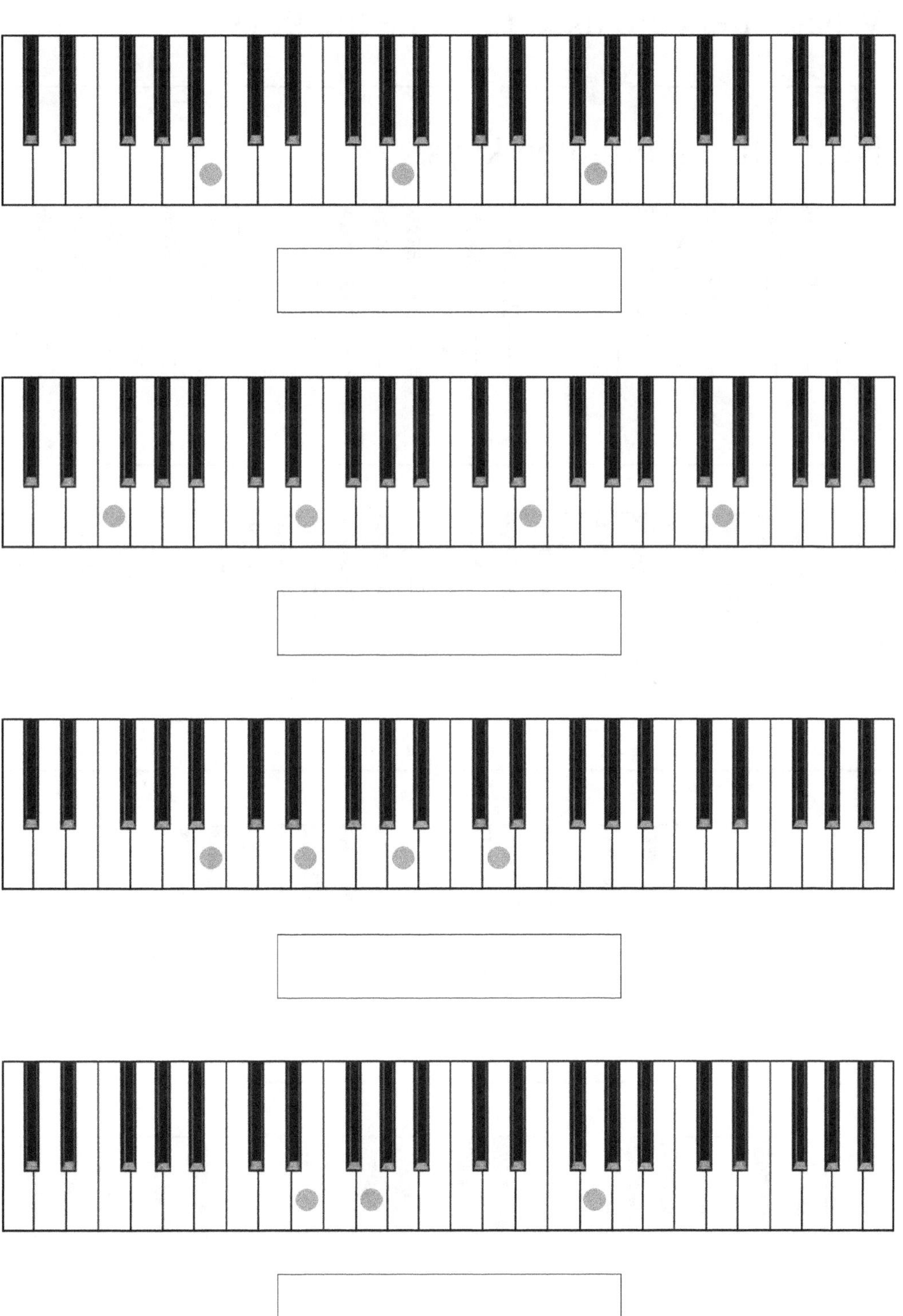

Review

1. What letters are used to name the keys?

_____ _____ _____ _____ _____ _____ _____

2. Name the highlighted keys.

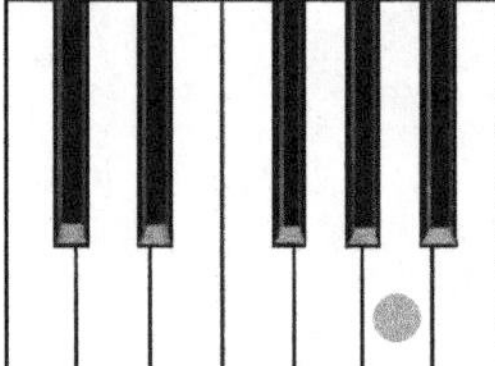
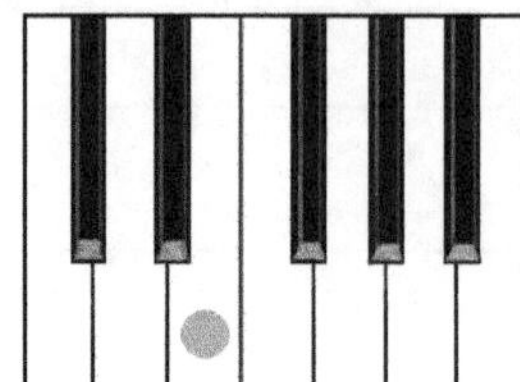
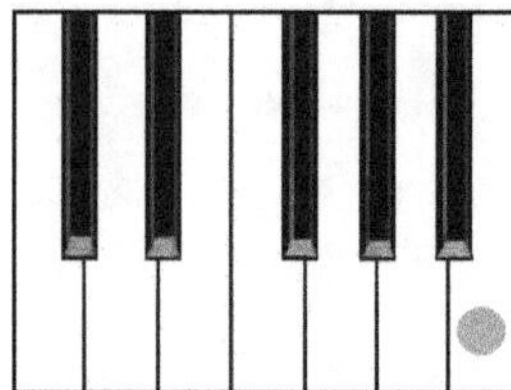

__________ __________ __________

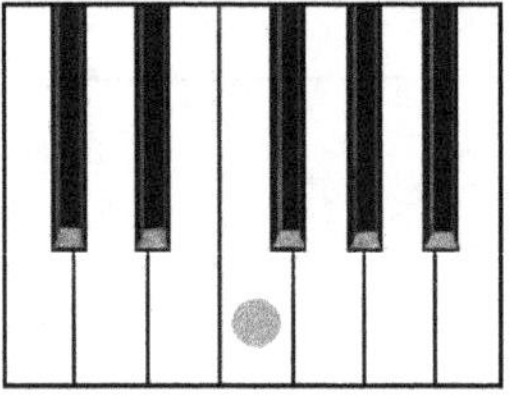
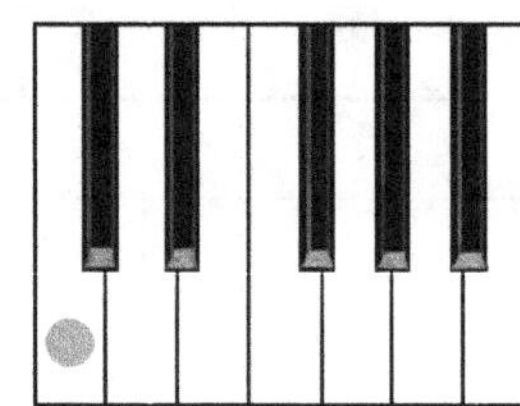
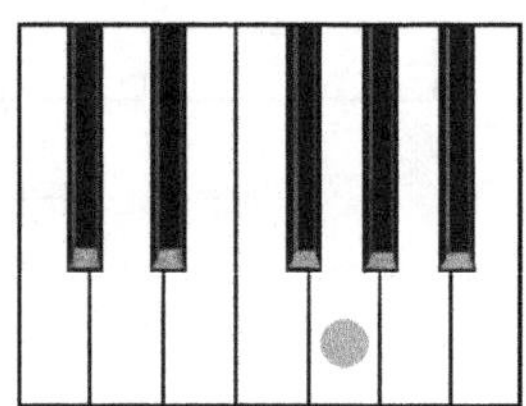
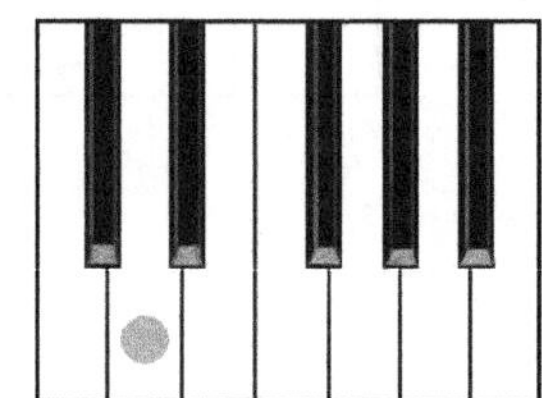

__________ __________ __________ __________

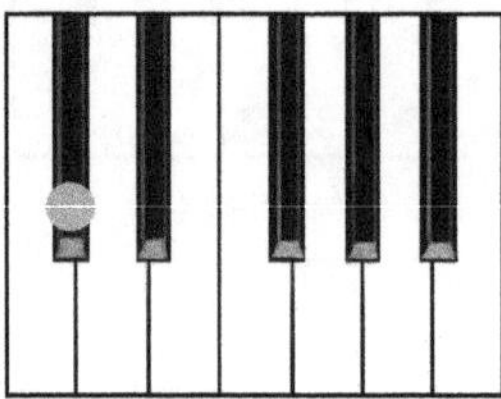
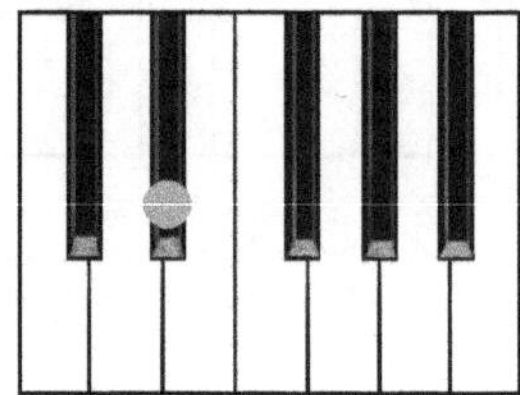

__________ __________

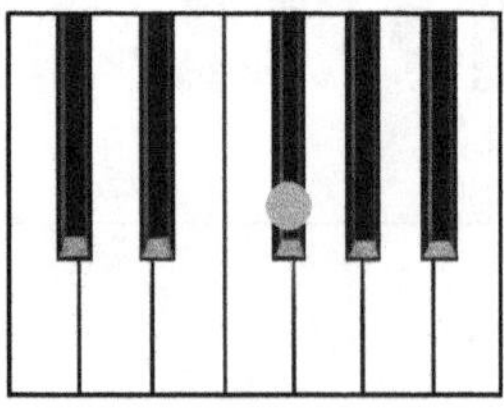
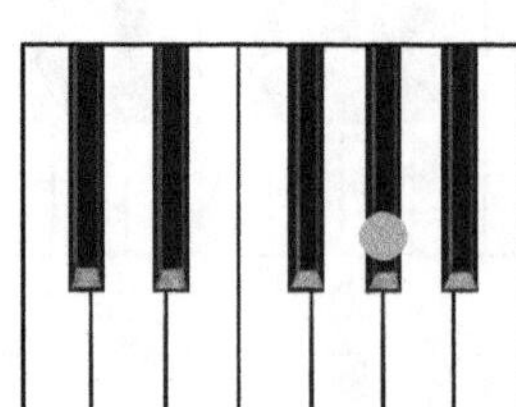
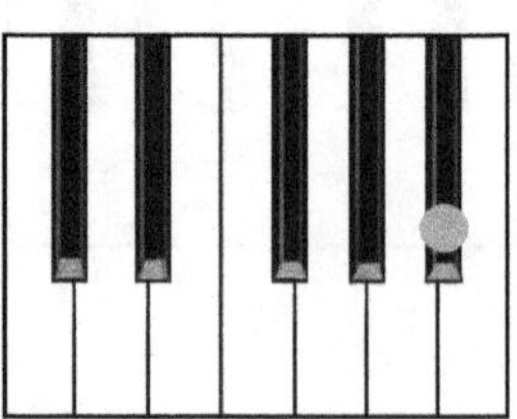

__________ __________ __________

Lesson Four

Reading Music (Part One)

Lesson Four: Reading Music (Part One)

Symbols

Music uses symbols to represent sound. The basic symbol for sound, an oval, is called a note.

Note

Note vs. Key: The symbol on the printed page is a note. The piano part used to make a sound is a key.

Sometimes the terms are used interchangeably as in "play the note," which is shorthand for "play the key represented by the note."

Notes are placed on a series of five lines called a staff.
Multiple staffs are called staves.

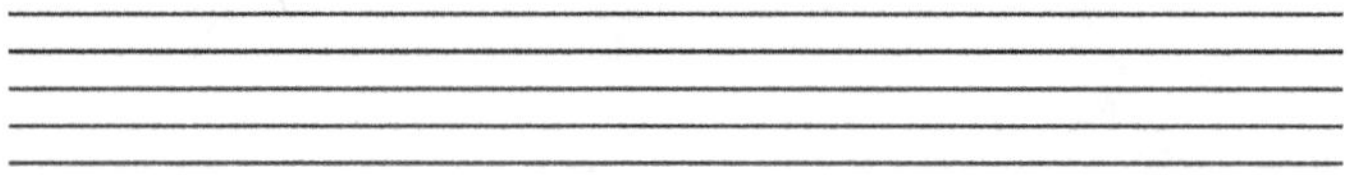

Staff

Notes may be on a line or in a space.

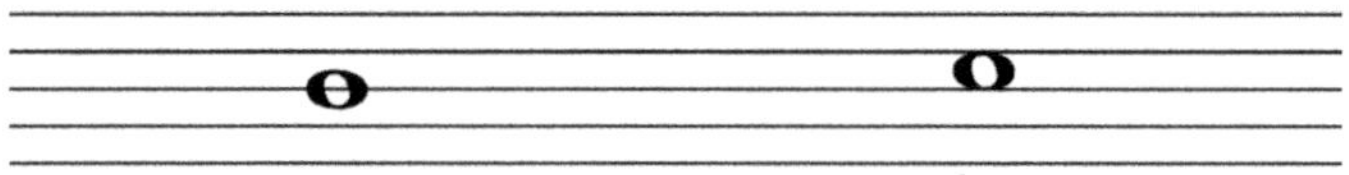

Each note on the staff represents one key on the keyboard.

Activity

Practice drawing some notes on a line.

Practice drawing some notes in a space.

Clefs

Every staff will have a clef at the beginning to indicate a region of the keyboard. Piano music uses two staves (plural for staff) for its notation grouped together with a curly brace. This grouping is collectively known as the grand staff.

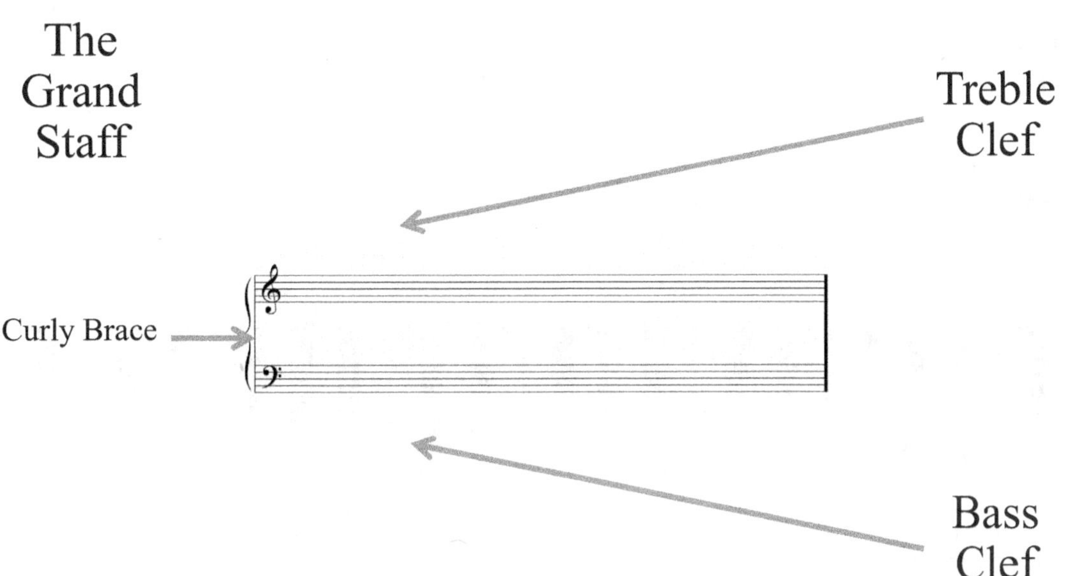

In general, the staff with a treble clef is used for notes that the right hand plays and the staff with a bass clef is used for notes that the left hand plays.

Activity

Practice drawing some treble clefs.

Start Here

Practice drawing some bass clefs.

Start Here

Ledger Lines: Short lines above or below a staff used for notes beyond the range of the current staff, as in the "C" between the treble and bass clefs.

One Note, One Key

Notes lower on the staff have a lower sound, and notes higher on the staff have a higher sound.

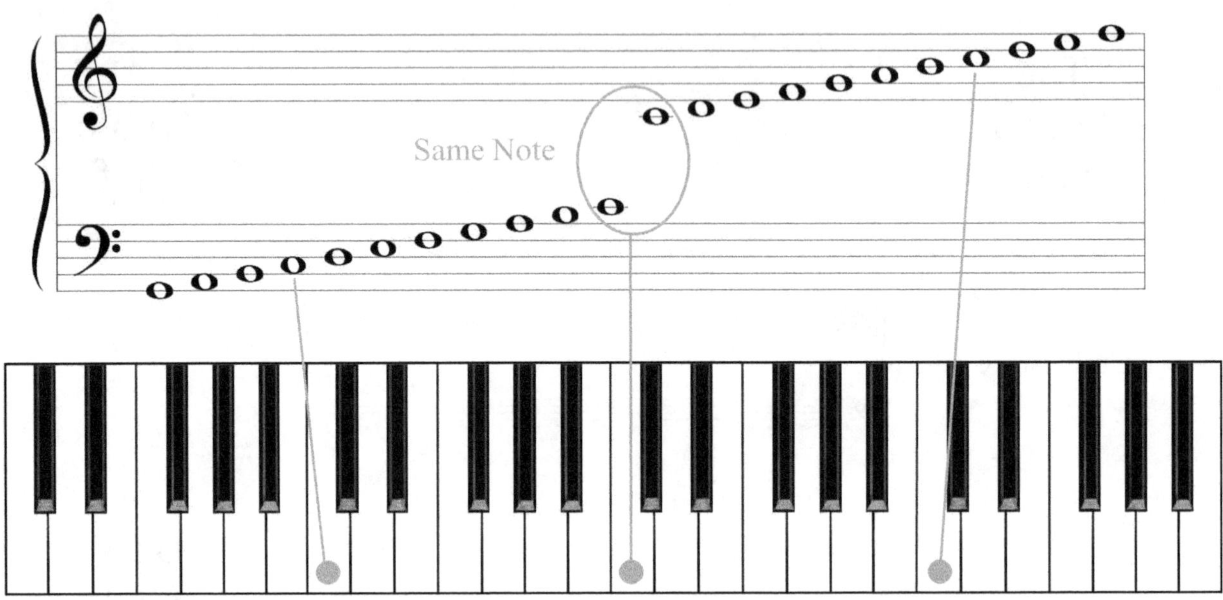

Memory Hints

To remember the names of the notes, think of the following:

Treble Clef Lines: (from the bottom up)

Elephants **G**et **B**igger **D**uring **F**all

Treble Clef Spaces: (from the bottom up)

Friendly **A**nimals **C**an **E**ntertain

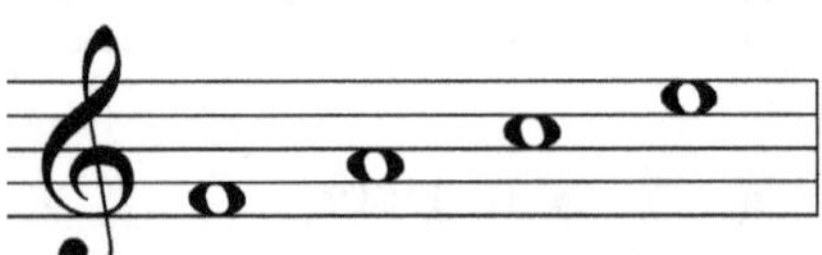

Bass Clef Lines: (from the bottom up)

Good **B**arking **D**ogs **F**etch **A**pples

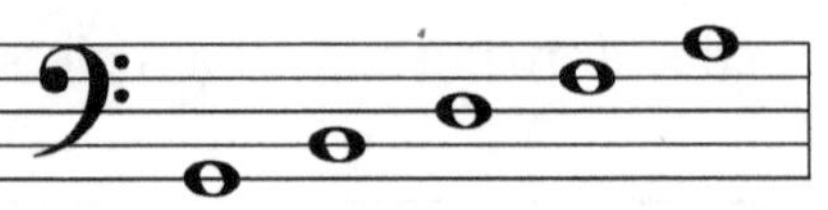

Bass Clef Spaces: (from the bottom up)

All **C**reatures **E**njoy **G**rass

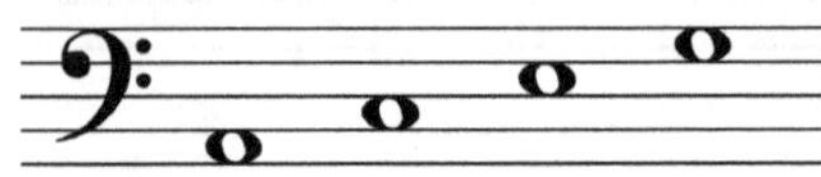

One Key, Two Notes

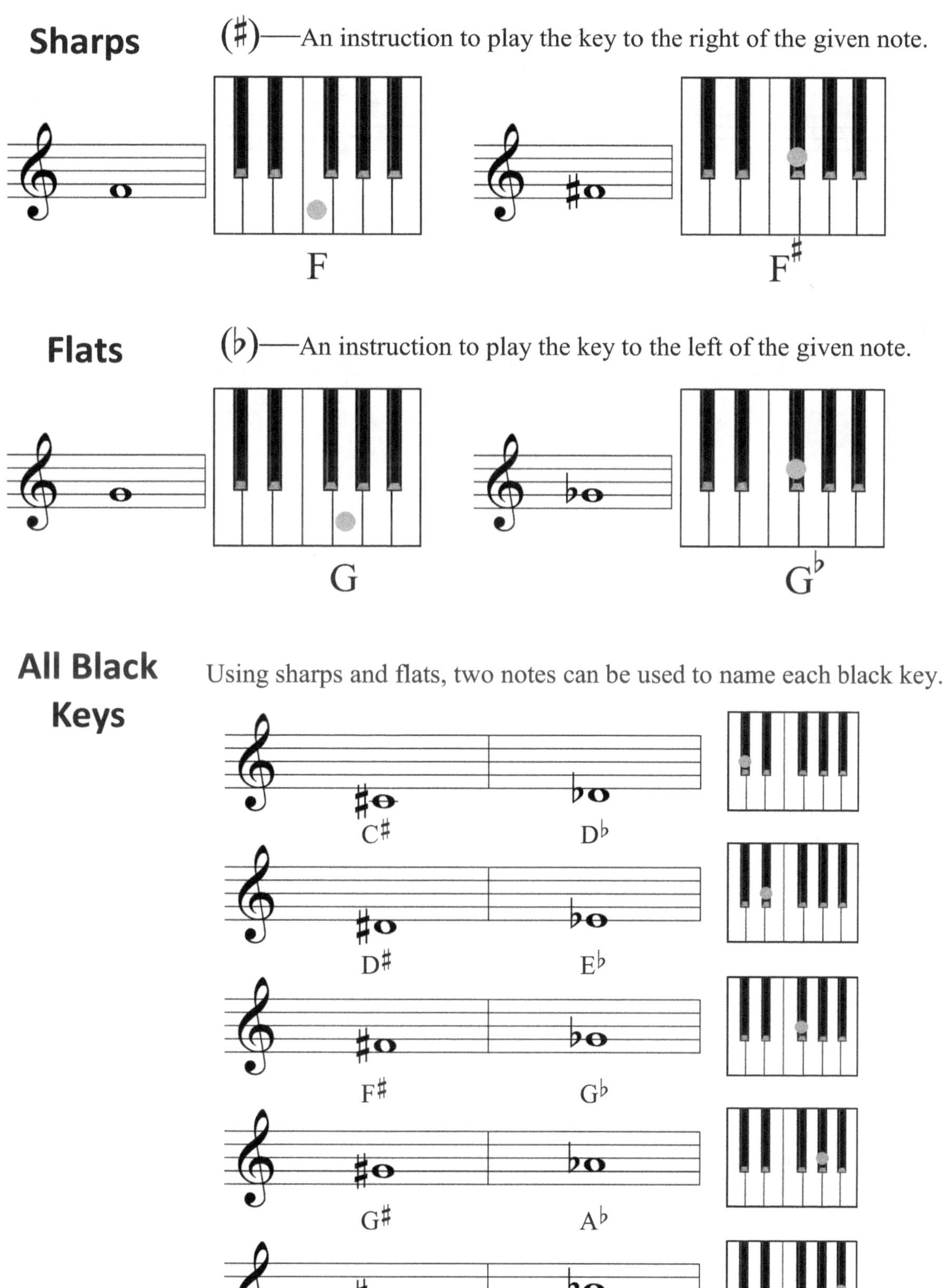

Refer to "More ABCs" in the previous lesson for a reminder on naming the black keys.

Lesson Four: Reading Music (Part One)

Spell the word below each staff by drawing the notes on the staff.

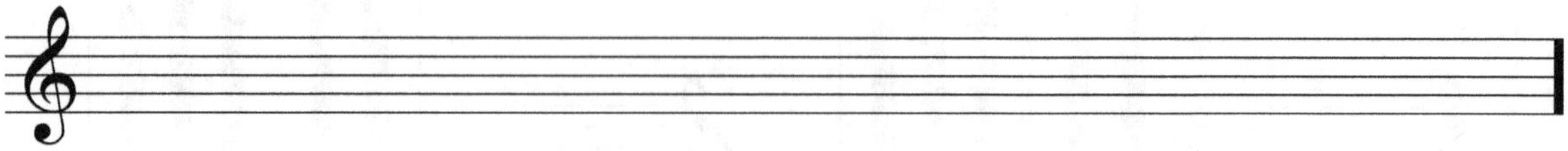

FACE

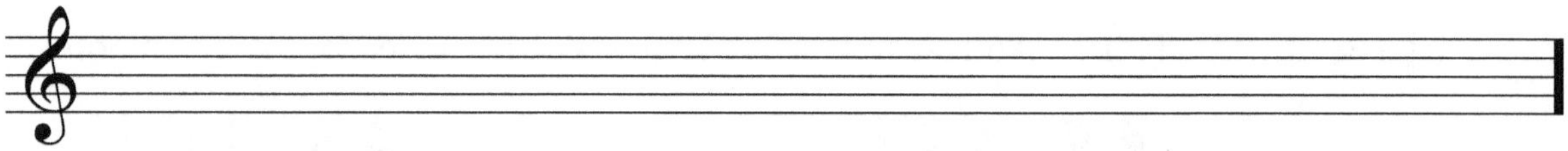

GABE

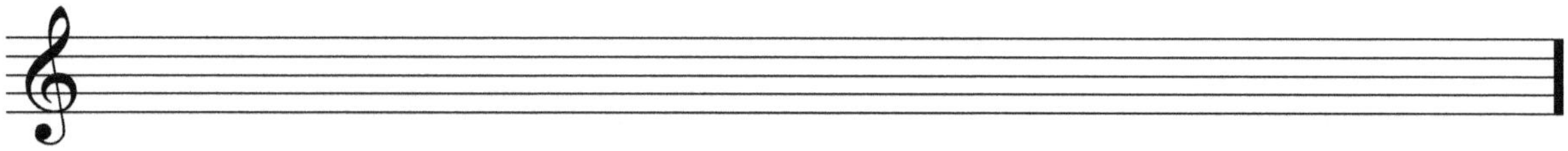

CAB

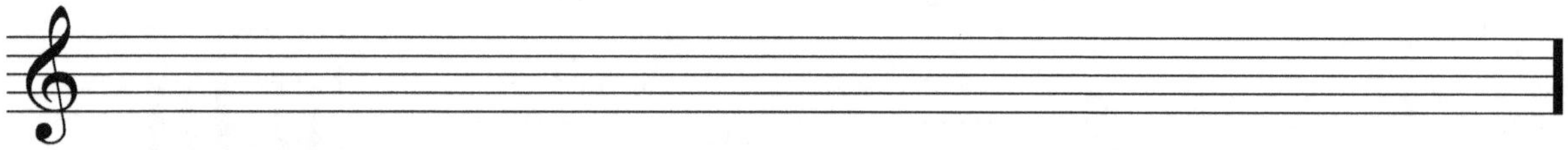

DEAF

What word do these notes spell?

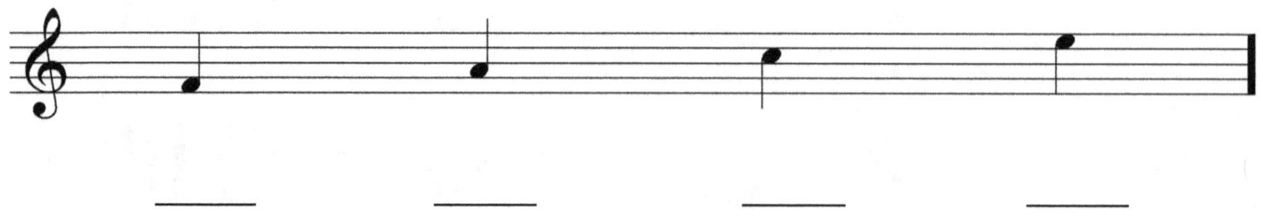

Spell the word below each staff by drawing the notes on the staff.

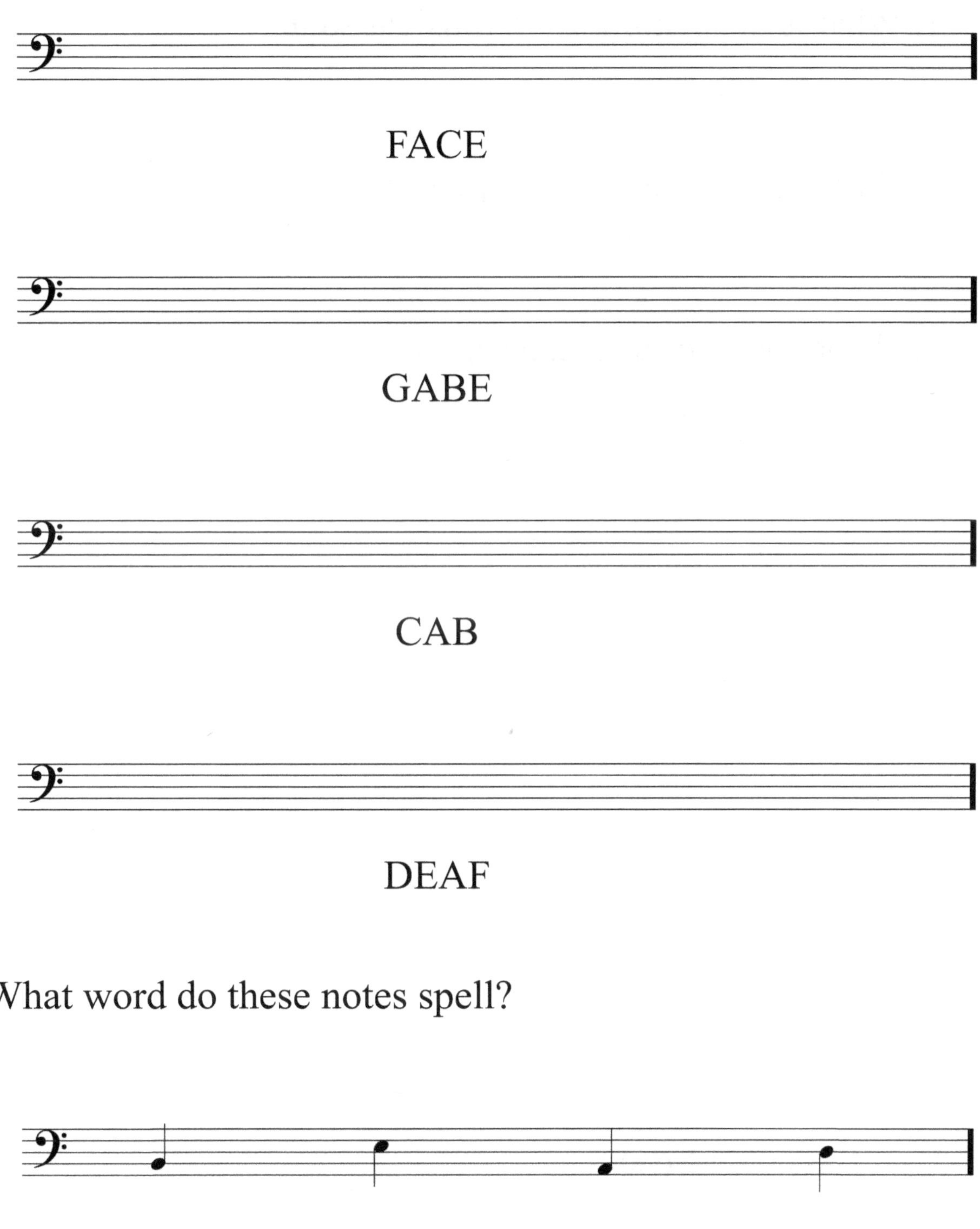

What word do these notes spell?

Review

1. What is the symbol for a musical sound?

2. Where are these symbols placed?

3. Name the lines and spaces:

Treble Clef Lines

_____ _____ _____ _____ _____

Treble Clef Spaces

_____ _____ _____ _____

Bass Clef Lines

_____ _____ _____ _____ _____

Bass Clef Spaces

_____ _____ _____ _____

Lesson Five

Reading Music (Part Two)

Lesson Five: Reading Music (Part Two)

Notes and Rests

Notes are symbols for sounds.

Rests are symbols for silence.

Beat:
A measured pulse like a heartbeat.

Notes and rests are equal in importance.

A steady beat is the foundation upon which we play notes and rests.

Duration

Duration is the length of a period of sound or silence relative to a predetermined beat. In the example below, each number represents the beginning of a beat and the dotted line the duration. In other words, notes and rests have starting and ending points.

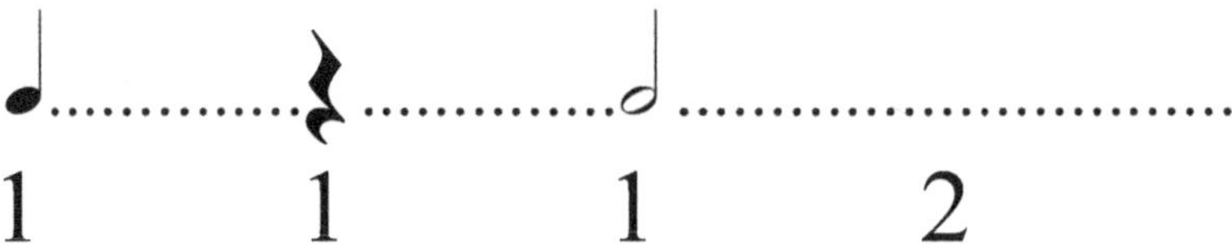

Basic Symbols

Sound		Beats		Silence
	Quarter Note	1	Quarter Rest	
	Half Note	2	Half Rest	
	Whole Note	4	Whole Rest	

Activity

Complete the following exercises as illustrated in this example.

1 1 1 2 1 2 1 1 1 2 3 4

1. Add notes and rests to complete the following exercise.

1 2 1 2 1 2 3 4 1 1 1 1

2. Write the number of beats for each note below.

Metronome

A metronome is a musician's tool to show the performer the general speed of a composition. It produces a ticking sound which can be set to any number of ticks per minute. The ticks are usually referred to as beats.

The following symbol is used to specify a metronome setting at the beginning of a piece of music:

♩= 60

This shows that the basic beat of the piece will consist of 60 quarter notes per minute, or one quarter note every second.

Lesson Five: Reading Music (Part Two)

Measures

Vertical lines known as measure lines break staves into measures. Measures are frames into which notes and rests are placed. They help organize music and make it easier to read.

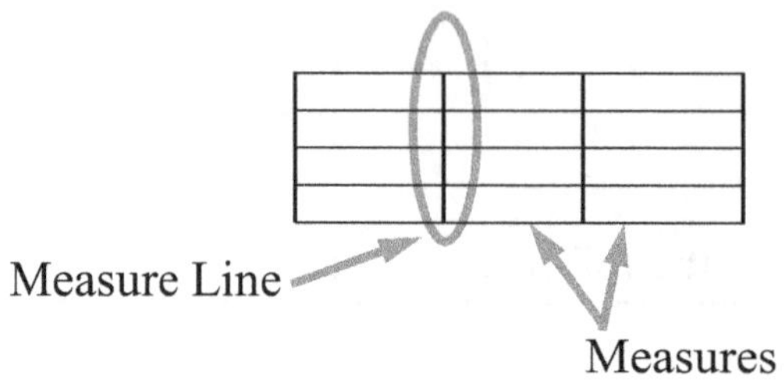

Time Signature

The time signature is a code at the beginning of a musical composition. It tells the performer the number of beats in a measure and the kind of note that will equal one beat. The number of notes and rests in a measure is governed by the time signature.

The top number represents the number of beats in a measure while the bottom number represents the kind of note that will equal one beat.

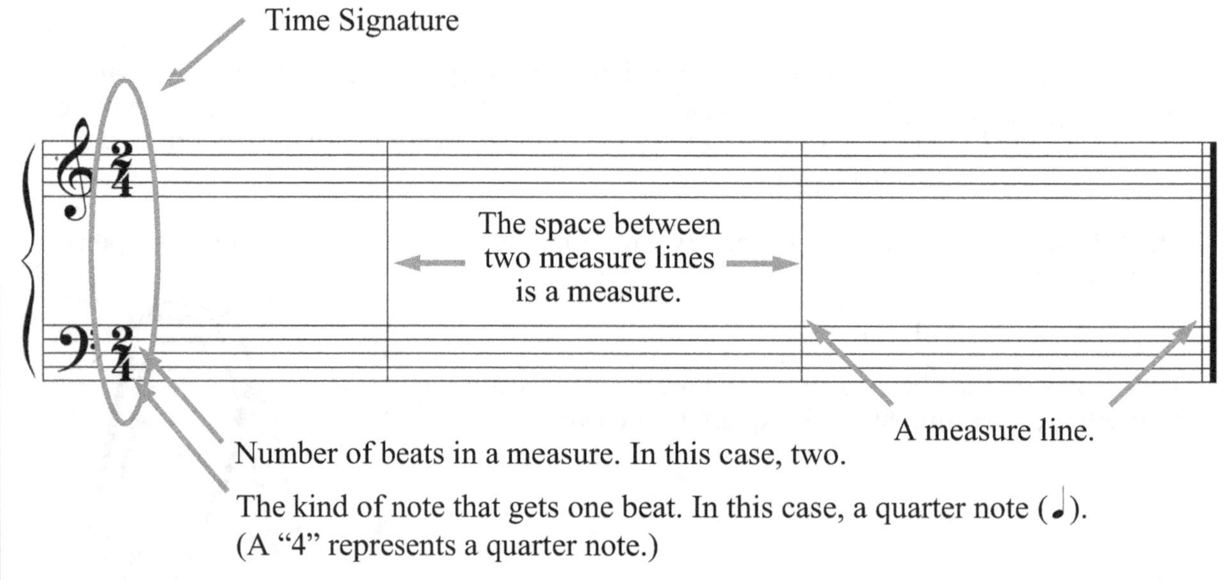

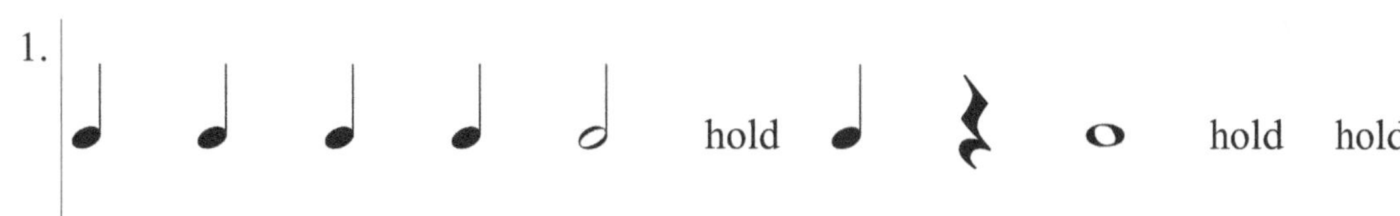

Clap the notes while counting. Hold your hands together when it says hold and apart when there is a rest.

1.

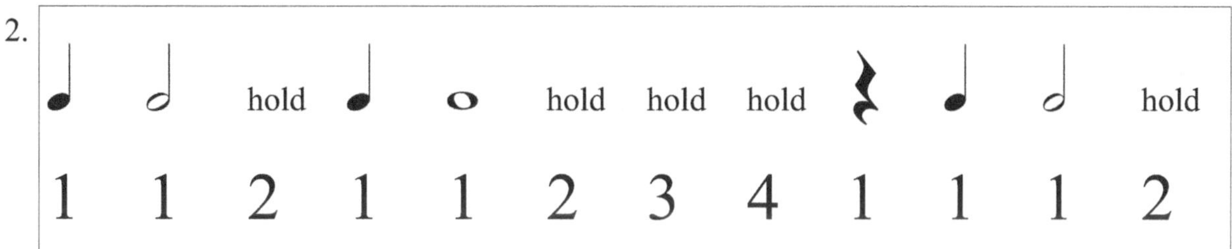

2.

hold hold hold hold hold

1 1 2 1 1 2 3 4 1 1 1 2

Play

Play the following exercises using the third finger on each hand. (See page 28 for help with the notes.)

Notes that align vertically are to be played at the same time.

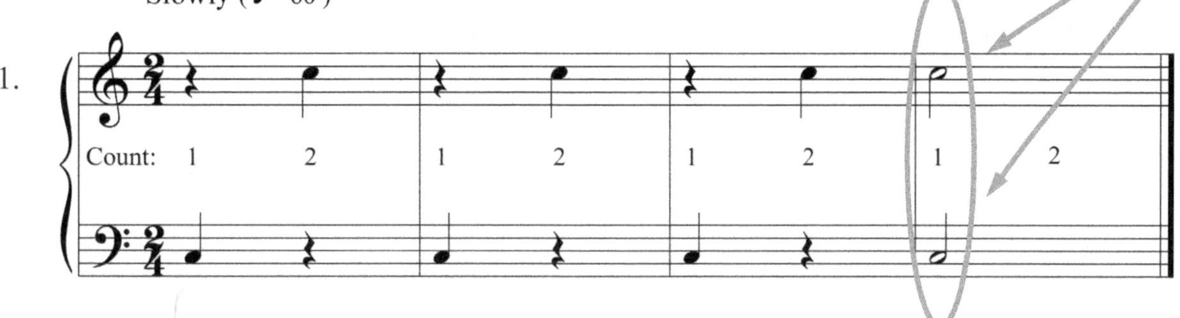

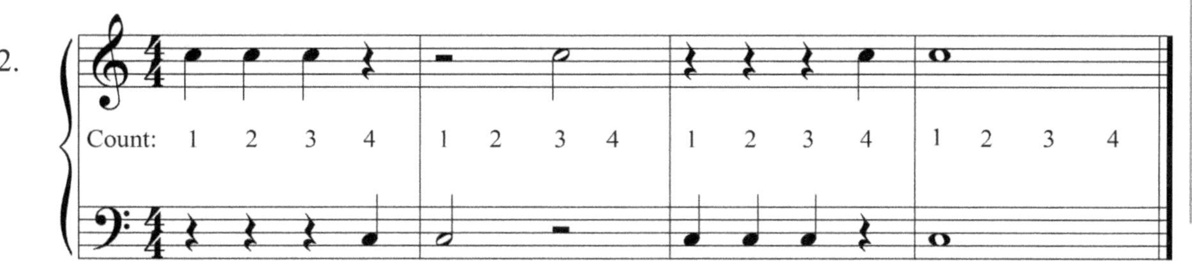

1. Place a 4/4 time signature on the staff below.
2. Using quarter notes, spell the words by drawing the notes on the staff.
3. Draw measure lines where needed.

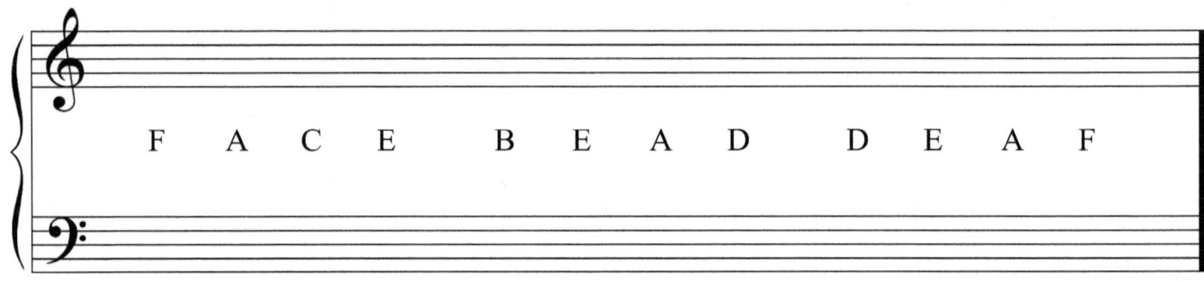

4. Place a 4/4 time signature on the staff below.
5. Using quarter notes and half notes, spell the words by drawing the notes on the staff.
6. Draw measure lines where needed.

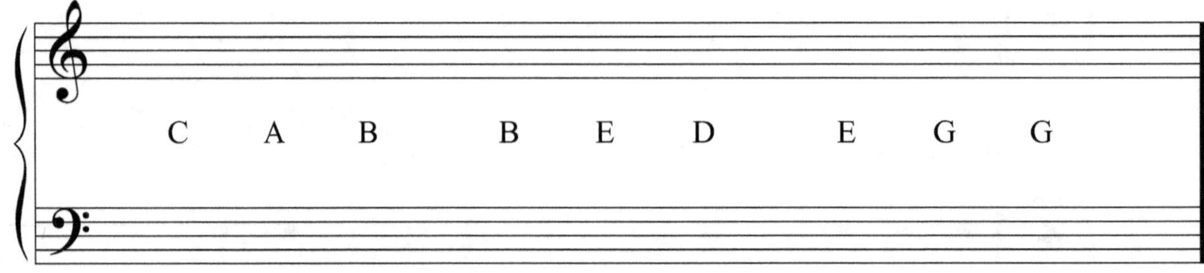

1. Place a 4/4 time signature on the staff below.
2. Spell three words of your own in the boxes below having four letters from A-G.
3. Using quarter notes, spell the words by drawing the notes on the staff.
4. Draw measure lines where needed.

5. Place a 4/4 time signature on the staff below.
6. Spell three words of your own in the boxes below having three letters from A-G.
7. Using quarter notes and half notes, spell the words by drawing the notes on the staff.
8. Draw measure lines where needed.

Review

1. Draw the symbols used for sound.

2. Draw the symbols used for silence.

3. Notes and rests are grouped into units called

   _______________.

4. What does the top number in a time signature represent?

5. What does the bottom number in a time signature represent?

6. What is a metronome and what is it used for?

Lesson Six

C Major / A Minor

Half Steps

A half step is the distance from one key to the key immediately next to it (either black or white).

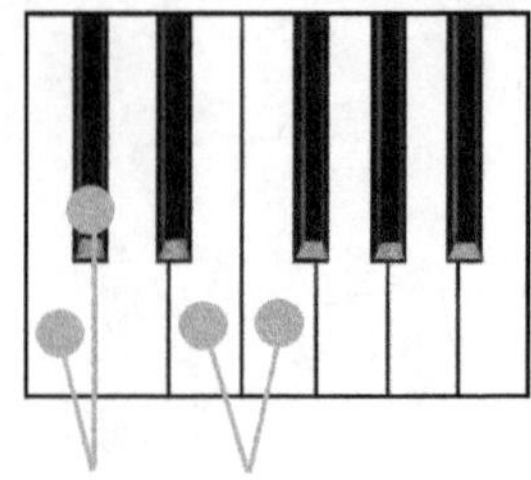

Whole Steps

A whole step is the distance from one key to another, skipping only one key (either black or white).

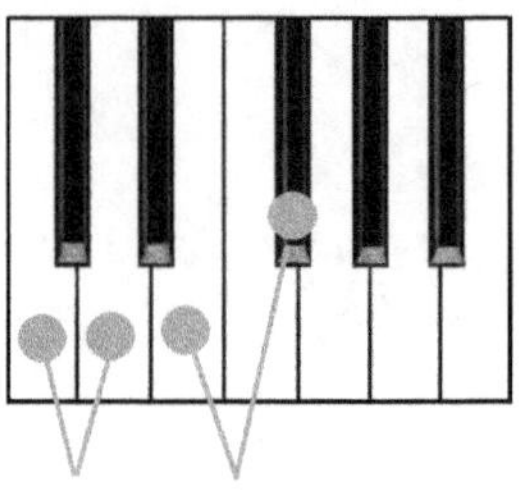

The notes we are using for the C-major position on the next page are the first five notes of the C-major scale.

Major Scale

A scale is a series of notes in a particular pattern of whole steps and half steps. The C-major scale consists of the following pattern of whole steps and half steps:

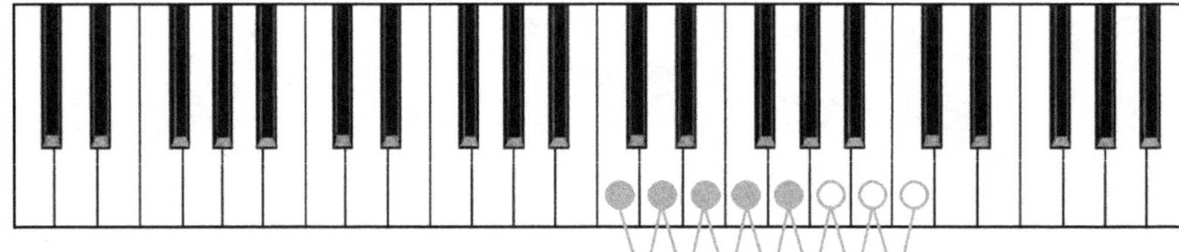

Whole Step | Whole Step | Half Step | Whole Step | Whole Step | Whole Step | Half Step

Major and minor scales that share the same notes are said to be related—A-minor is the relative minor of C-major.

The notes we are using for the A-minor position on the next page are the first five notes of the A-minor scale.

Minor Scale

Minor scales are related to major scales because they share the same notes but begin on a different note and follow their own sequence of whole steps and half steps. The A-minor scale consists of the following pattern of whole steps and half steps:

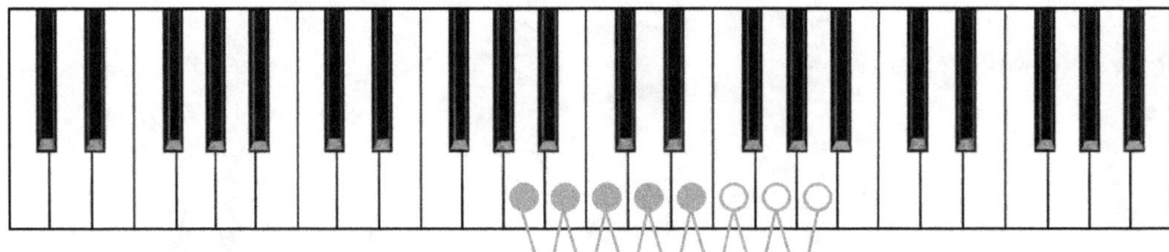

Whole Step | Half Step | Whole Step | Whole Step | Half Step | Whole Step | Whole Step

C-Major Position, Chord, and Warm-up

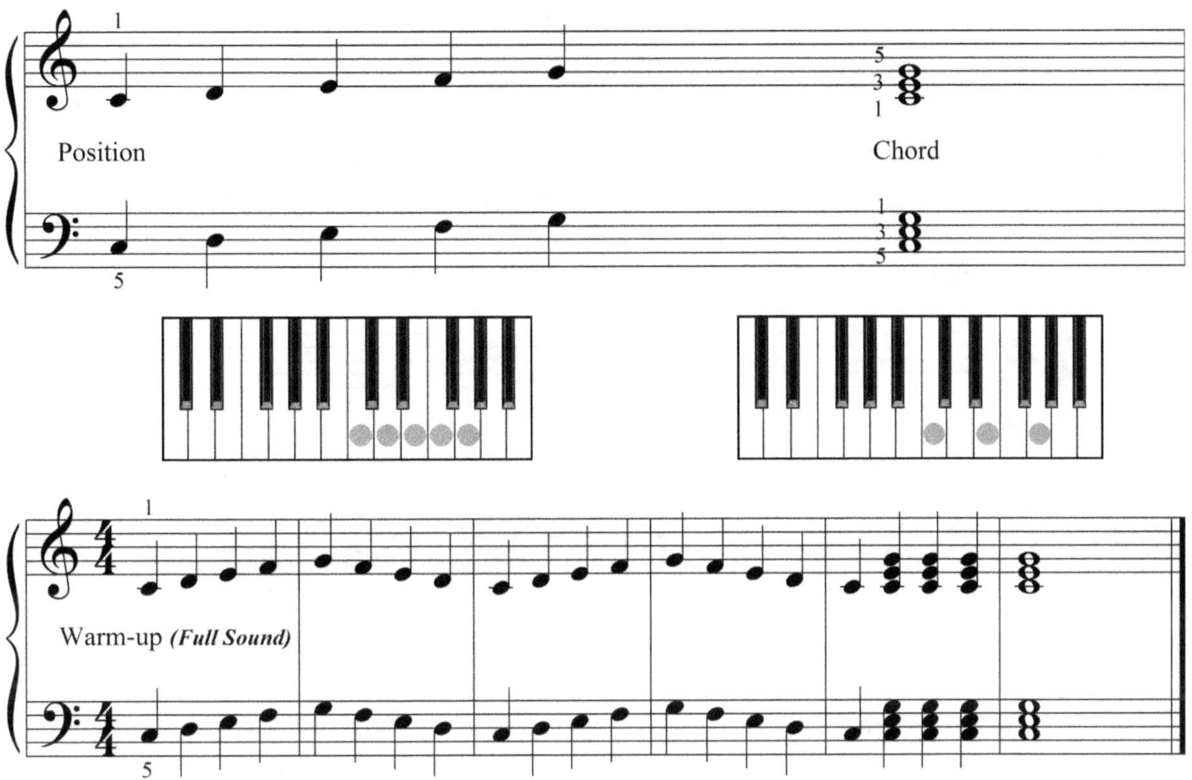

If needed, refer to Lesson Four for the exact key to play.

The small number close to a note indicates which finger to use.

A chord is a group of three or more notes that align vertically on the staff and are played at the same time.

Another way to say "in C-major position" is, "in the key of C major."

A-Minor Position, Chord, and Warm-up

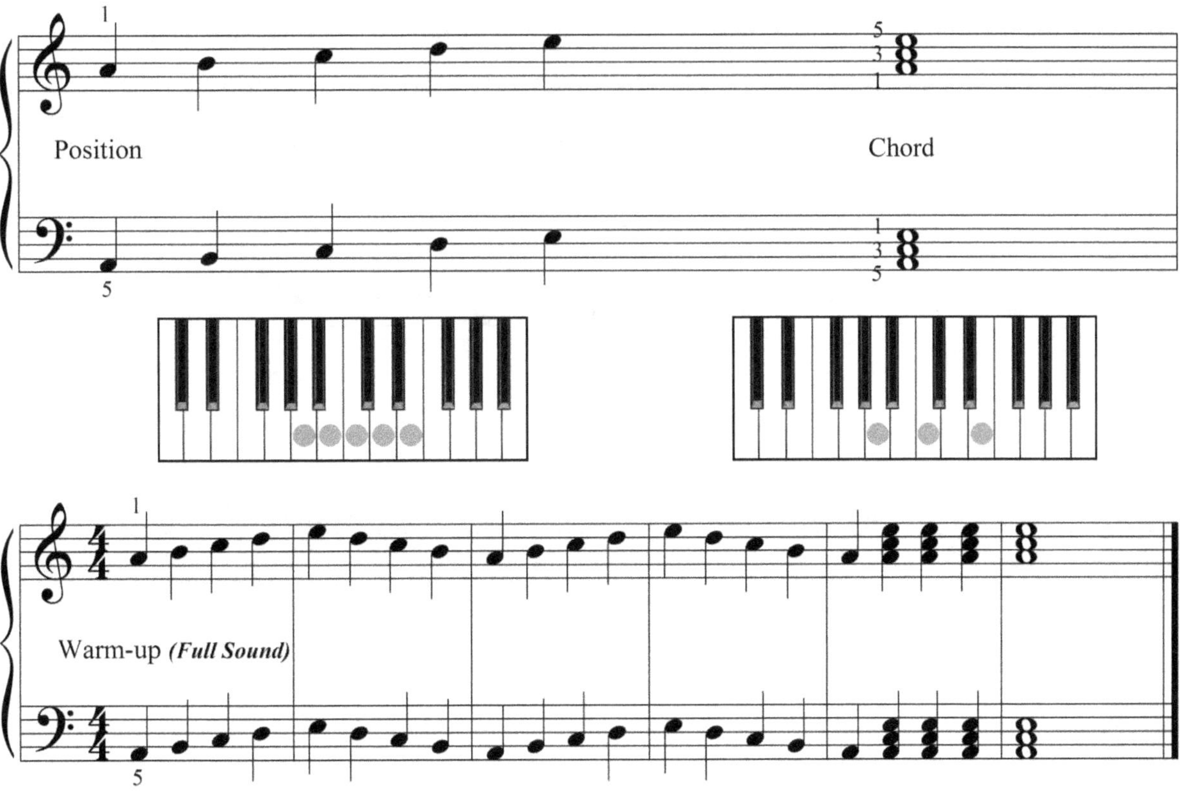

Another way to say in "A-minor position" is, "in the key of A minor."

Play the warm-ups with a full sound by pressing each key with one smooth motion all the way to the bottom of the keybed.

Lesson Six: C-Major Position

Practice Tip: Always practice each hand separately before playing both hands together.

Italian terms are used in music to give the performer instructions on how something should be played. One of these terms is *Andante*.

The term *Andante* indicates that the piece should be played at a walking speed. (♩ = 56-88)

Steps

Andante (♩ = 56-88)

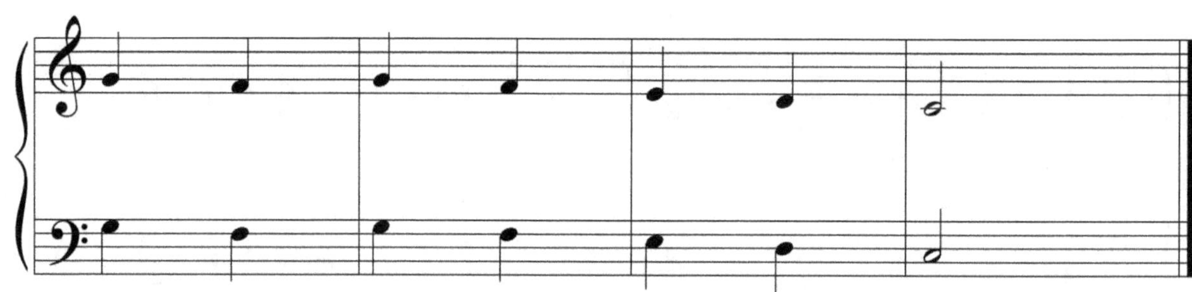

Skips

Andante (♩ = 56-88)

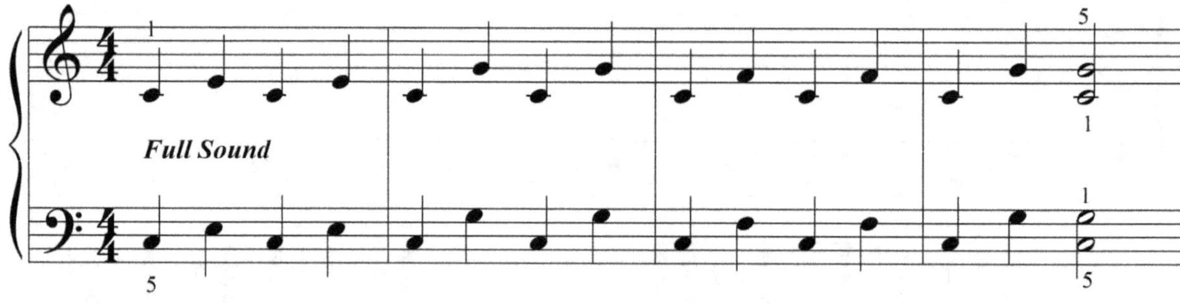

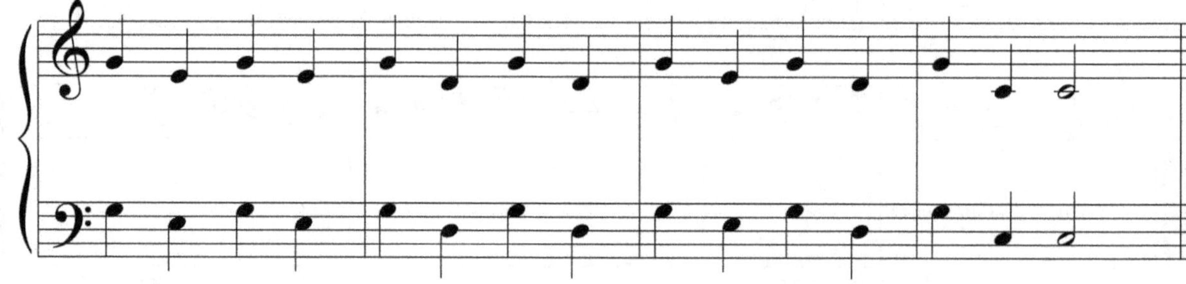

My title for this piece:

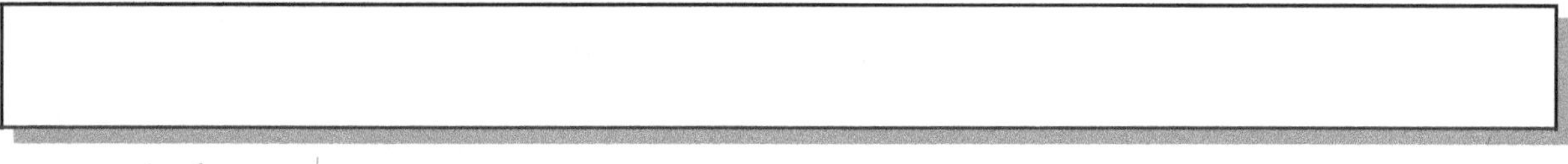

Performance Tip:
Think about your speed before you begin to play. Use a metronome if desired.

The four grand staffs in this piece can also be referred to as four lines of music.

Andante (♩ = 56-88)

Full Sound

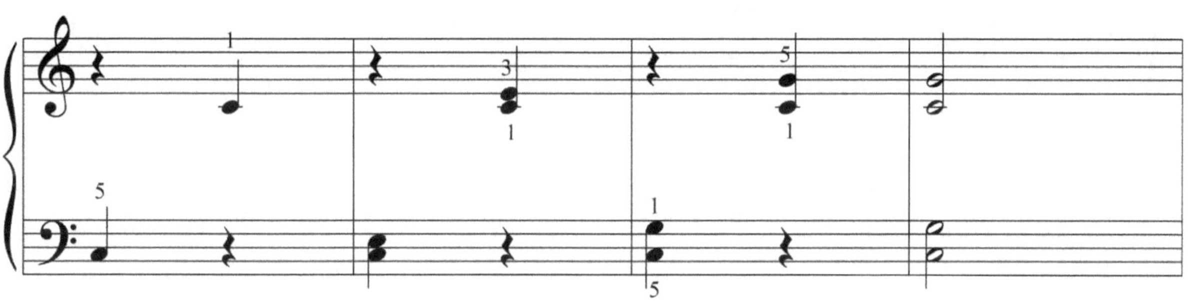

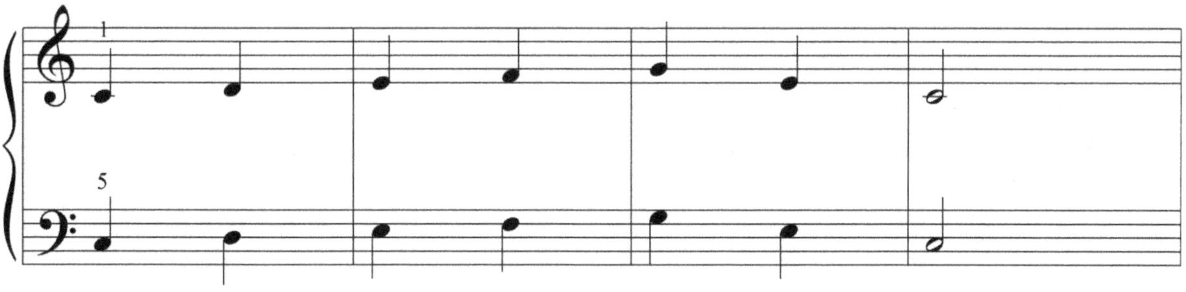

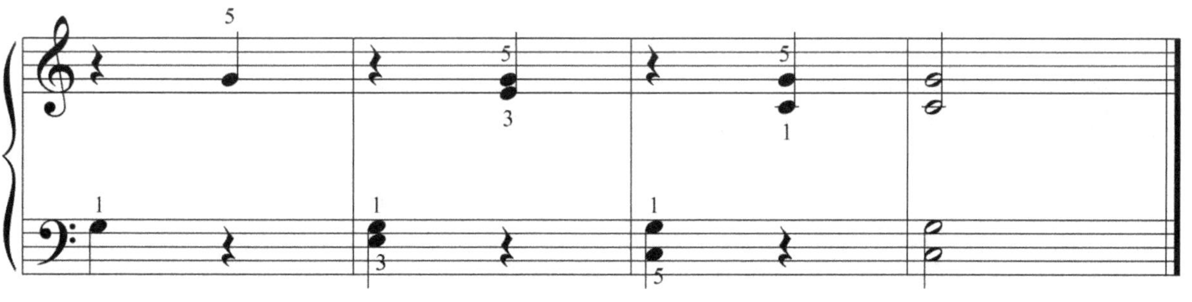

The term *Moderato* indicates that a piece or passage should be played at a moderate speed. (♩ = 88-126)

Practice each exercise with a full sound.

More Steps

More Skips

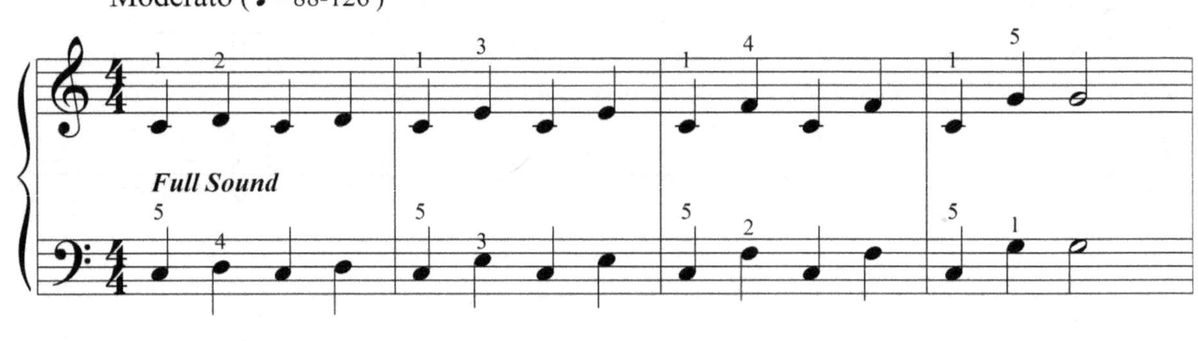

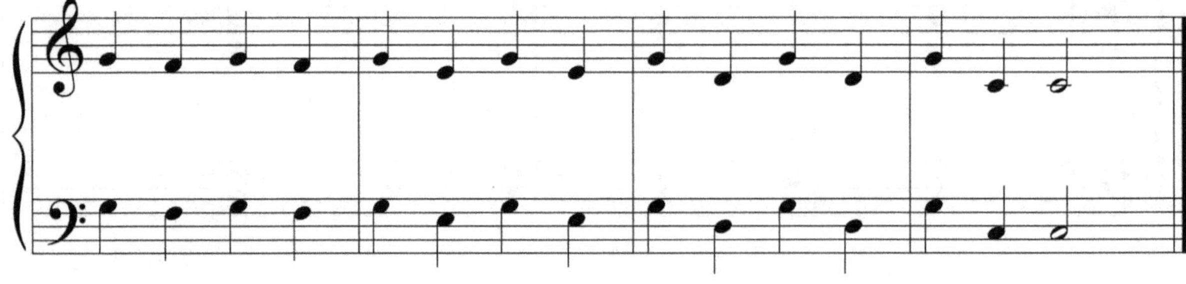

Harmony

Moderato (♩ = 88-126)

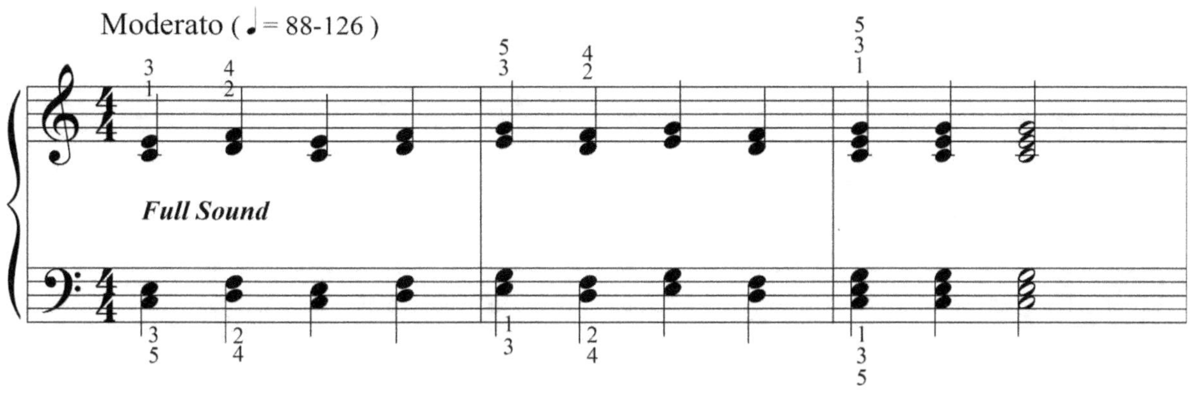

Harmony is the playing of different sounds at the same time.

Remember to always practice each hand separately before playing both hands together.

Leaps

Moderato (♩ = 88-126)

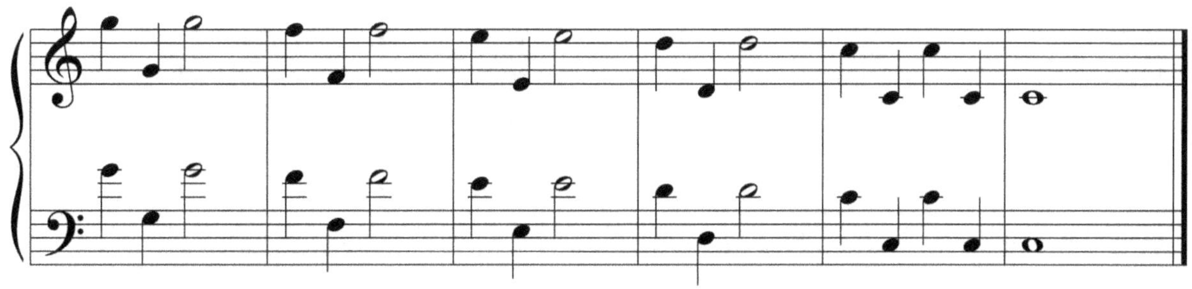

A leap is the movement of the hand from one position to another.

Don't be overwhelmed by all of the notes in this exercise. All of the notes in each measure have the same letter name. For example, in the first measure, every note is a C. In the second measure, every note is a D. And so forth through all five notes of the C-major position. All you have to do is leap up to the next key with the same name and back.

To "transpose" is to play the same piece of music in a different key.

The musical selections in the A-minor position are a transposition of the pieces in the C-major position.

Steps

Andante (♩ = 56-88)

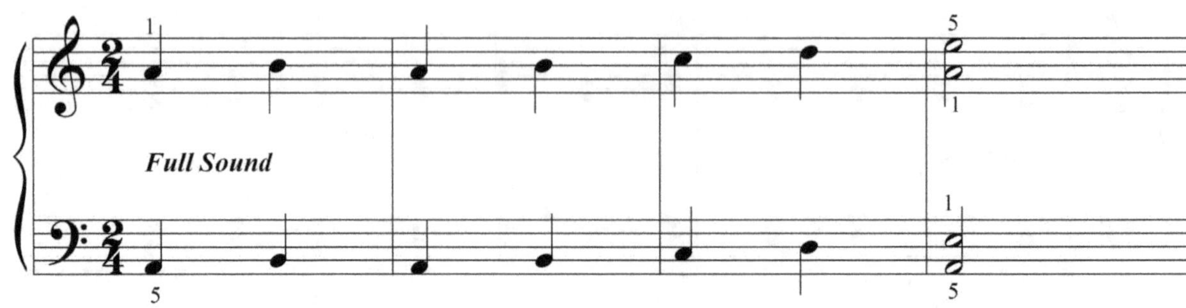

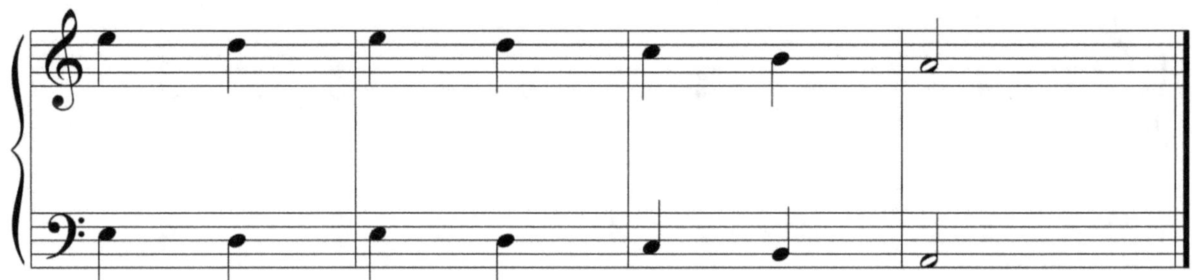

Skips

Andante (♩ = 56-88)

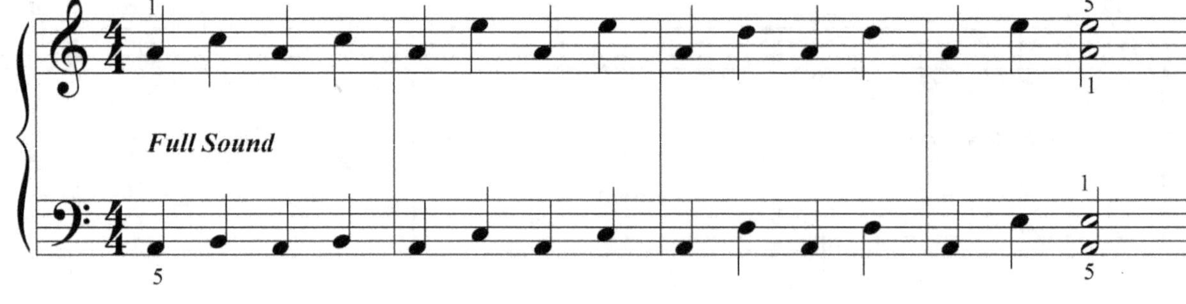

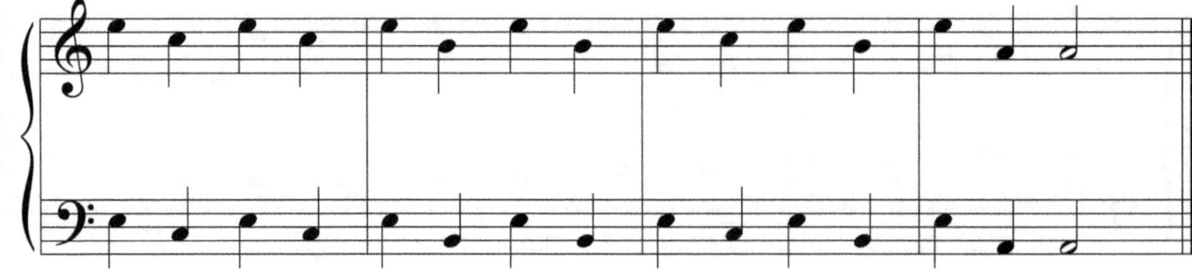

My title for this piece:

Andante (♩ = 56-88)

Full Sound

More Steps

Moderato (♩ = 88-126)

More Skips

Moderato (♩ = 88-126)

Harmony

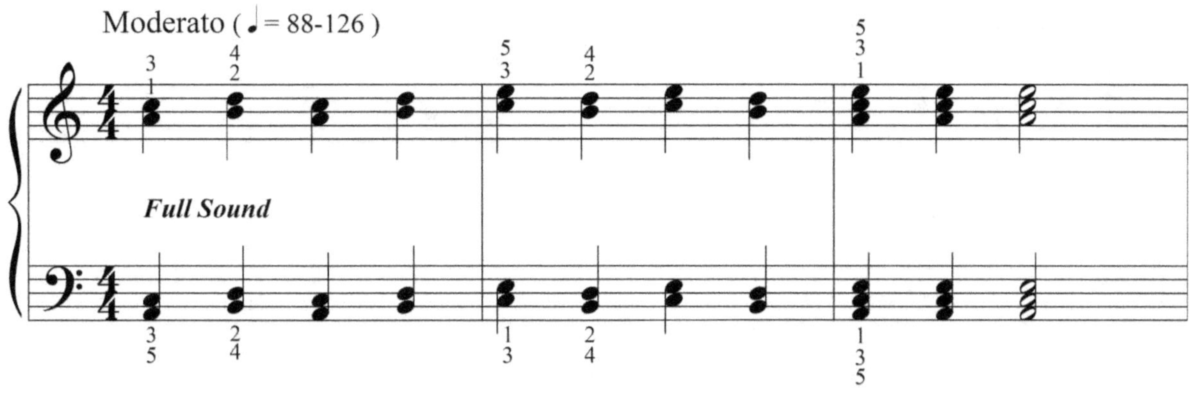

Remember to always practice each hand separately before playing both hands together.

Leaps

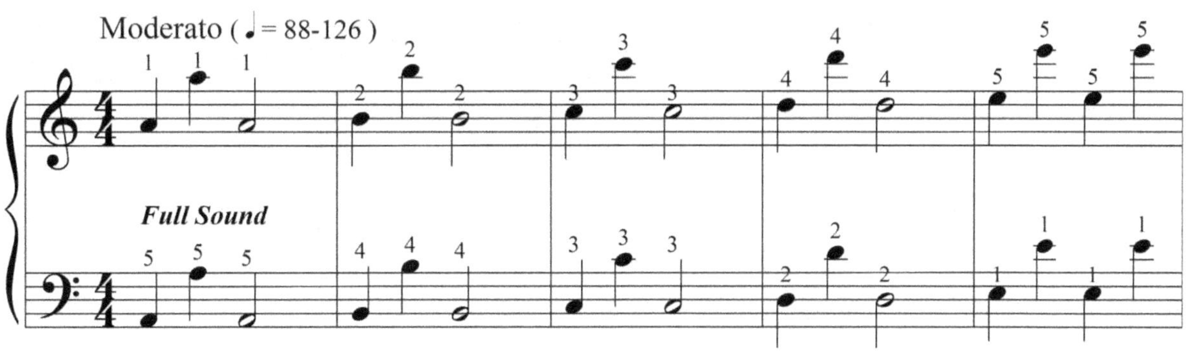

Don't be overwhelmed by all of the notes in this exercise. All of the notes in each measure have the same letter name. For example, in the first measure, every note is an A. In the second measure, every note is a B. And so forth through all five notes of the A-minor position. All you have to do is leap up to the next key with the same name and back.

Recital Piece No. 1

Moderato (♩ = 100)

Full Sound

The numbers in the squares show measure numbers. These are helpful when referring to specific places in the music.

17

21

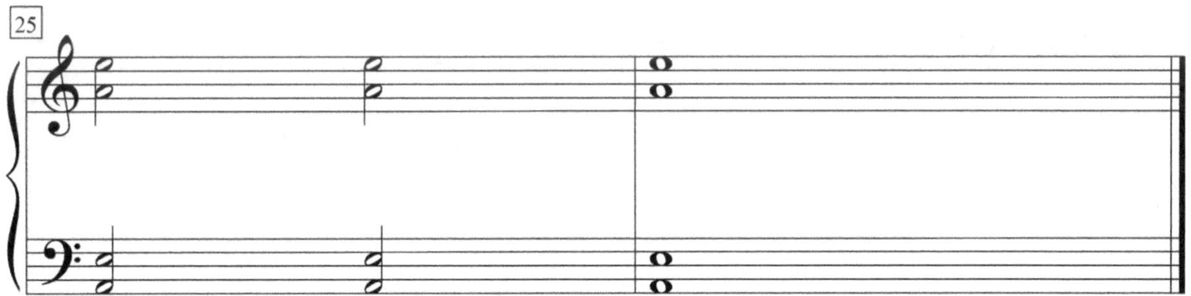
25

C-Major Position, Chord, and Warm-up

If needed, refer to page 43 to complete the exercise.

1. Draw the notes to the C-major position and chord, and label the keys.

2. Draw the time signature and notes to the C-major warm-up.

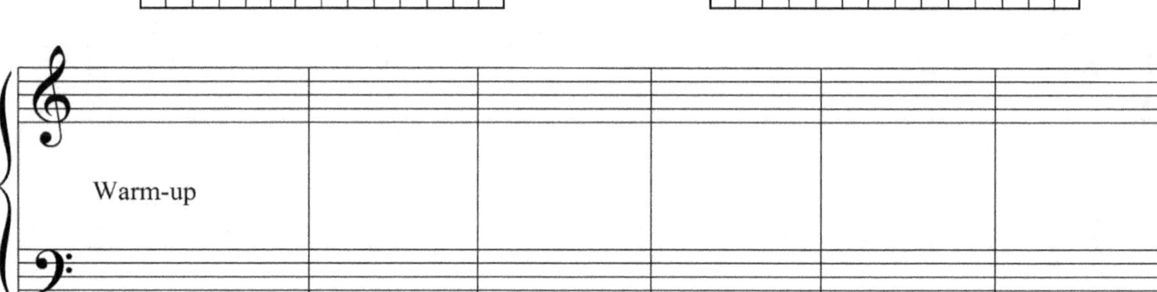

A-Minor Position, Chord, and Warm-up

3. Draw the notes to the A-minor position and chord, and label the keys.

4. Draw the time signature and notes to the A-minor warm-up.

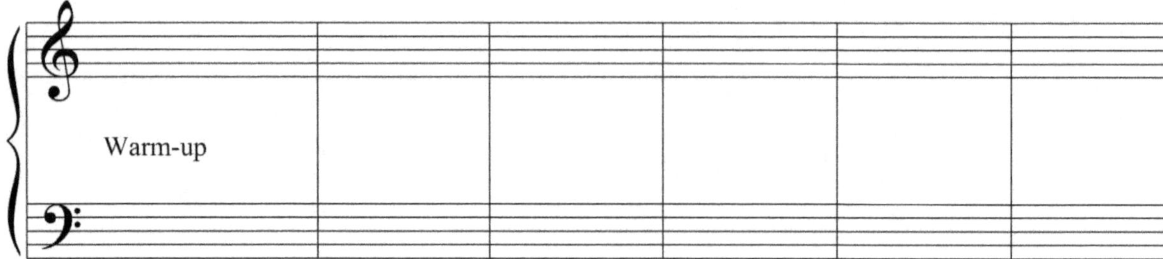

1. On the keyboard below draw a circle around the following:

- A whole step that goes from a black key to a white key
- A whole step that goes from a white key to a black key
- A whole step that goes from a black key to another black key
- A whole step that goes from a white key to another white key

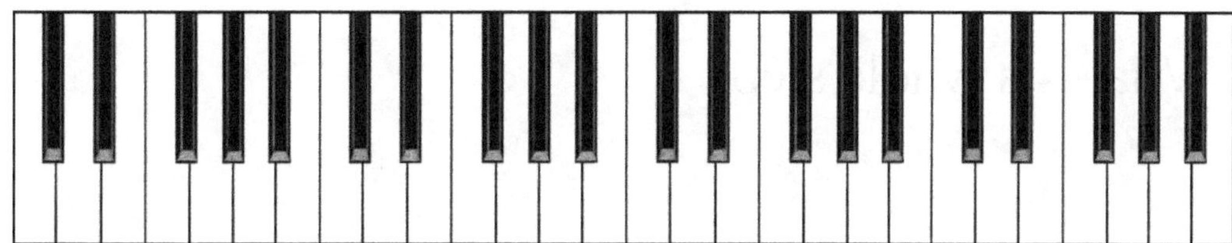

2. On the keyboard below draw a circle around the following:

- A half step that goes from a black key to a white key
- A half step that goes from a white key to a black key
- A half step that goes from a white key to another white key

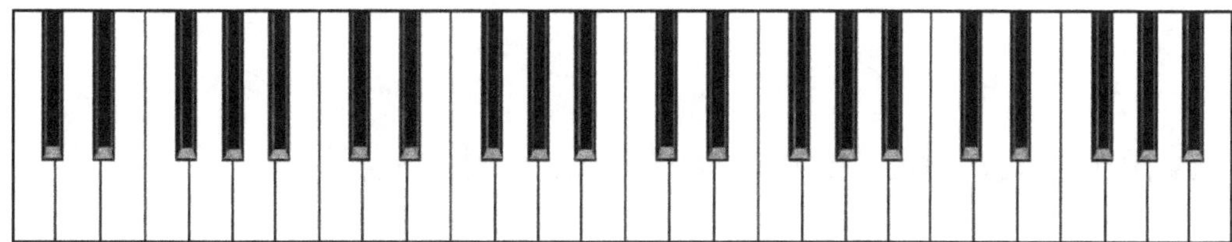

Review

1. What is a chord?

2. What is a whole step?

3. What is a half step?

4. What is a scale?

5. What does the term *Andante* indicate?

Lesson Seven

G Major / E Minor

Lesson Seven: Musical Concepts

Eighth notes may be grouped together using a bar instead of individual flags.

Note: Be sure to count as you clap and tap,

Eighth Notes and Rests

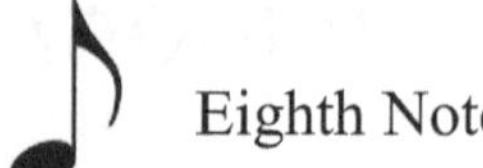

Eighth Rest

One eighth note (♪) is equal to half the value of a quarter note (♩).

One eighth rest (𝄾) is equal to half the value of a quarter rest (𝄽).

One quarter note = two eighth notes ♩ = ♪♪ or ♫

One quarter rest = two eighth rests 𝄽 = 𝄾𝄾

Clap the top line while tapping the bottom line with your foot.

Staccato

An Italian term used to describe sounds that are detached from each other. The symbol used to indicate this is a dot over or under a note. This is accomplished by pressing a key and releasing it immediately after it is played thus playing the note shorter than its given value.

Legato

An Italian term used to describe sounds that are connected to each other. The symbol used to indicate this is a curved line over or below two or more notes. This is accomplished by pressing a key, holding it, pressing another key, holding it and releasing the first key. There should be no silence between them.

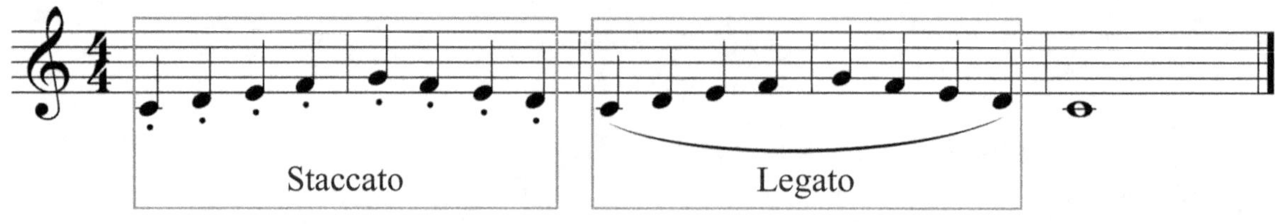

Lesson Four review:

♯ — An instruction to play the given note a half step higher.

Key Signature

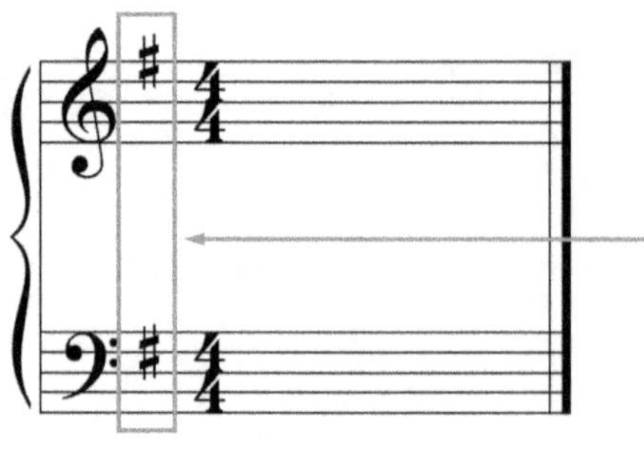

A key signature is a convenient way to let you know which notes will be altered throughout the piece. In this case, every time an F appears, an F-sharp should be played.

G-Major Position, Chord, and Warm-up

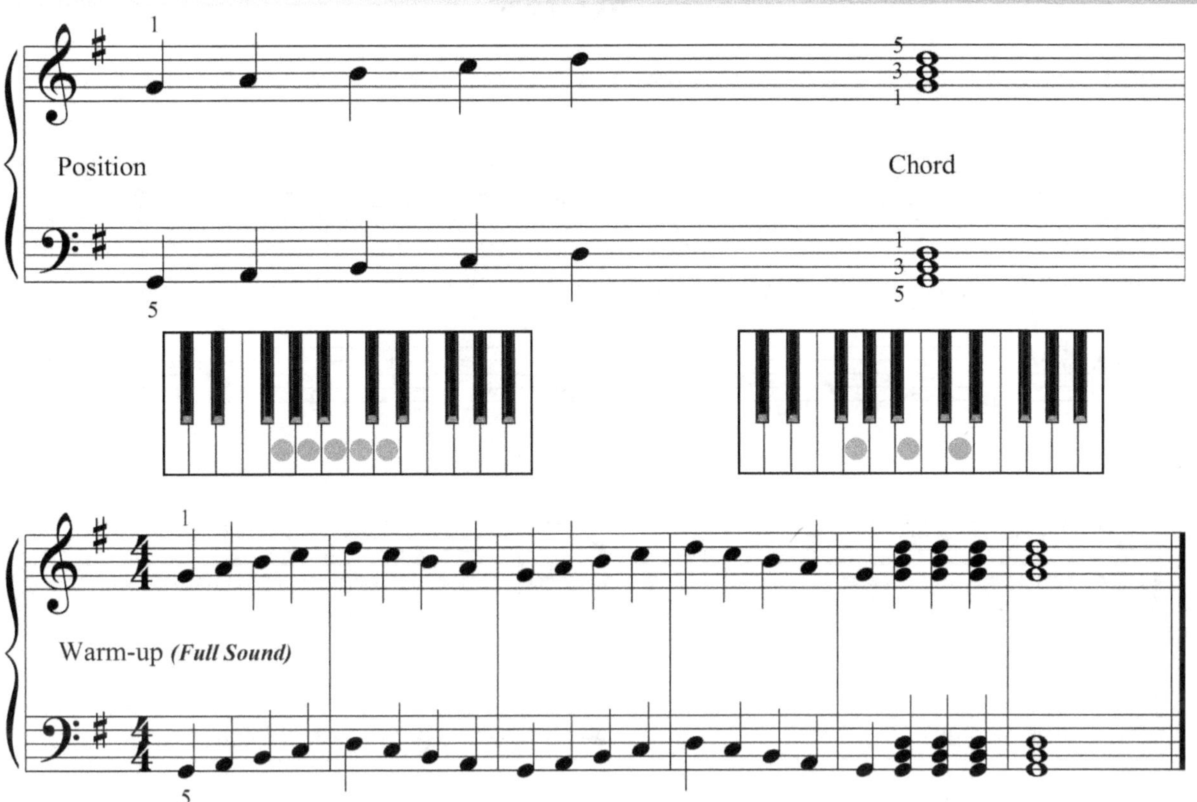

If needed, refer to Lesson Four for the exact key to play.

While there are no Fs in the G-major position, it is appropriate to have the sharps in the key signature, because the G-major scale does have an F-sharp.

Another way to say "in G-major position" is, "in the key of G major."

E-Minor Position, Chord, and Warm-up

Another way to say in "E-minor position" is, "in the key of E minor."

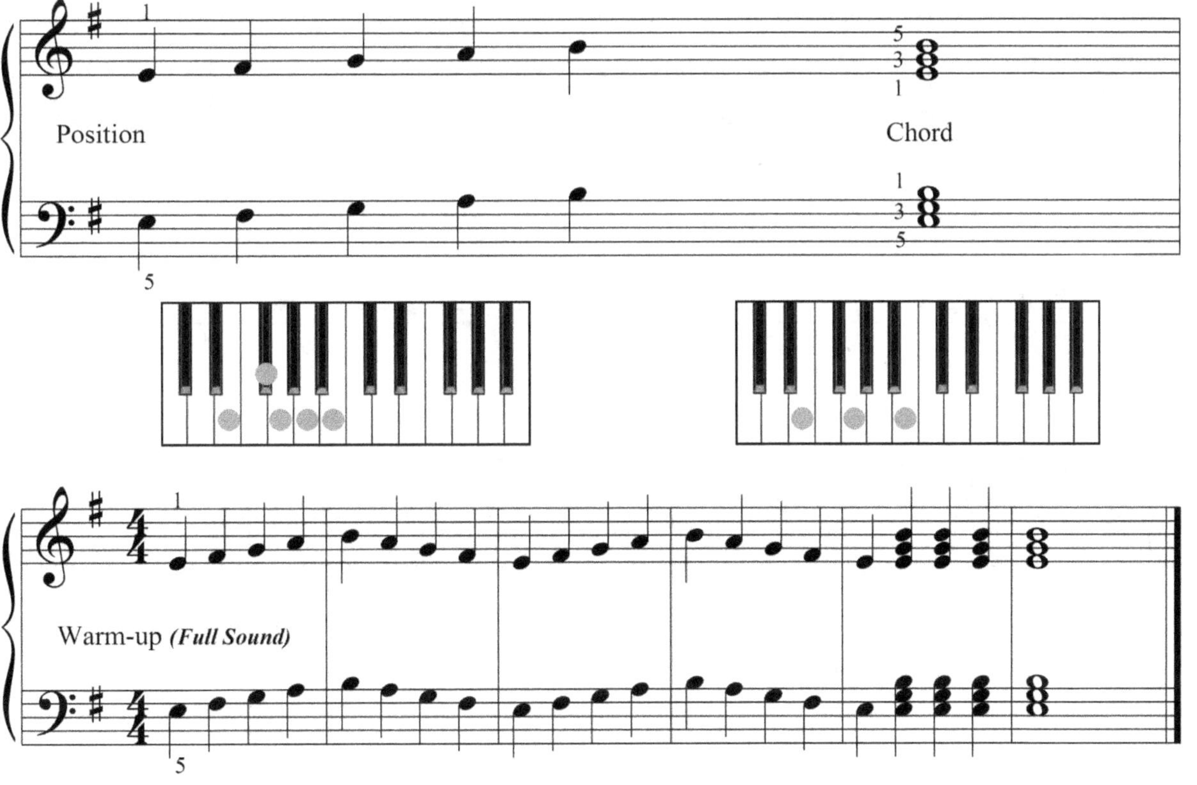

Note that the key signature is the same for G major and E minor.

Play "Steps" using a loud or soft sound throughout.

Loud Sound: slightly more sound than full sound.

Soft Sound: slightly less sound than full sound.

Loud and soft sounds are achieved by varying the amount of force used to strike the key—more force for more sound and less force for less sound.

Don't forget to relax the finger after striking the key—applying pressure on the key after producing the sound has no effect.

Steps

Skips

My title for this piece:

Allegro (♩ = 84-144)

Soft

Loud

Soft

Loud

Allegro indicates that a piece or passage should be played at a fast speed or *tempo*.

Tempo is an Italian word related to how fast a composition is to be played. The *tempo* marking for this piece is *Allegro*.

Practice each exercise using a *legato* touch with a loud or soft sound followed by a *staccato* touch with a loud or soft sound.

More Steps

More Skips

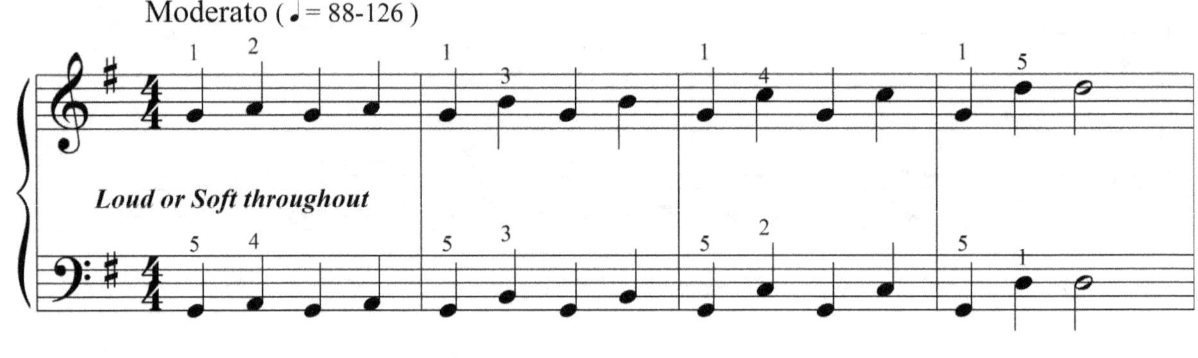

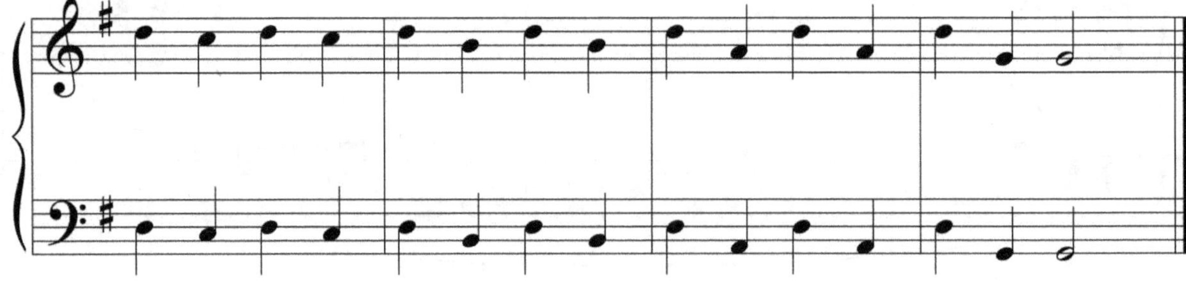

Harmony

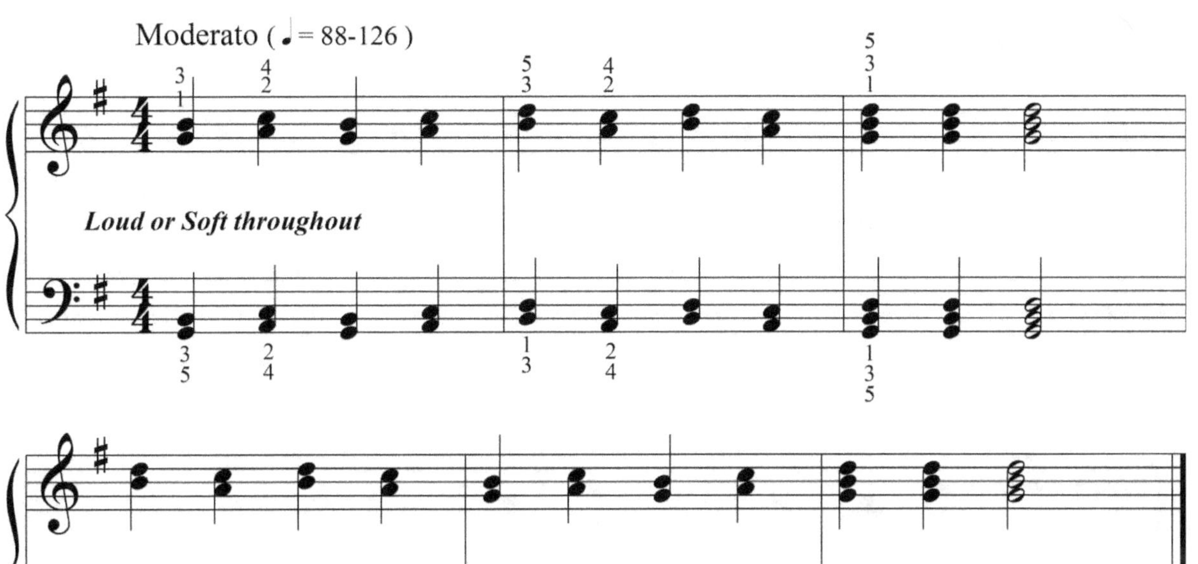

Leaps

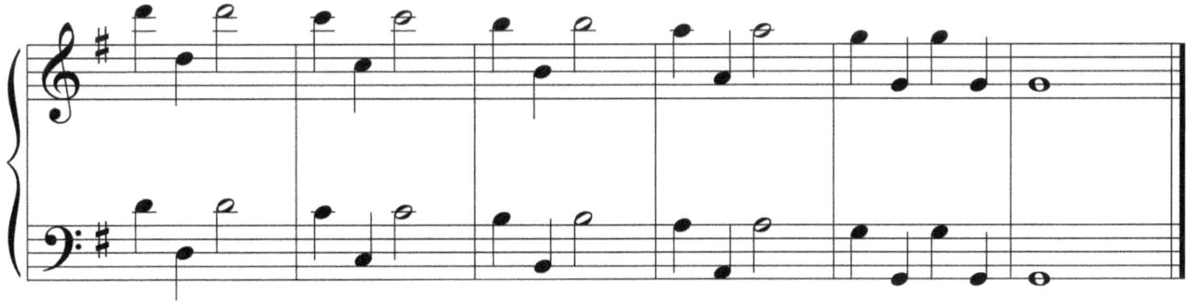

Steps

Moderato (♩ = 88-126)

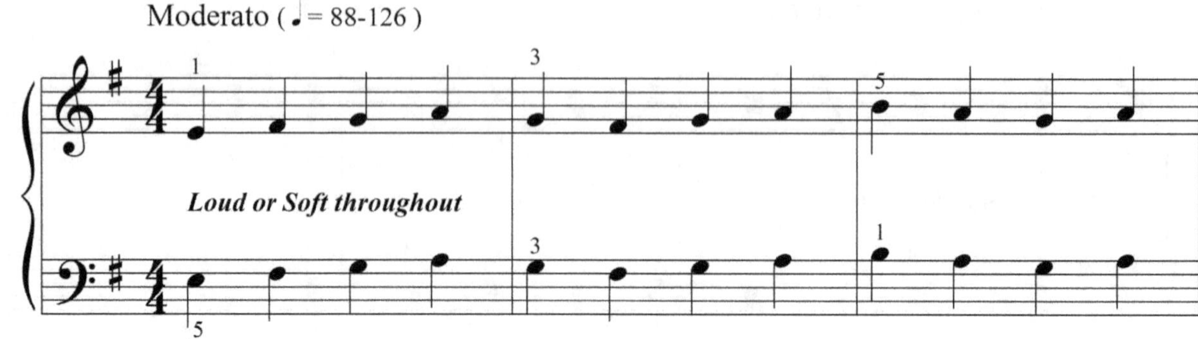

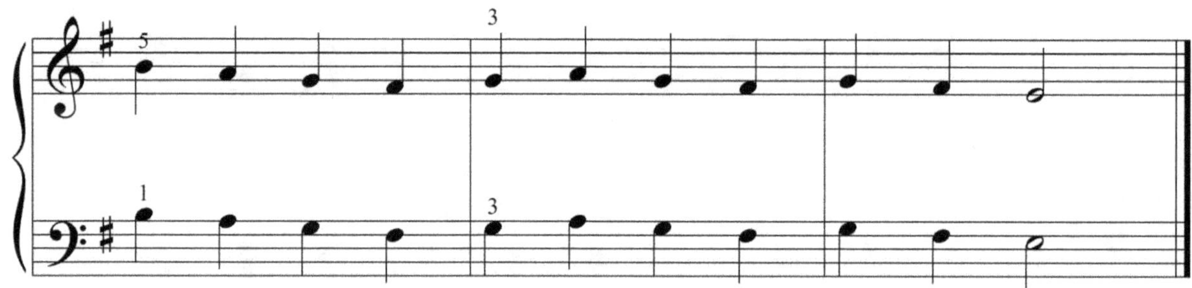

Skips

Moderato (♩ = 88-126)

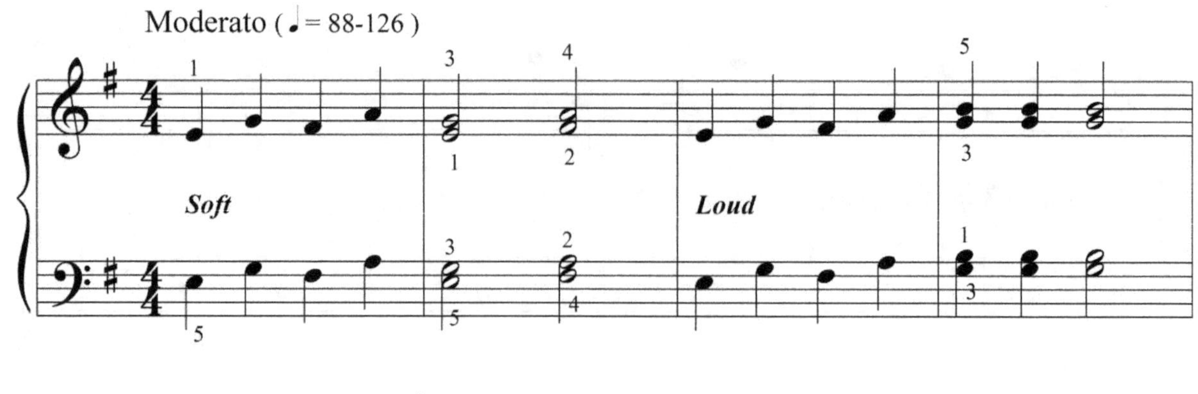

My title for this piece:

Allegro (♩ = 84-144)

Soft

Loud

Soft

Loud

Practice each exercise using a *legato* touch with a loud or soft sound followed by a *staccato* touch with a loud or soft sound.

More Steps

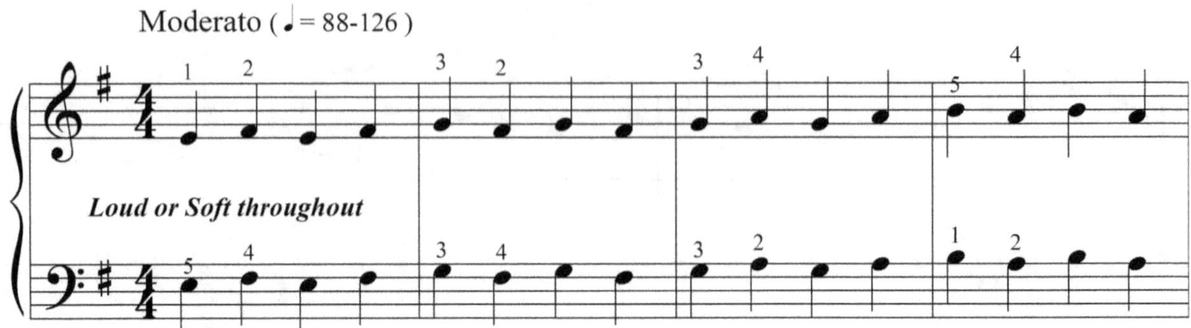

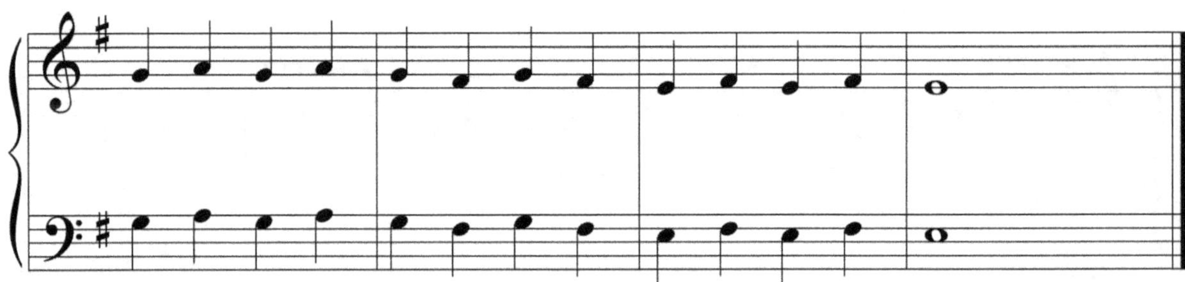

More Skips

Harmony

Moderato (♩ = 88-126)

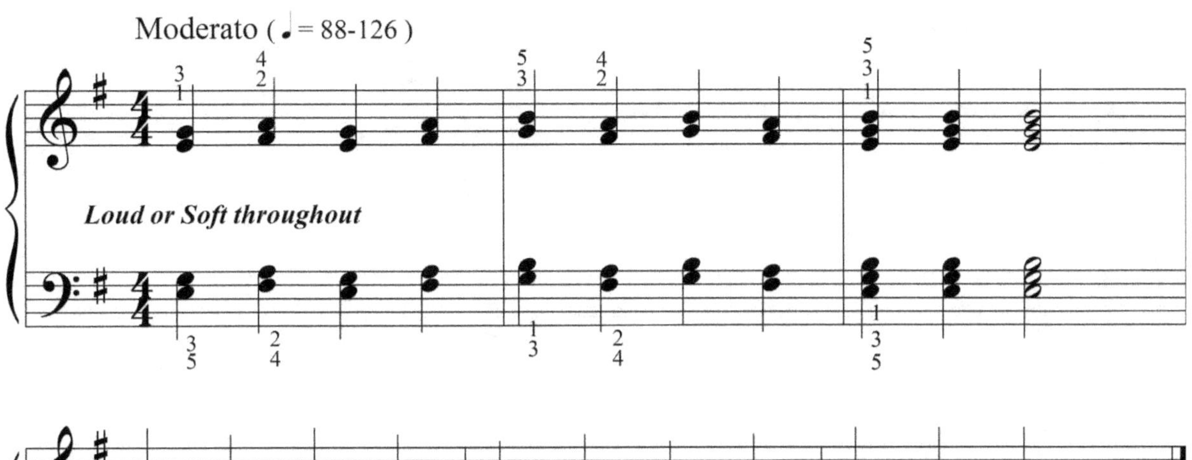

Leaps

Moderato (♩ = 88-126)

Recital Piece No. 2

Moderato (♩= 100)

17
21

25
Loud

G-Major Position, Chord, and Warm-up

If needed, refer to page 59 to complete the exercise.

1. Draw key signature and the notes to the G-major position and chord, and label the keys.

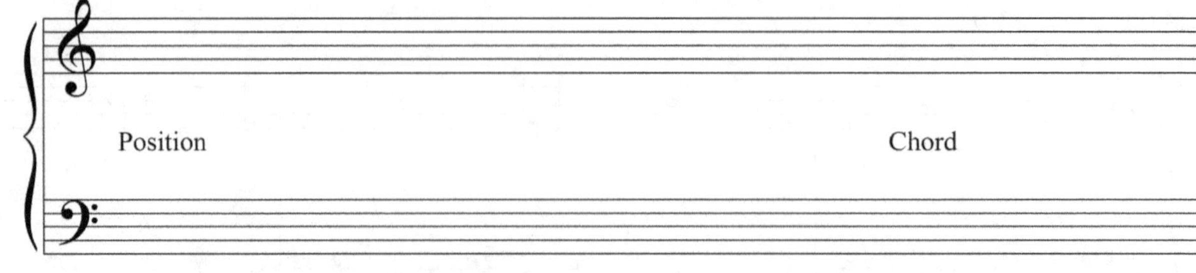

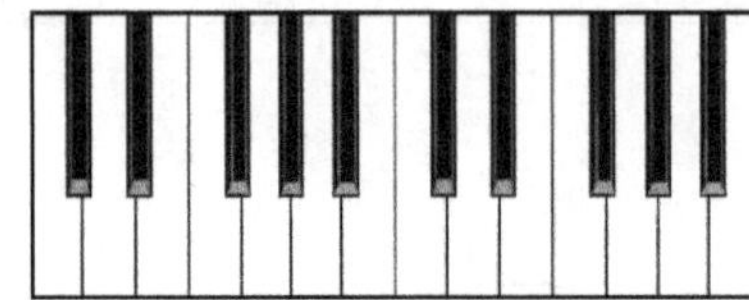

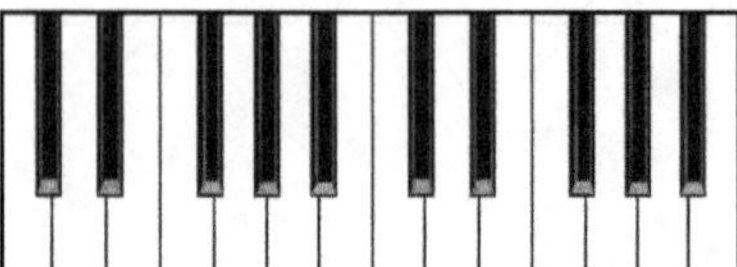

2. Draw the key signature, time signature, and notes to the G-major warm-up.

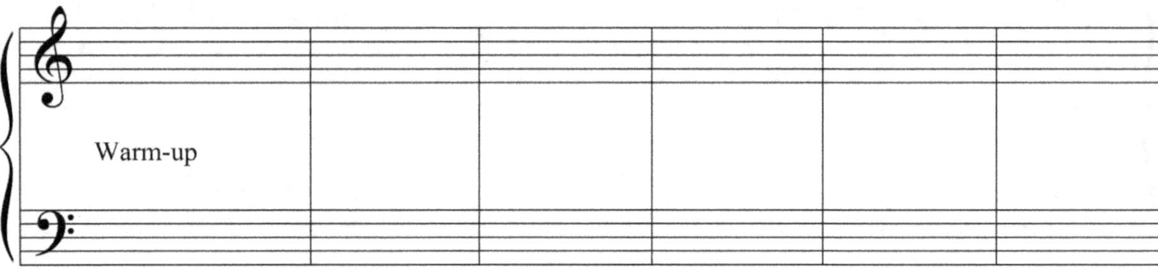

E-Minor Position, Chord, and Warm-up

3. Draw the key signature and notes to the E-minor position and chord, and label the keys.

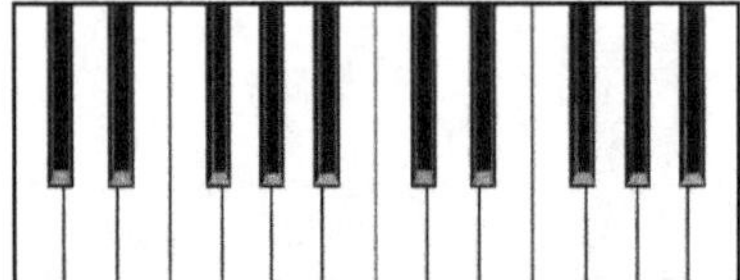

4. Draw the key signature, time signature, and notes to the E-minor warm-up.

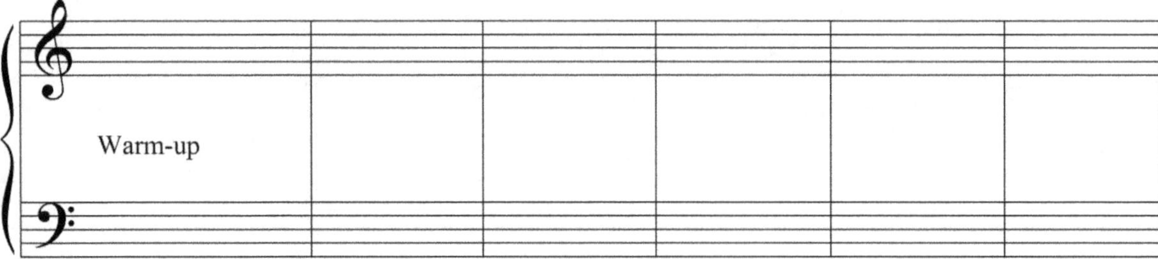

1. Draw eighth notes (♪) as necessary to complete the measures.

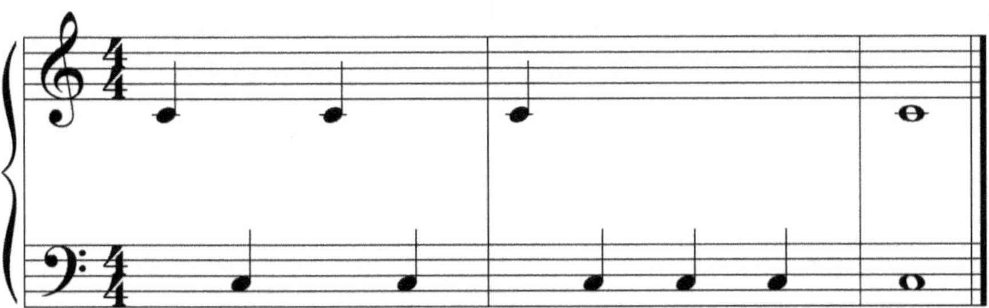

2. Add staccato symbols to measures one and two.
3. Add legato symbols to measures three and four.

4. Name the part of the staff.

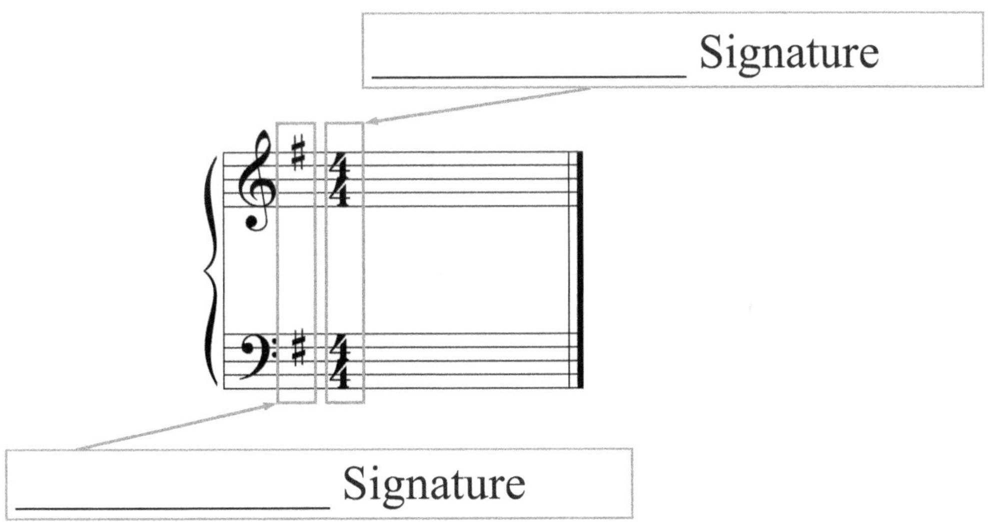

Review

1. What do the terms *Allegro* and *Moderato* mean?

2. What do the terms *Staccato* and *Legato* mean?

3. What is a key signature?

4. How many eighth notes equal the note on the left?

𝅘𝅥 = ___ eighth notes

𝅗𝅥 = ___ eighth notes

𝅝 = ___ eighth notes

Lesson Eight

D Major / B Minor

Lesson Eight: Musical Concepts

Ledger Lines

Ledger lines are shorthand for the continuation of lines above and below a staff.

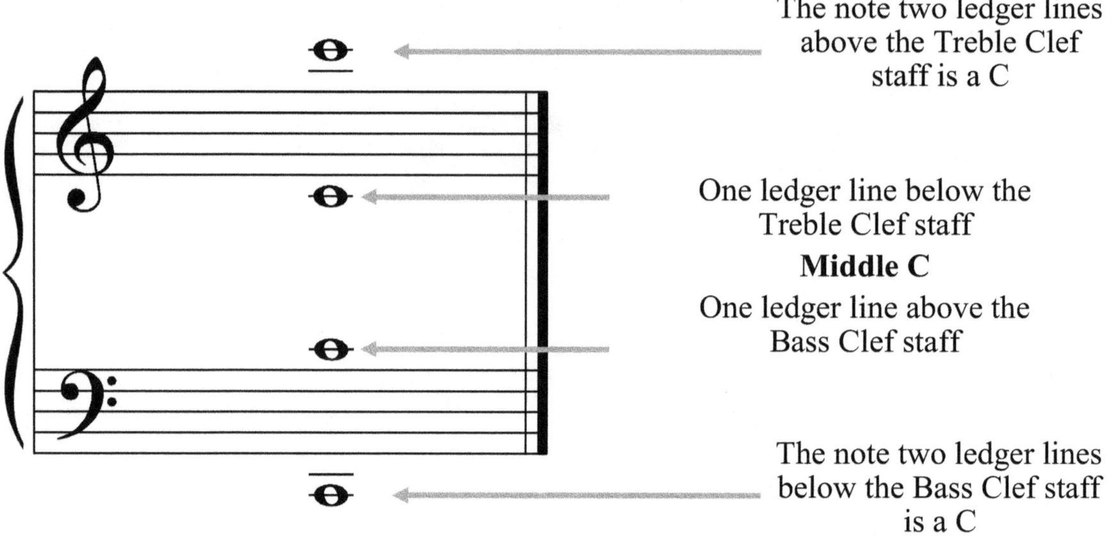

Incomplete Measure

A partial measure found at the beginning of a piece. The rhythmic remainder of the measure is usually found at the end of the piece.

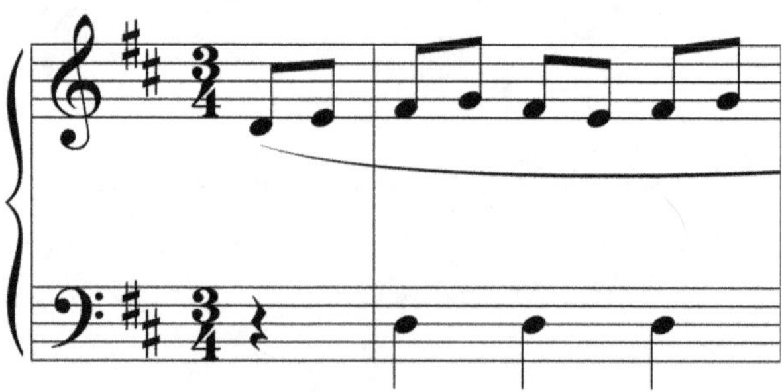

Note: The two notes (D and E) before the first full measure are sometimes referred to as "anacrusis" or "pickup notes".

Notice the time signature in the example above. There are three beats to a measure and the quarter-note gets one beat. The first note begins on beat three.

D-Major Position, Chord, and Warm-up

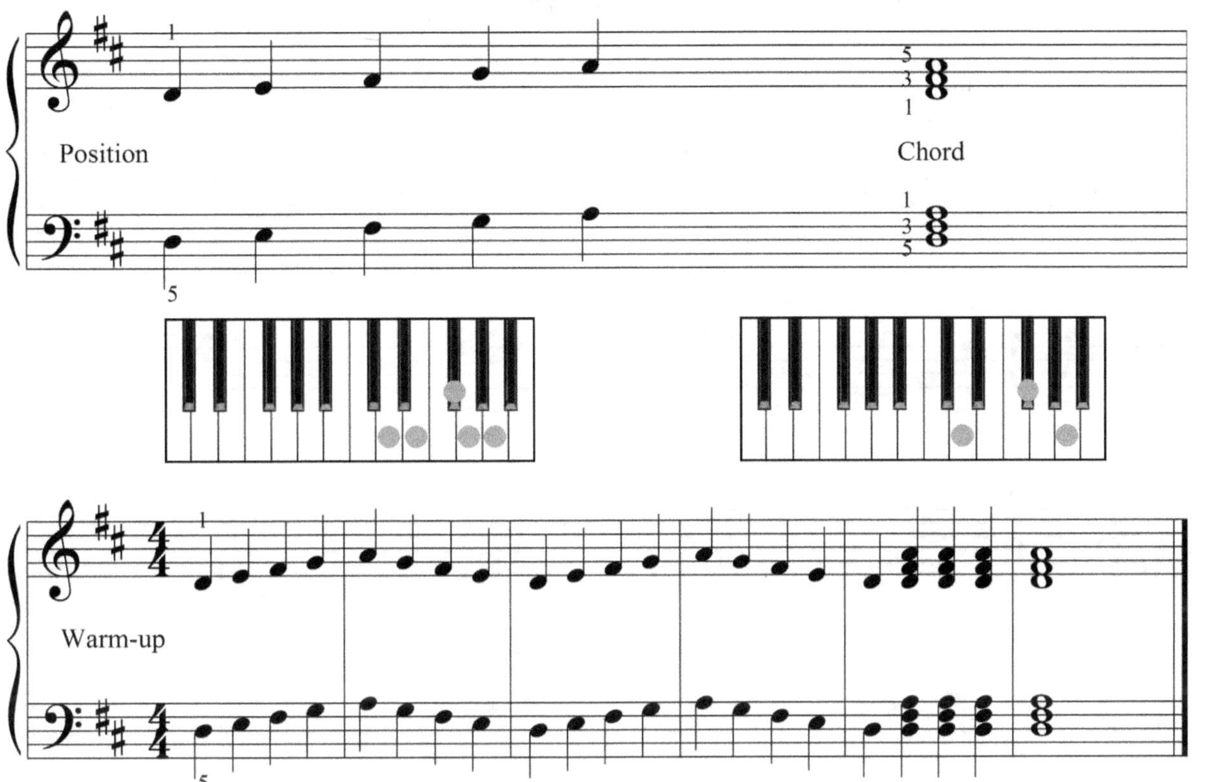

If needed, refer to Lesson Four for the exact key to play.

Another way to say "in D-major position" is, "in the key of D major."

Another way to say in "B-minor position" is, "in the key of B minor."

B-Minor Position, Chord, and Warm-up

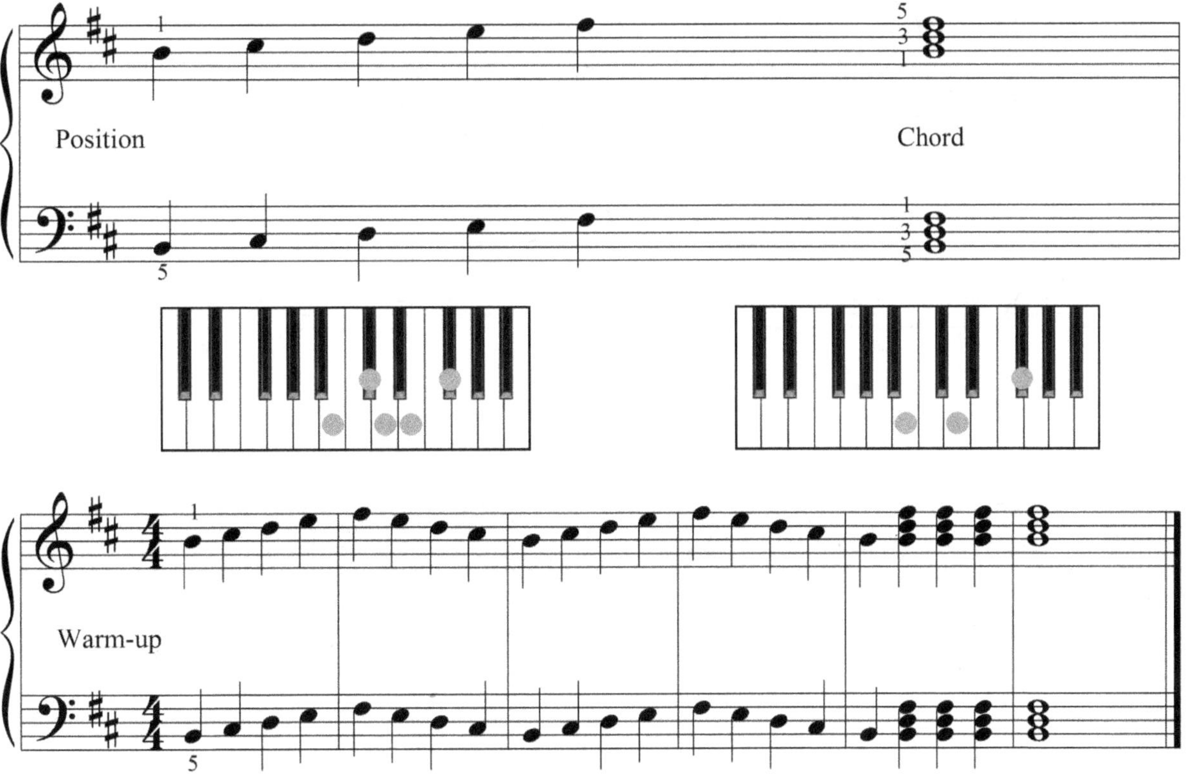

Steps

Moderato (♩ = 88-126)

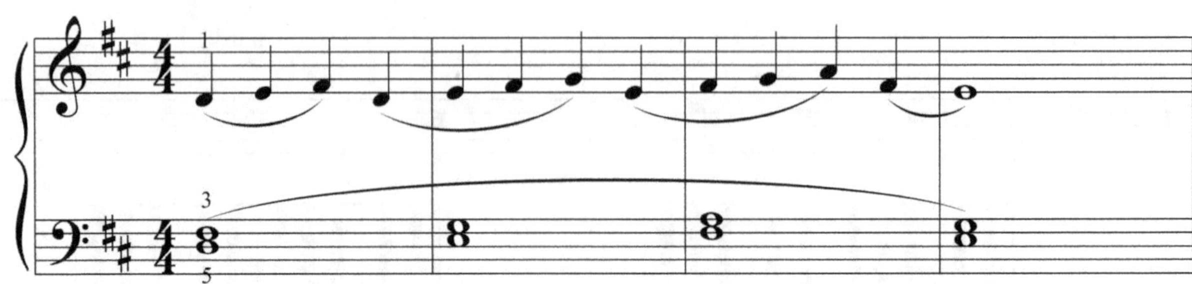

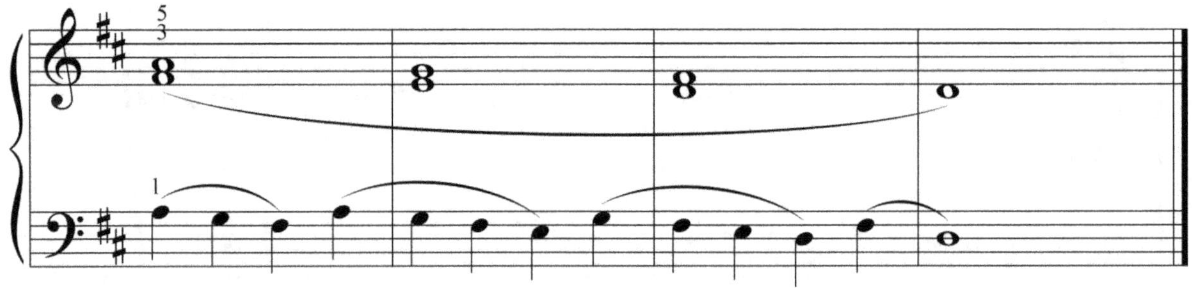

Skips

Moderato (♩ = 88-126)

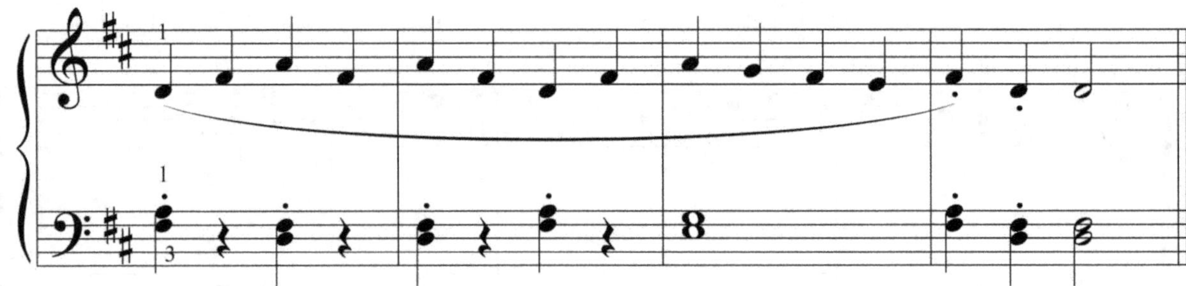

My title for this piece:

Andante (♩ = 66-88)

More Steps

Moderato (♩ = 88-126)

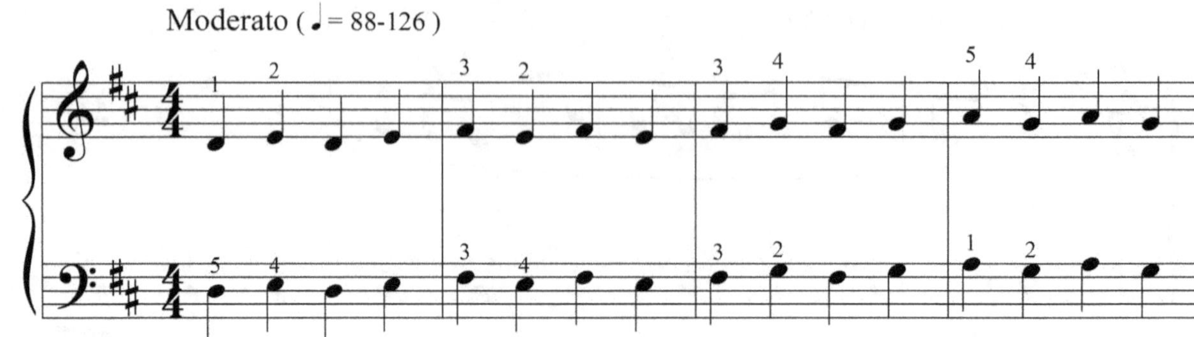

More Skips

Moderato (♩ = 88-126)

Harmony

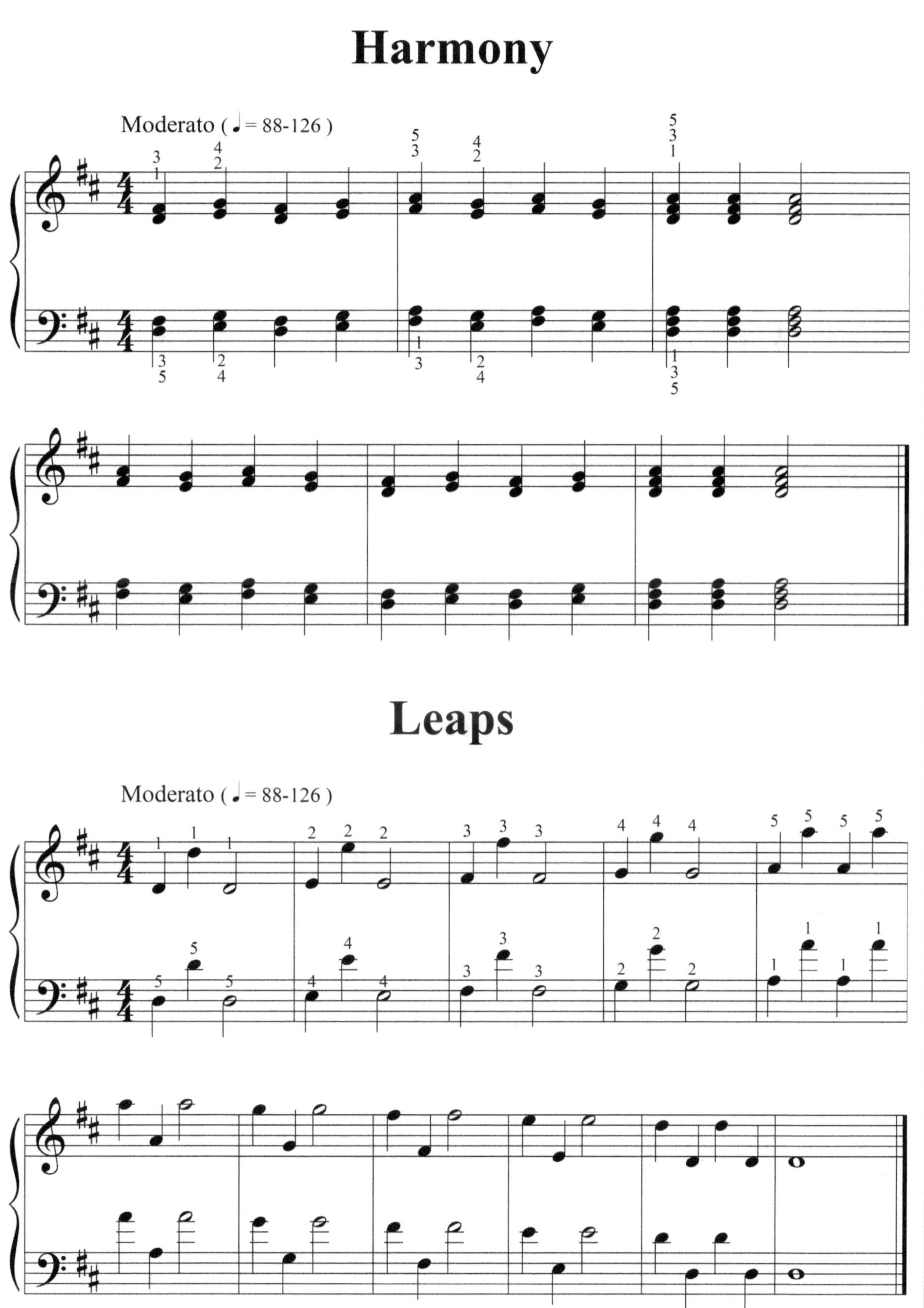

Steps

Moderato (♩ = 88-126)

Skips

Moderato (♩ = 88-126)

My title for this piece:

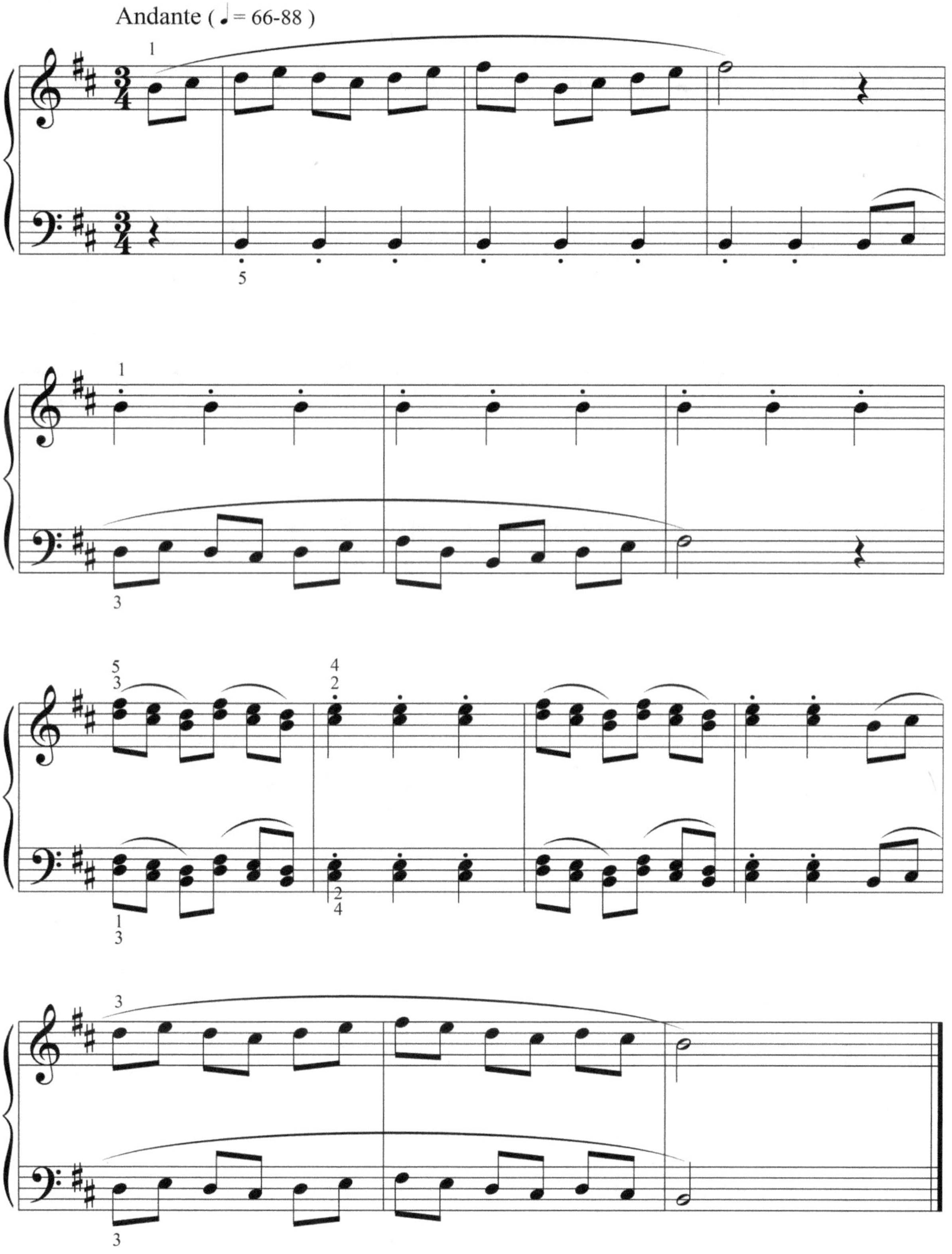

Andante (♩ = 66-88)

More Steps

Moderato (♩ = 88-126)

More Skips

Moderato (♩ = 88-126)

Harmony

Recital Piece No. 3

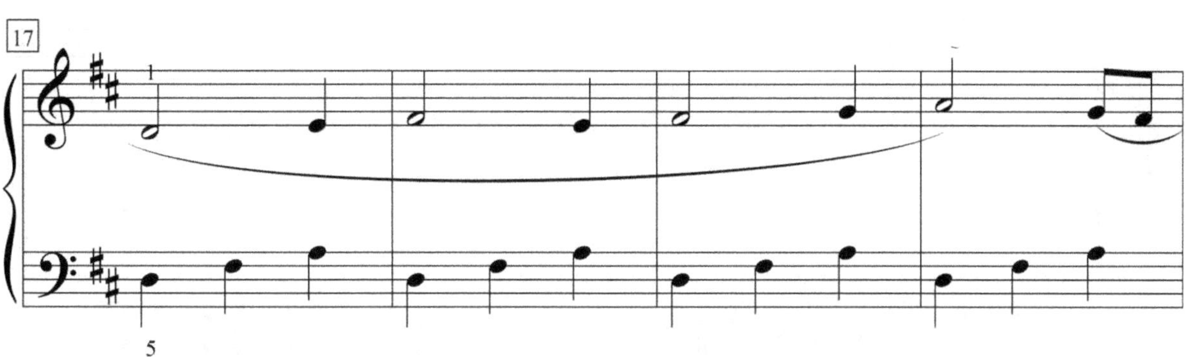
17
1
5

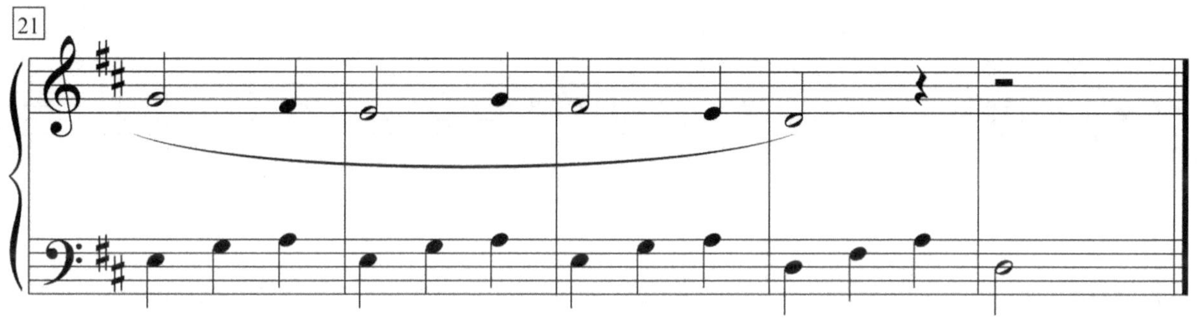
21

D-Major Position, Chord, and Warm-up

If needed, refer to page 75 to complete the exercise.

1. Draw the notes to the D-major position and chord, and label the keys.

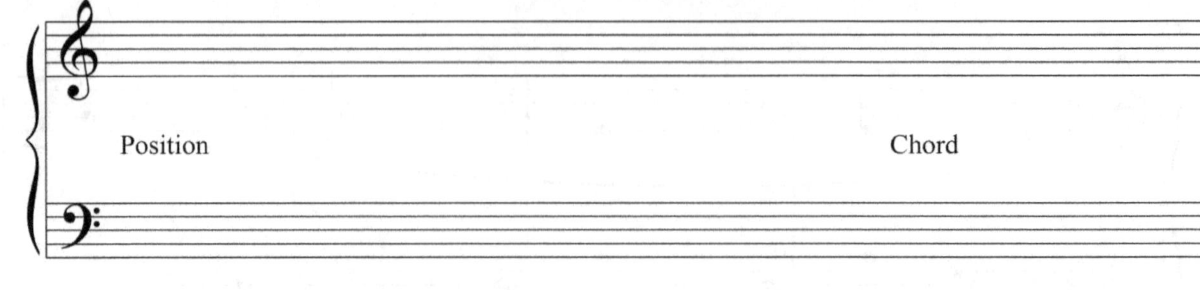

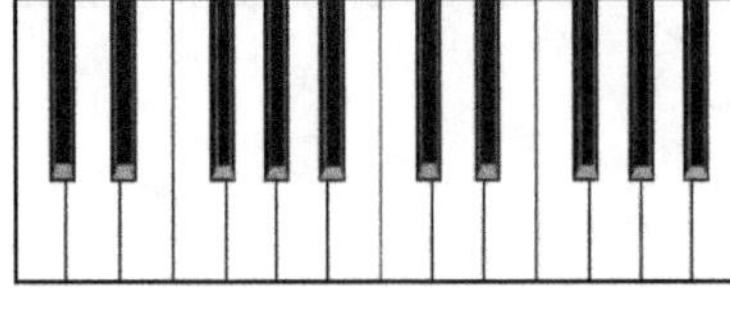

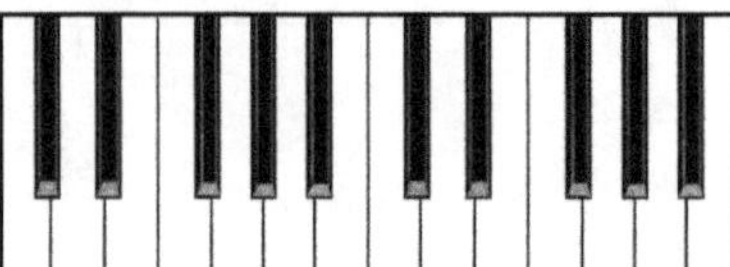

2. Draw the notes to the D-major warm-up.

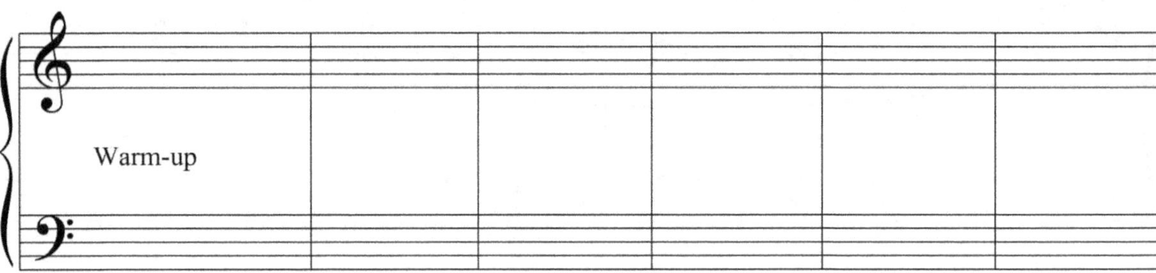

B-Minor Position, Chord, and Warm-up

3. Draw the notes to the B-minor position and chord, and label the keys.

Position

Chord

4. Draw the notes to the B-minor warm-up.

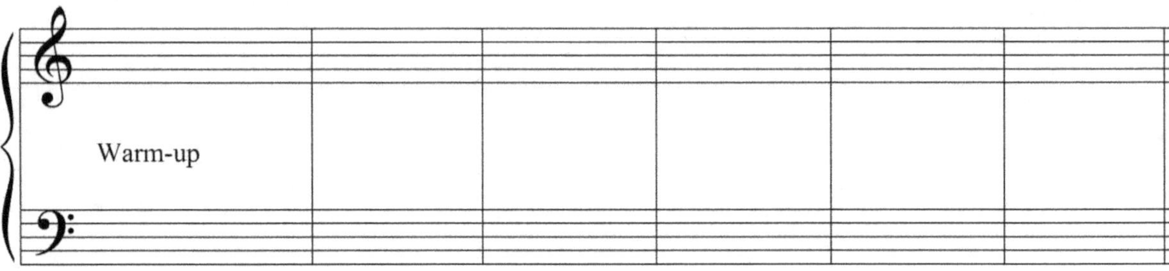

1. Beginning with the C in the third space, draw the notes to the C-major scale up to two lines above the Treble Clef. Add ledger lines as needed.

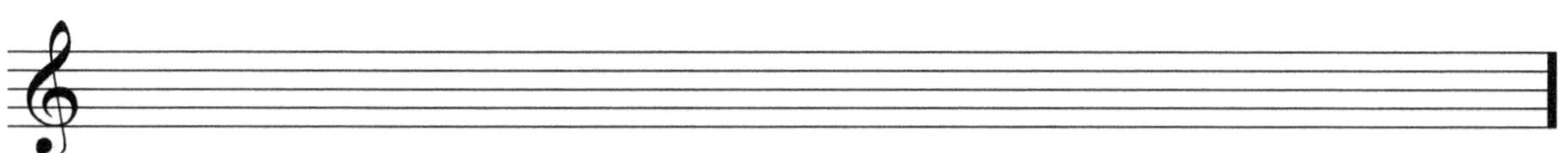

2. Beginning with the C in the second space, draw the notes to the C-major scale down to two lines below the Bass Clef. Add ledger lines as needed.

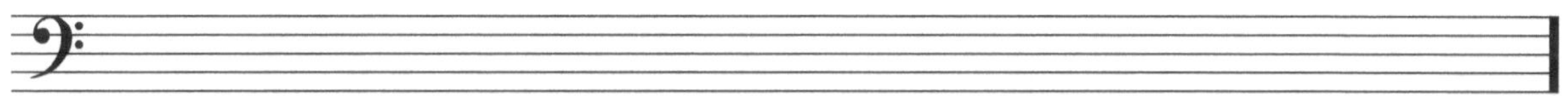

3. Name the notes below.

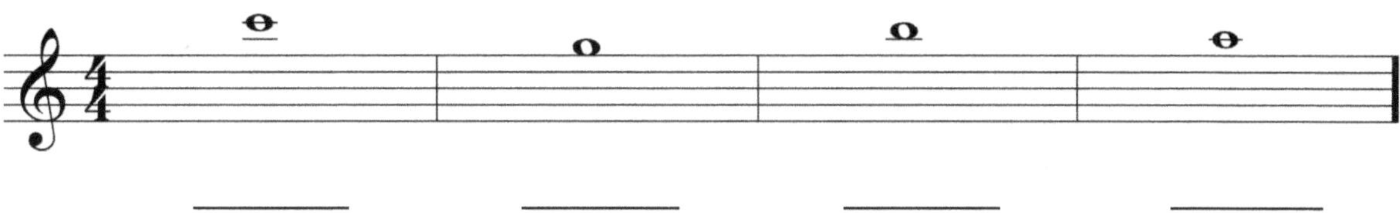

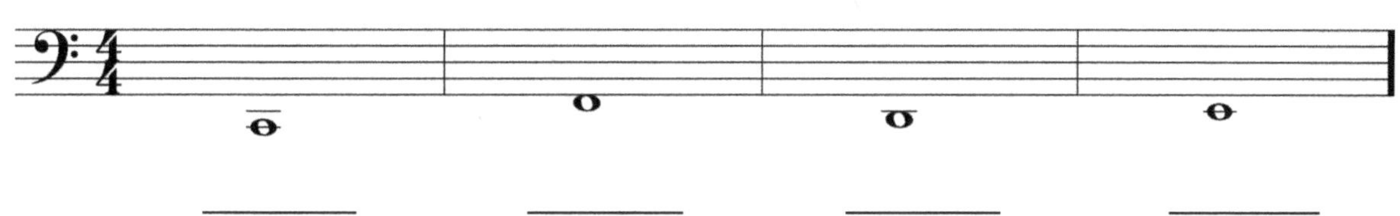

Review

1. What are ledger lines?

2. What is name of the note located two ledger lines above the Treble Clef?

3. What is the name of the note located two ledger lines below the Bass Clef?

4. What is an incomplete measure?

Lesson Nine

A Major / F♯ Minor

Lesson Nine: Musical Concepts

Pedals

Pianos usually have three pedals. The pedals may differ depending on the type of piano, make, and model, but the pedals usually have the functions and placement described below.

On grand pianos the three pedals are known as:

- Sustaining Pedal *(always on the right)* - Lifts all the dampers (pads to keep the string from vibrating) so that the sound continues after a key is released.
- Sostenuto Pedal *(middle)* - Applying this pedal after a key is played will lift the damper for that key only.
- Una Corda Pedal *(left)* - On most grand pianos, this pedal will shift the entire keyboard to the right so the treble hammers will strike two of the three strings reducing the volume of sound. That is why it is also known as the soft pedal.

On upright pianos the three pedals are known as:

- Sustaining Pedal *(always on the right) - same as above*
- Practice Pedal *(left or middle)* - Applying this pedal will either move the hammers closer to the strings or put a piece of felt between the hammers and strings. Both have the effect of softening the sound.
- Bass Sustaining Pedal *(left or middle)* - Works the same as the sustaining pedal except that the effect is applied only to the lower bass strings.

Successive pedal marks are shown in the following manner: The goal is to lift and reapply the pedal quietly.

Using the sustaining pedal

Two-note slurs consist of two distinct sounds connected using finger legato in the manner described on this page.

Two-Note Slurs

Two-note slurs should be played in the following manner:

1. The first note should be louder than the second
2. There should be no silence between the two notes
3. A slight lifting of the finger or hand after the second note will produce a silence and a feeling of a graceful lift

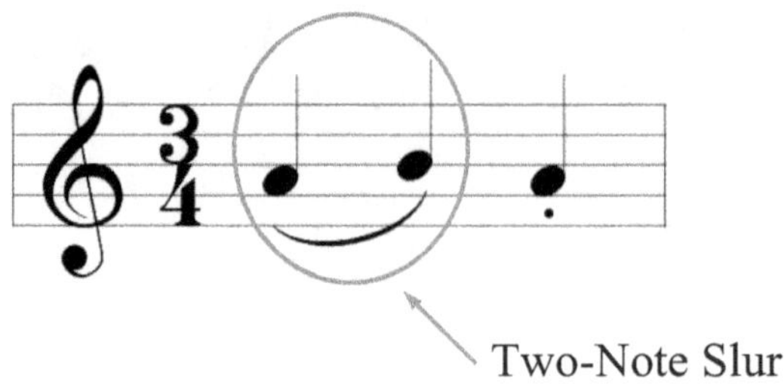

A-Major Position, Chord, and Warm-up

If needed, refer to Lesson Four for the exact key to play.

Another way to say "in A-Major position" is, "in the key of A major."

F♯-Minor Position, Chord, and Warm-up

Another way to say in "F♯-Minor position" is, "in the key of F♯ minor."

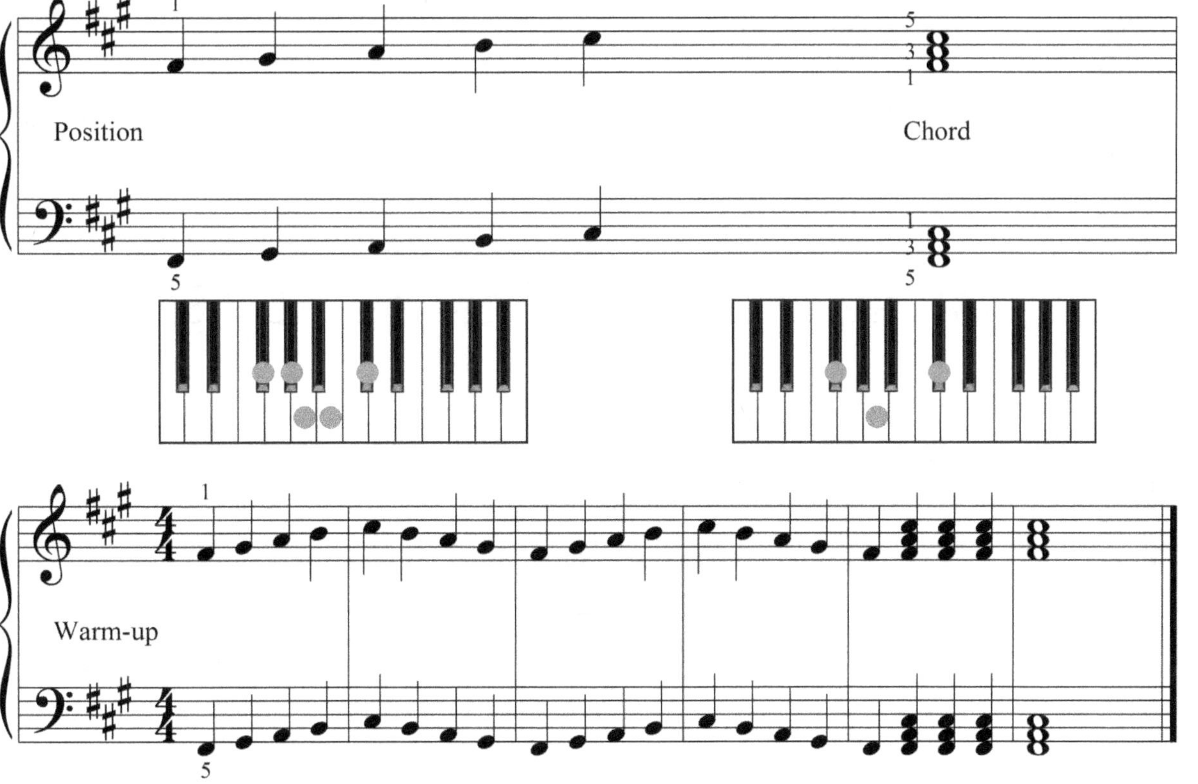

Lesson Nine: A-Major Position

Crescendo is the Italian term for gradually increasing the volume of sound.

This is indicated by placing the word *crescendo,* the abbreviation *cresc*, or the symbol

<

on the musical score.

(This symbol is used in the piece on the next page.)

Steps

Skips

My title for this piece:

Allegretto (♩ = 104-132)

Position Change*

Position Change*

Position Change*

Position Change*

Allegretto is an Italian tempo marking indicating a speed a little slower than *allegro*.

Decrescendo and *diminuendo* are the Italian terms for gradually decreasing the volume of sound.

This is indicated by placing the word de*crescendo* or *diminuendo*, the abbreviation de*cresc* or *dim*, or the symbol

on the musical score.

*Position Change—a courtesy reminder that the hand position moves to the A below middle C.

More Steps

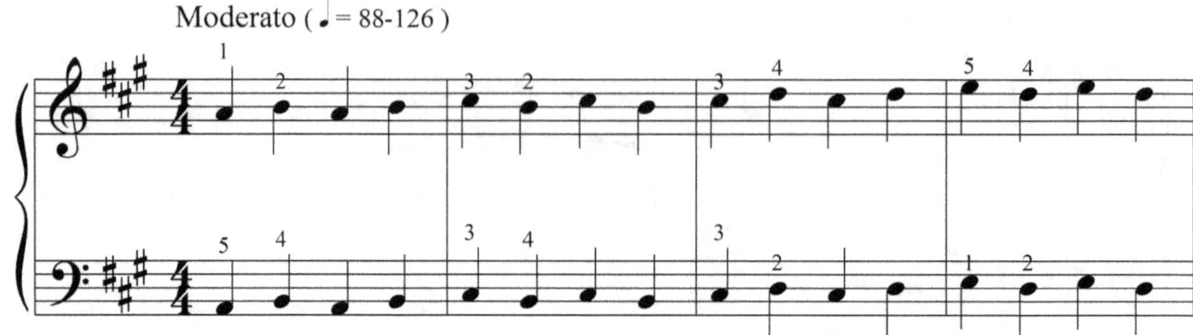

More Skips

Harmony

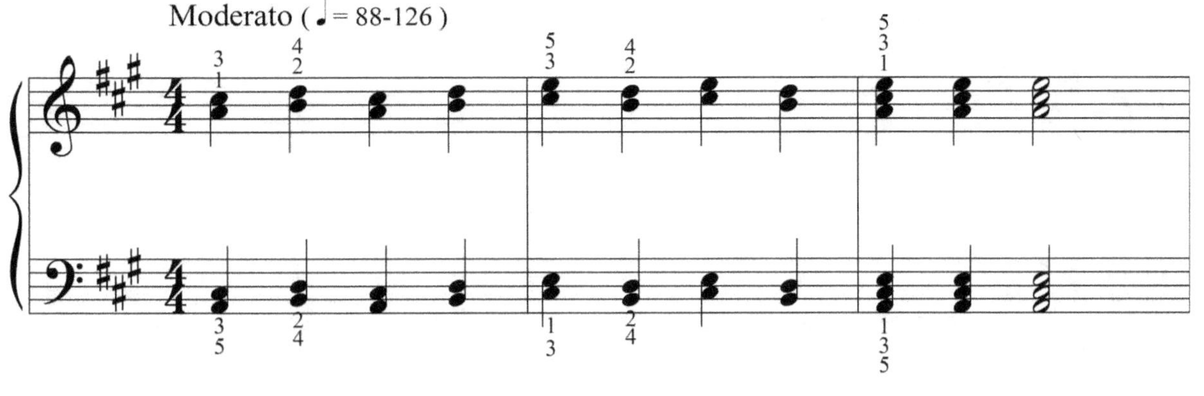

Leaps

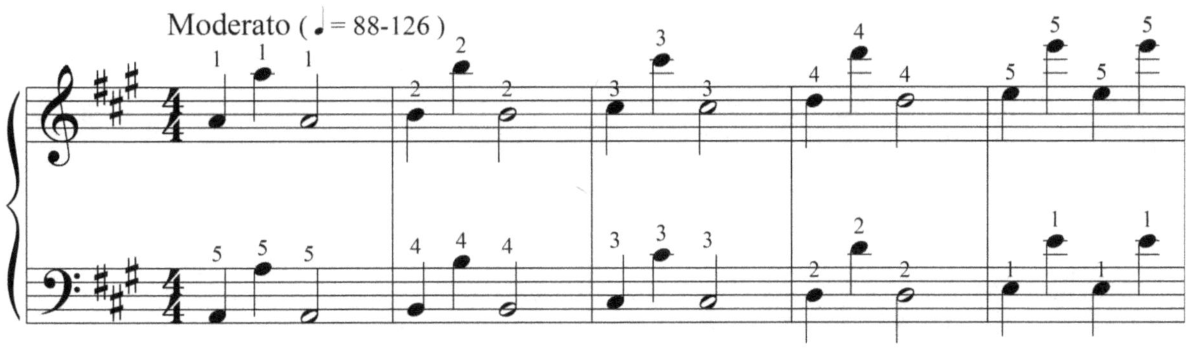

Skips

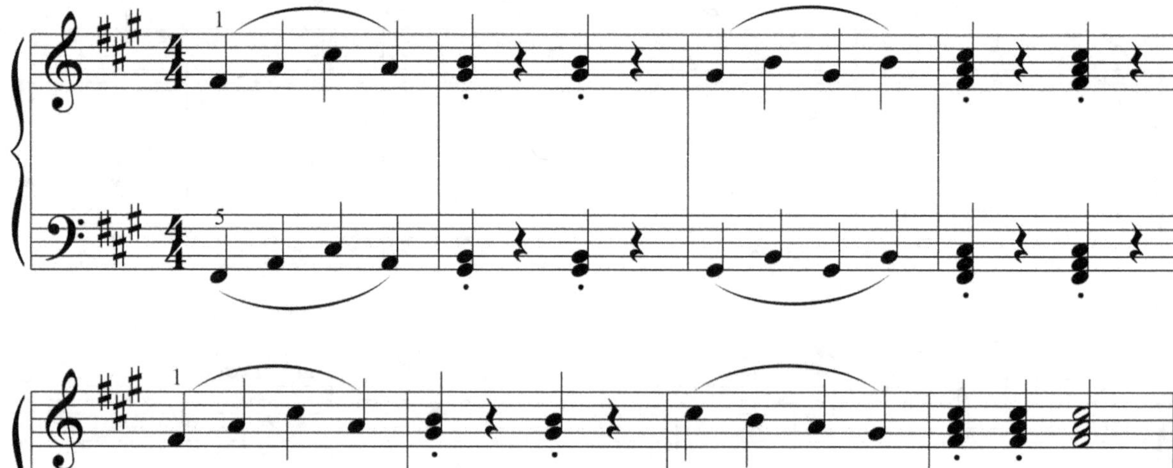

My title for this piece:

Allegretto (♩ = 104-132)

1

3

Position Change*

1

1

5

5

Position Change*

5

Position Change*

5

1

1

Position Change*

1

3

*Position Change—a courtesy reminder that the hand position moves to the F♯ below middle C.

More Steps

Moderato (♩ = 88-126)

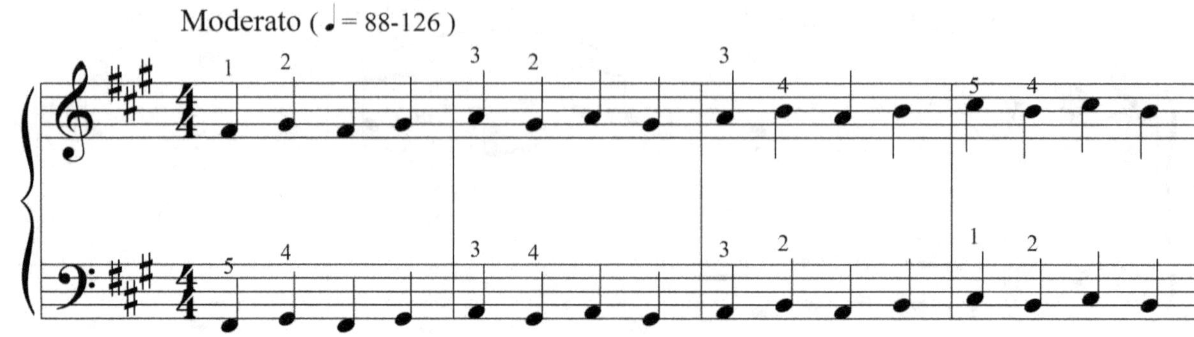

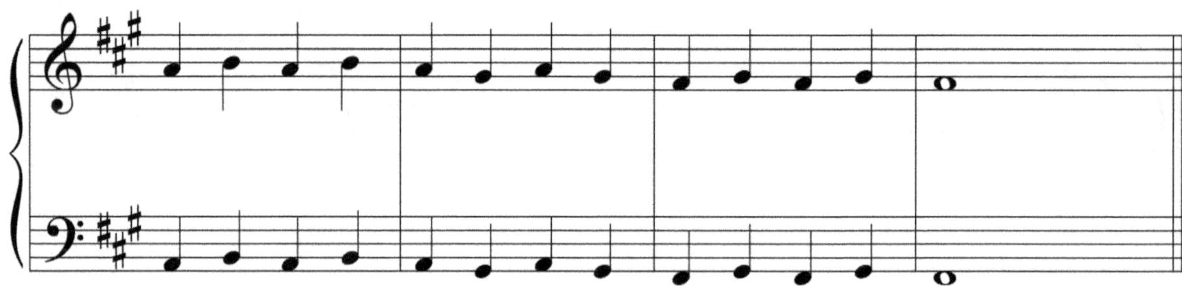

More Skips

Moderato (♩ = 88-126)

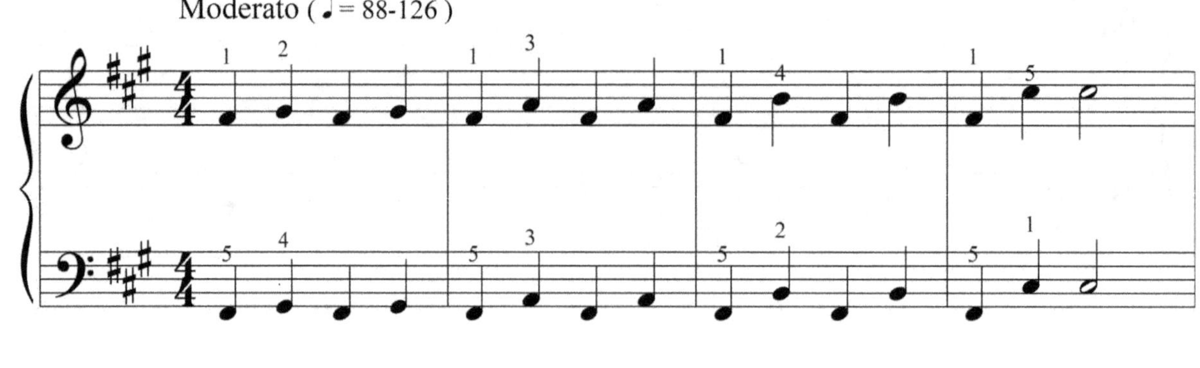

Harmony
Moderato (♩ = 88-126)
Leaps
Moderato (♩ = 88-126)

*Position Change—the right hand position moves to the A below middle C in measures 9, 12, and 25, and to the F♯ below middle C in measures 13 and 17. The left hand position moves to the A below middle C in measures 10, 11, and 26, and to the F♯ below middle C in measures 14 and 15.

Recital Piece No. 4

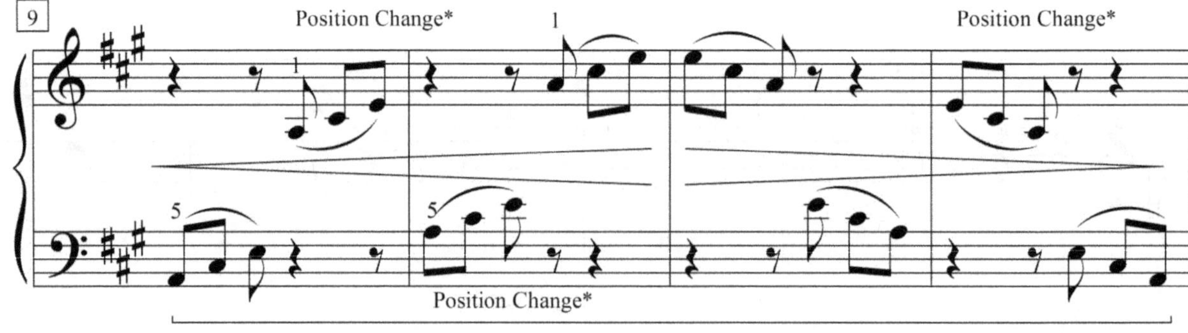

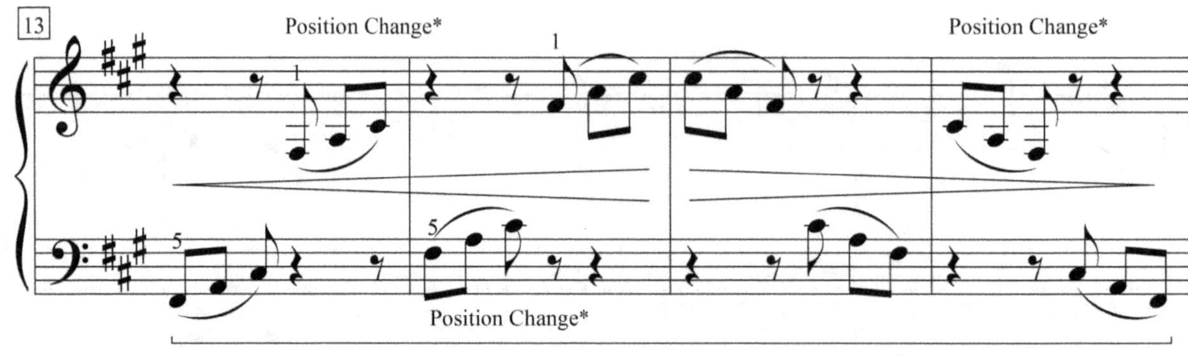

17

21

25

Position Change*

L. H.

Position Change*

A-Major Position, Chord, and Warm-up

If needed, refer to page 91 to complete the exercise.

1. Draw the notes to the A-Major position and chord, and label the keys.

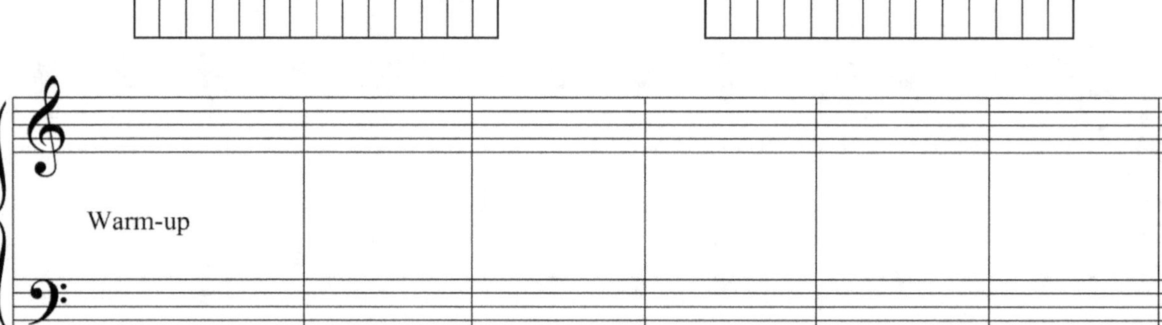

2. Draw the notes to the A-Major warm-up.

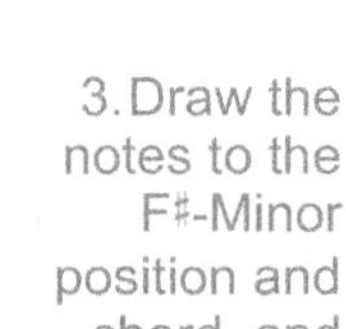

F♯-Minor Position, Chord, and Warm-up

3. Draw the notes to the F♯-Minor position and chord, and label the keys.

Position

Chord

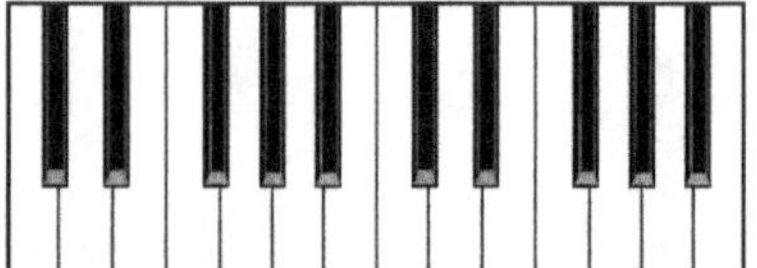

4. Draw the notes to the F♯-Minor warm-up.

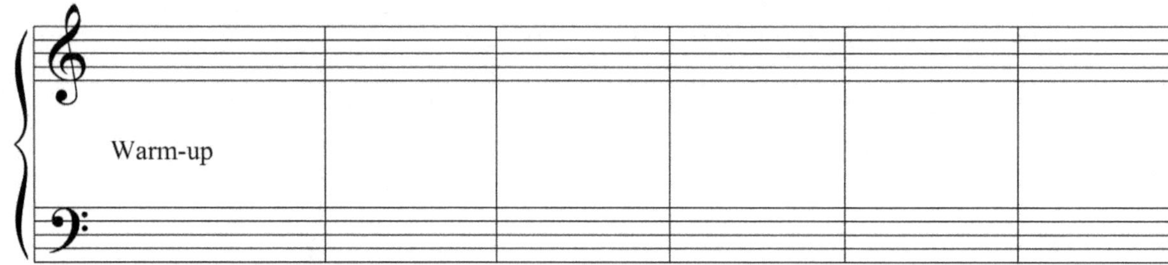

1. Add one pedal marking so that the first sound continues until the end of the stave.

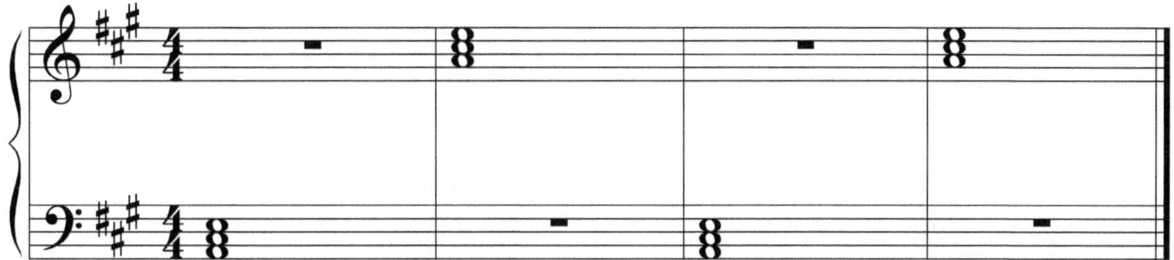

2. Add connected pedal markings so that the sounds are connected using the pedal and only one chord sounds in each measure.

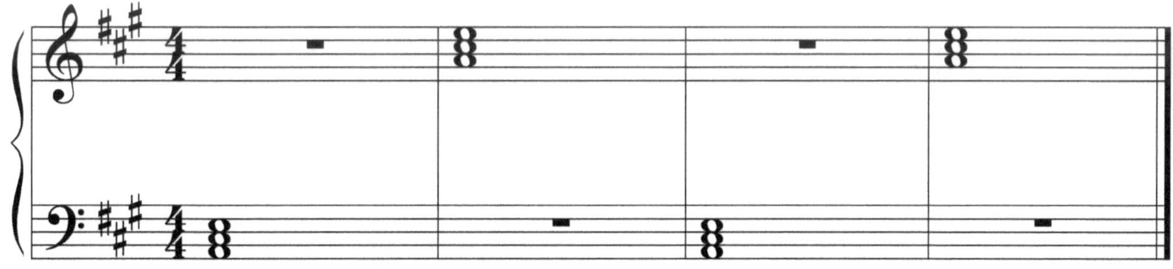

3. Create as many two-note slurs as you can.

Review

1. How many pedals does your piano have?

2. Experiment with the pedals and write down your discoveries.

   Pedal on the left:

   Pedal in the middle:

   Pedal on the right:

3. How is a two-note slur to be played?

4. Define and draw the crescendo symbol.

5. Define and draw the decrescendo symbol.

Lesson Ten

E Major / C♯ Minor

Dotted Notes and Rests

Notes and rests with a dot next to them are called dotted. The dot adds half the value of the note or rest. For example, a dotted quarter note equals one and a half quarter notes.

Assume a quarter note equals 1 beat.

Notes		Beats		Rests
𝅝.	=	6	=	𝄻.
𝅗𝅥.	=	3	=	𝄼.
♩.	=	1½	=	𝄽.

Clap the top line while tapping the bottom line with your foot.

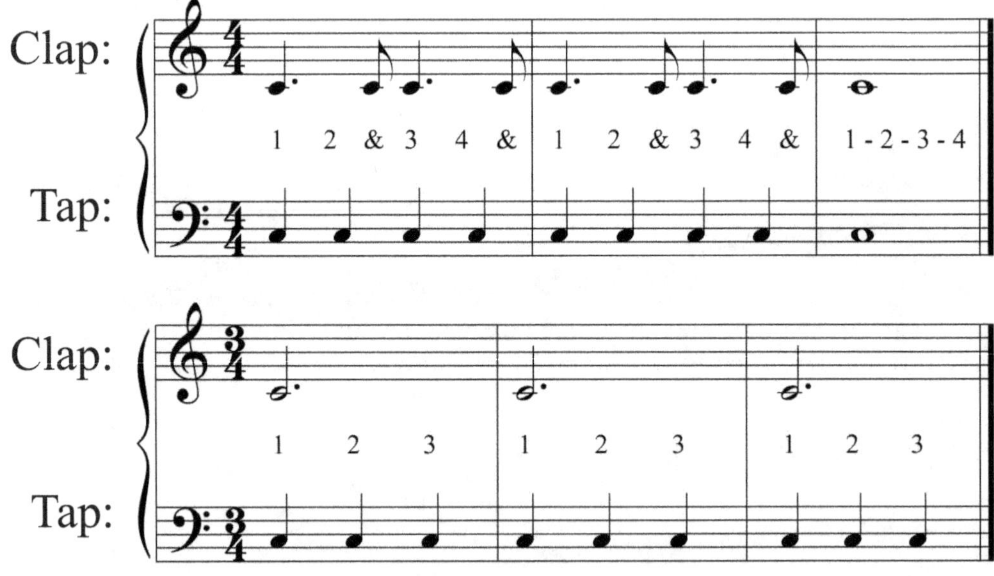

Accents

An accent is a symbol that directs the performer to emphasize a note or chord. For example, the > symbol directs the performer to play a note or chord louder than those without the > symbol.

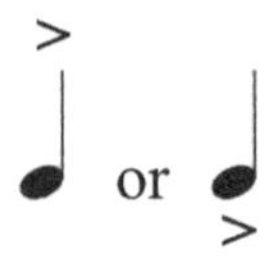

E-Major Position, Chord, and Warm-up

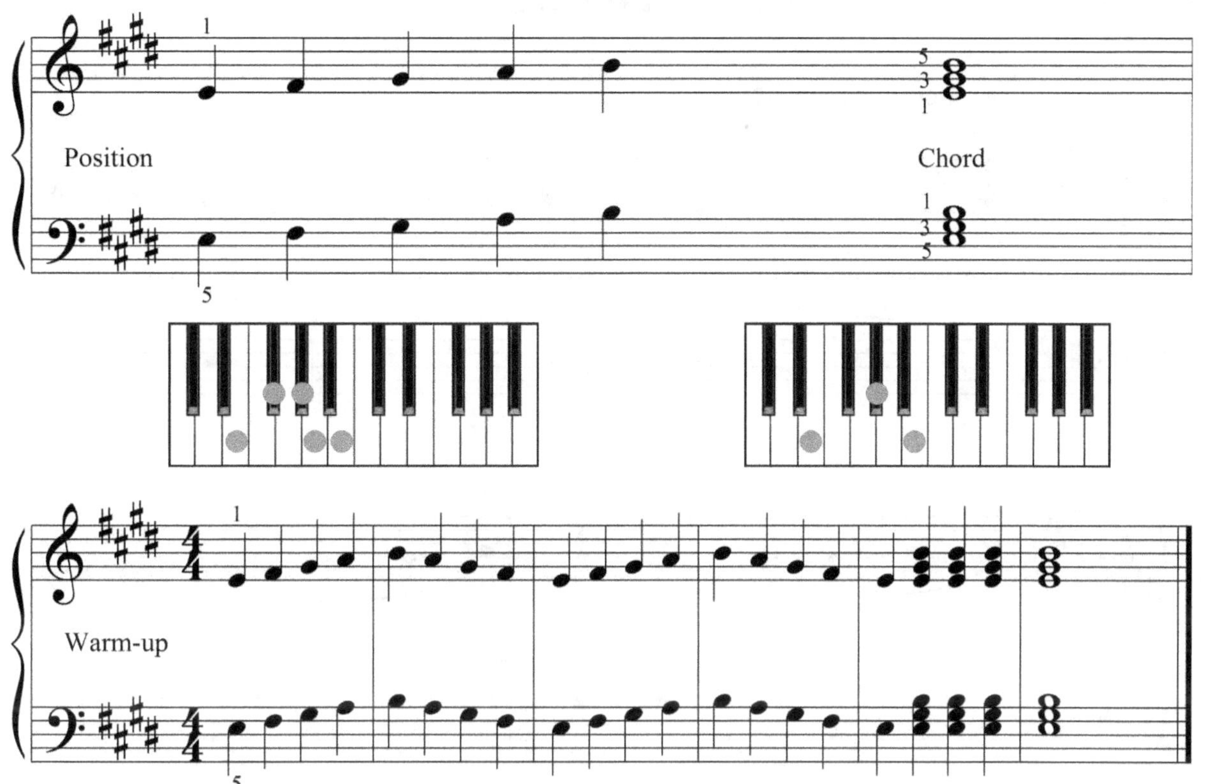

If needed, refer to Lesson Four for the exact key to play.

Another way to say "in E-Major position" is, "in the key of E major."

C♯-Minor Position, Chord, and Warm-up

Another way to say in "C♯-Minor position" is, "in the key of C♯ minor."

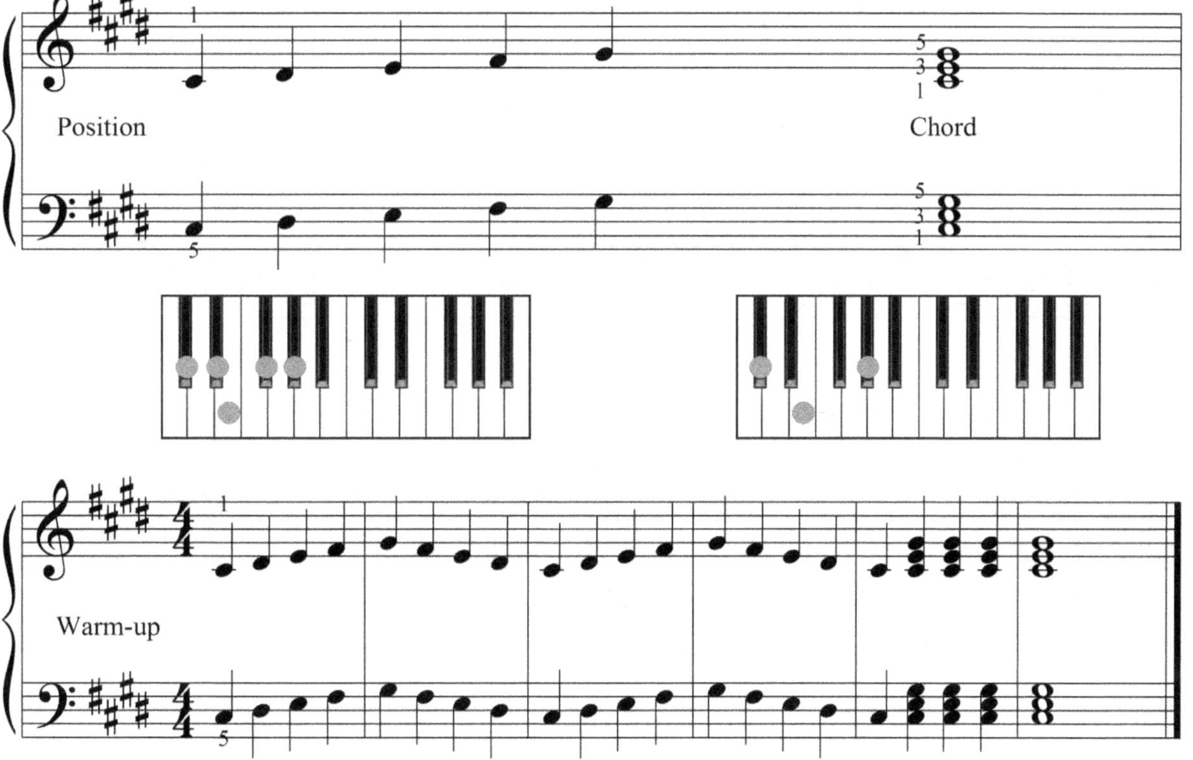

Steps

Moderato (♩ = 88-126)

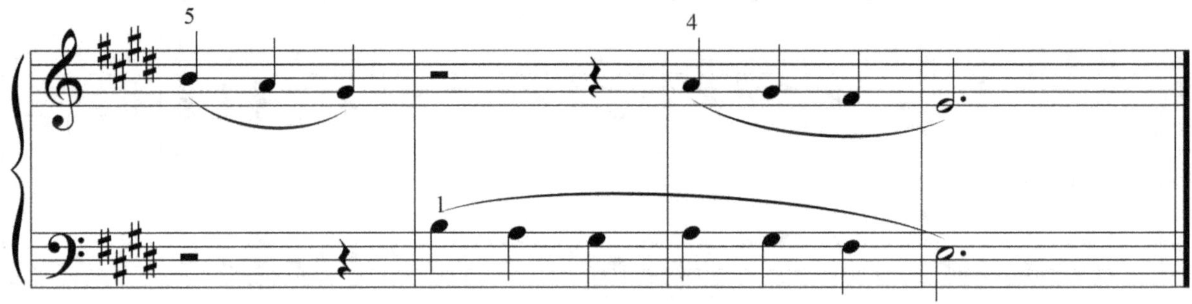

Skips

Moderato (♩ = 88-126)

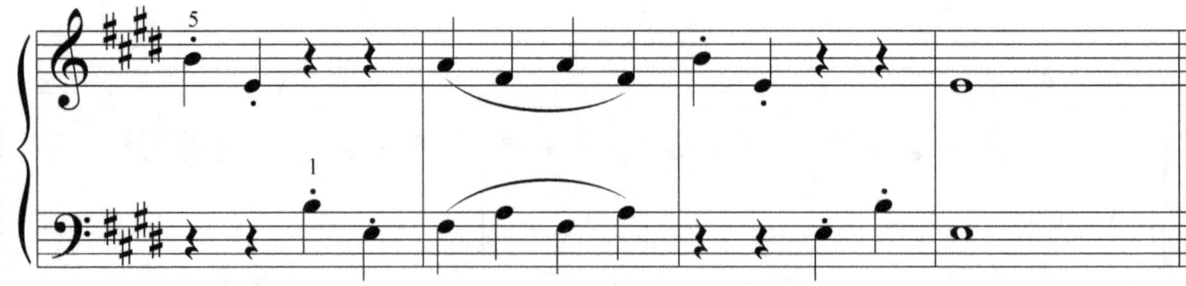

My title for this piece:

Presto (♩ = 100-152)

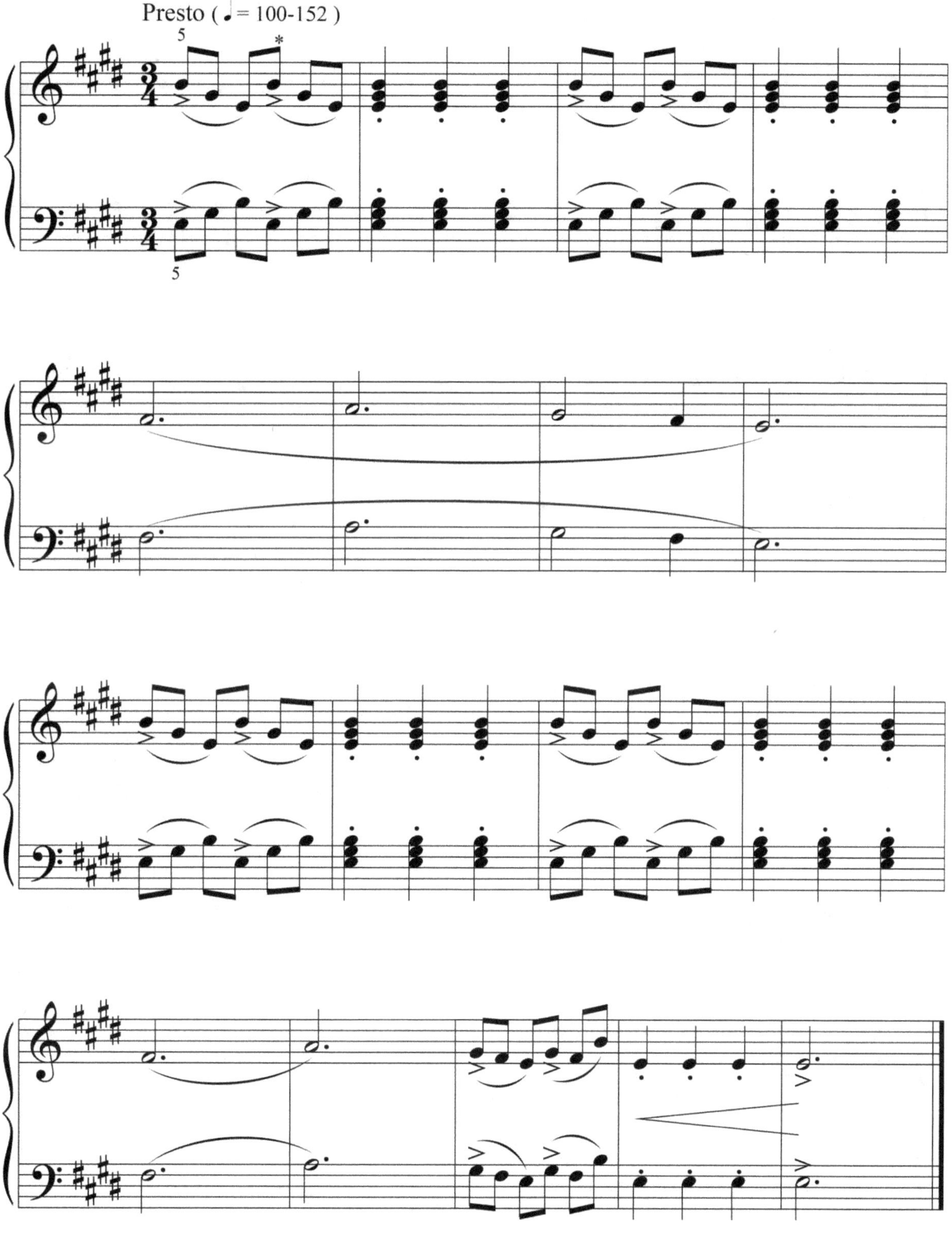

Presto is an Italian tempo marking indicating that the speed of the piece should be very fast.

* Syncopation—an accented note on a beat where it does not ordinarily occur such as the first beat of the measure. In this piece, syncopation occurs in the middle of the first measure and other measures like it.

More Steps

Moderato (♩= 88-126)

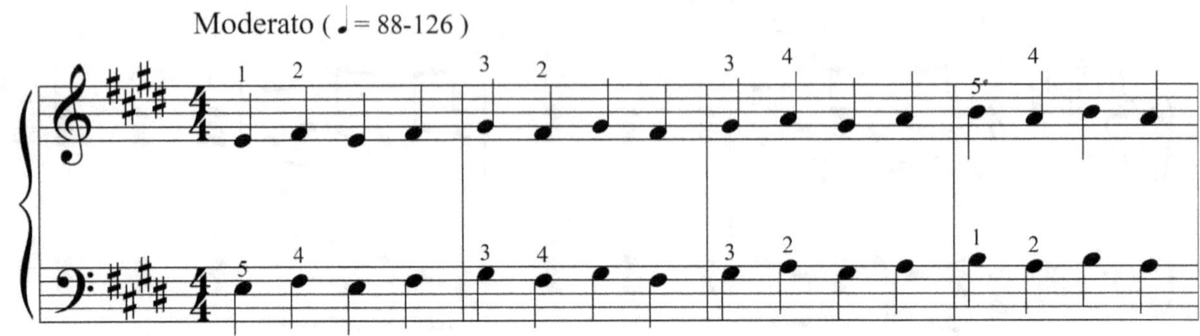

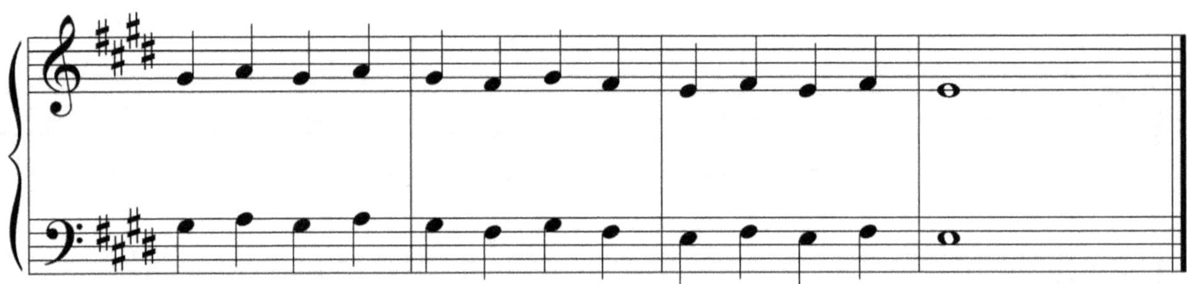

More Skips

Moderato (♩= 88-126)

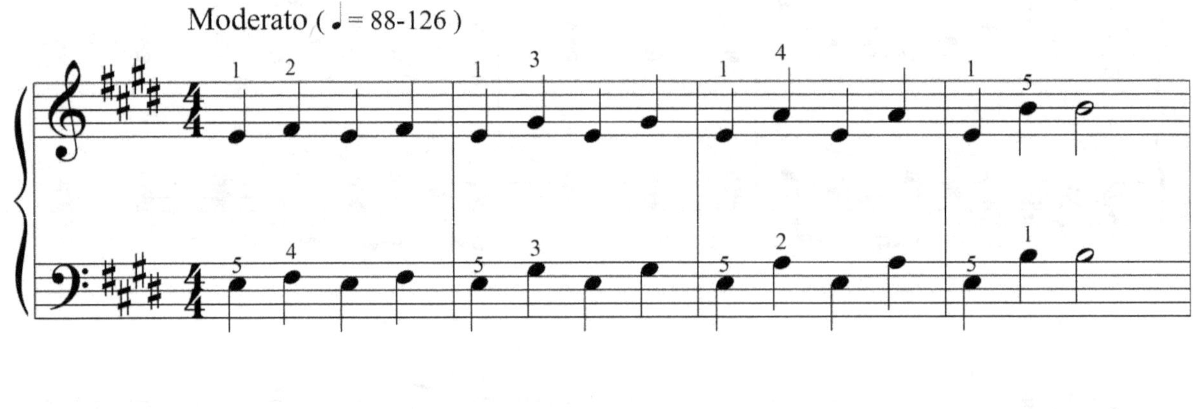

Harmony

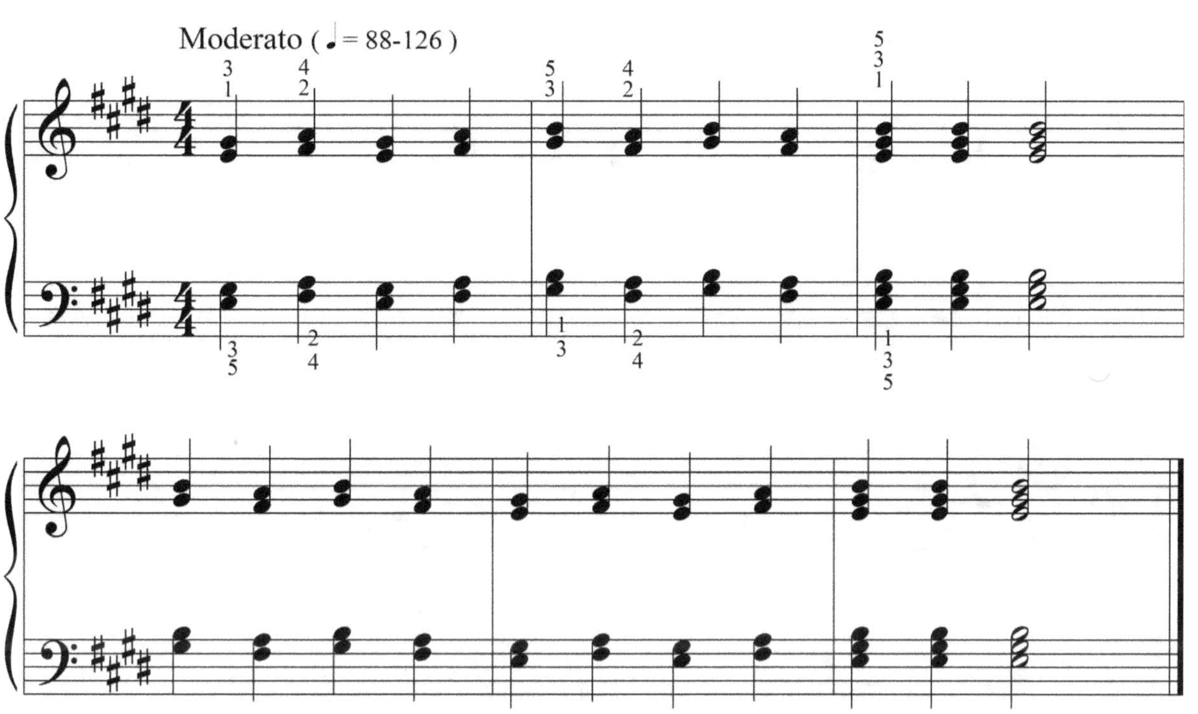

Leaps

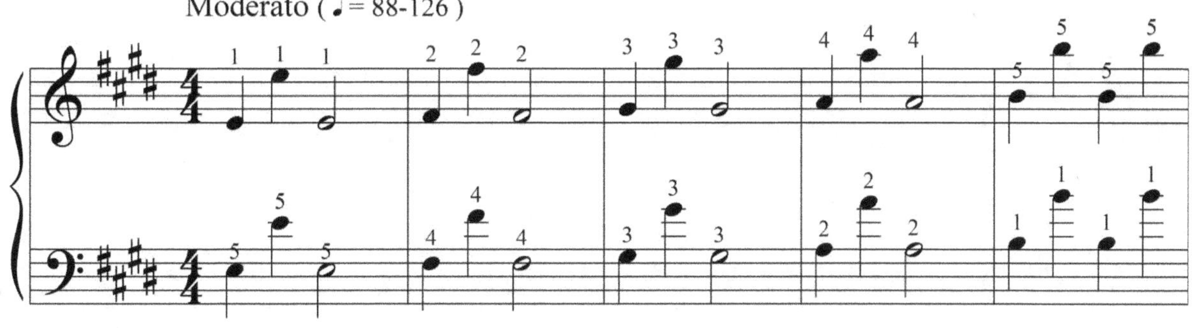

Lesson Ten: C♯-Minor Position

Steps

Moderato (♩ = 88-126)

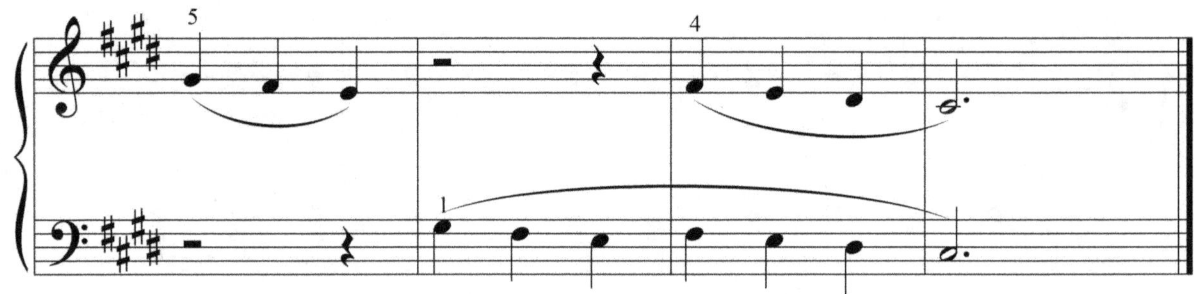

Skips

Moderato (♩ = 88-126)

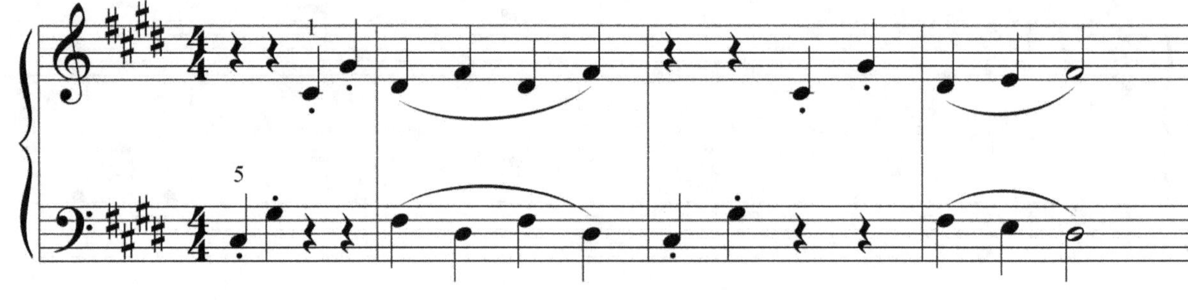

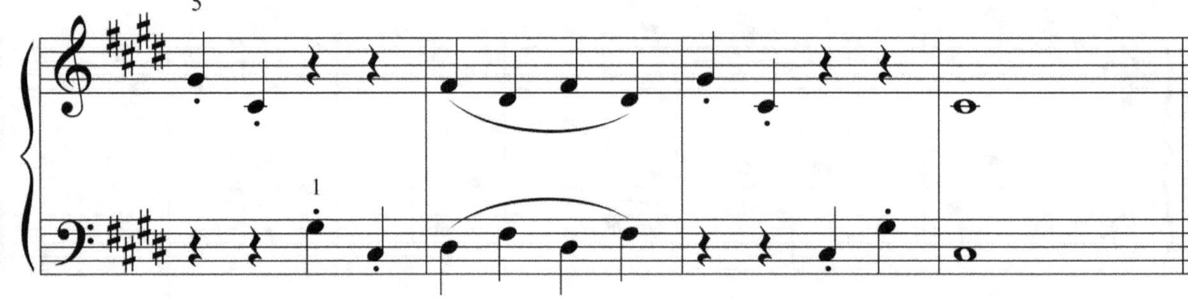

My title for this piece:

Presto (♩ = 100-152)

5

5

More Steps

Moderato (♩ = 88-126)

More Skips

Moderato (♩ = 88-126)

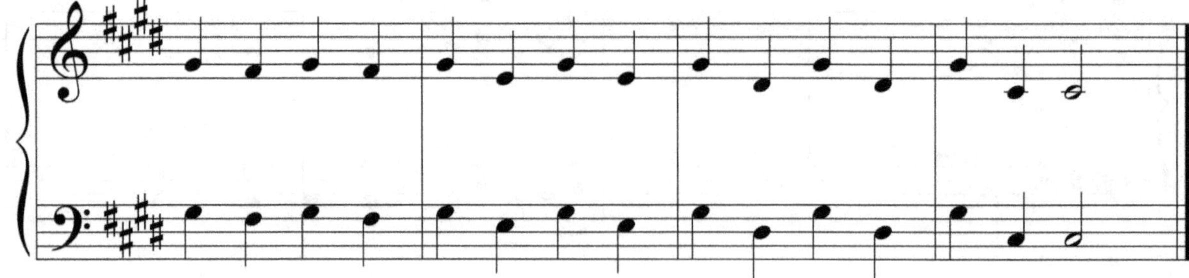

Harmony

Moderato (♩ = 88-126)

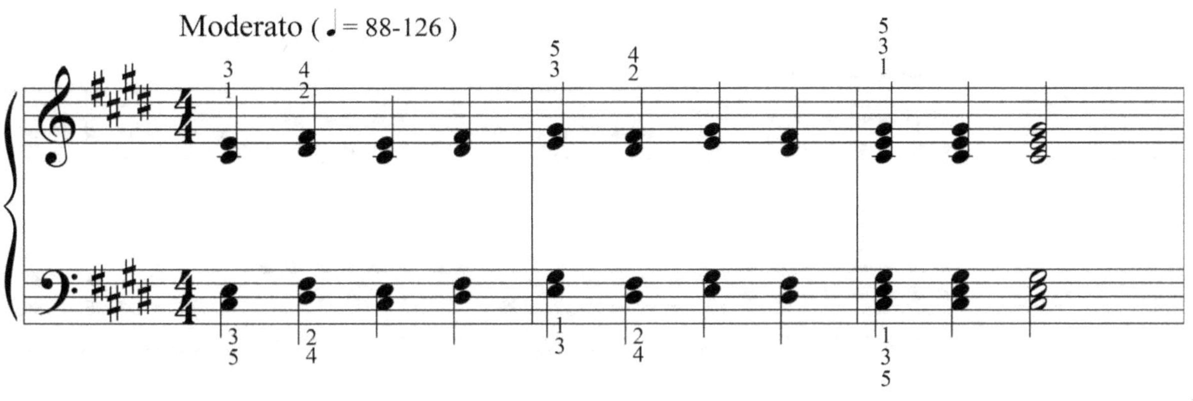

Leaps

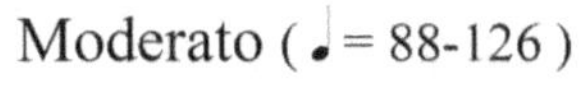

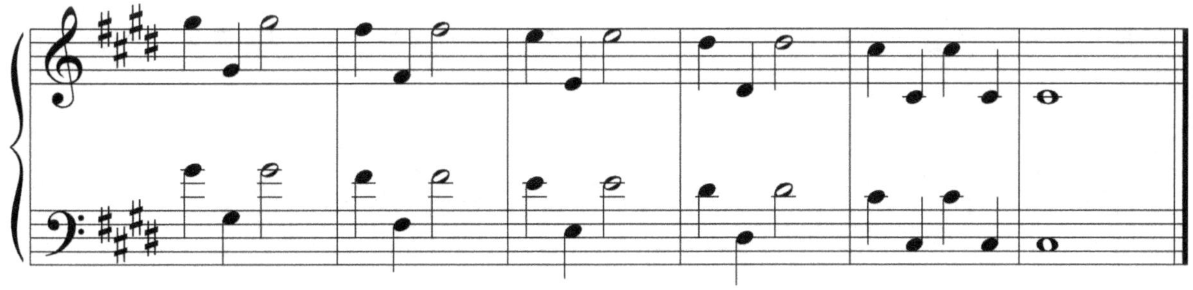

Recital Piece No. 5

17

21

25

E-Major Position, Chord, and Warm-up

If needed, refer to page 107 to complete the exercise.

1. Draw the notes to the E-major position and chord, and label the keys.

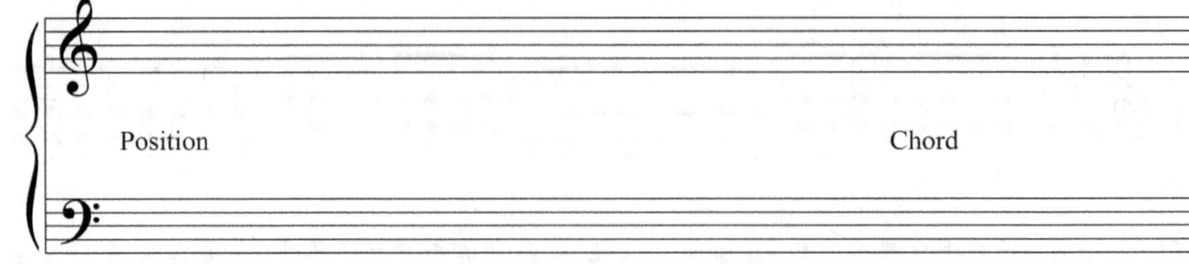

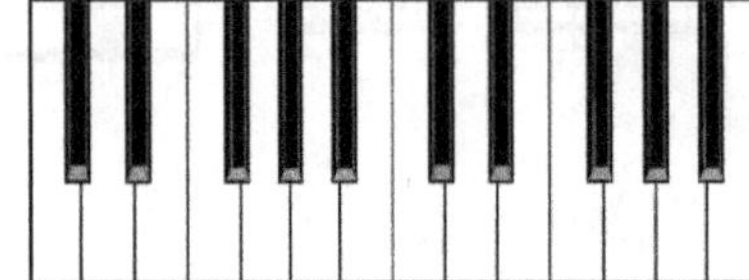

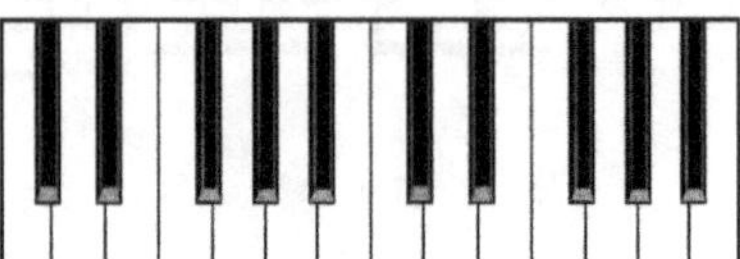

2. Draw the notes to the E-major warm-up.

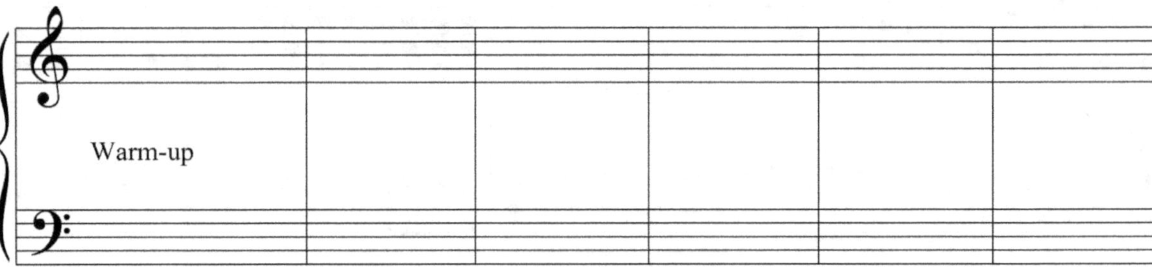

C♯-Minor Position, Chord, and Warm-up

3. Draw the notes to the C♯-minor position and chord, and label the keys.

Position

Chord

4. Draw the notes to the C♯-minor warm-up.

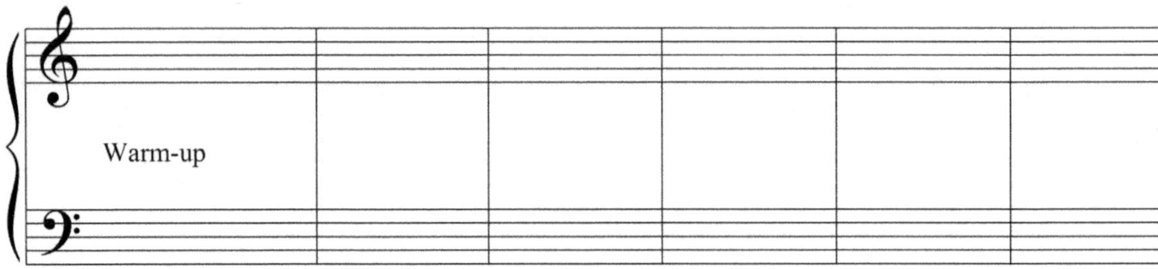

1. Complete the following measures by adding dots where needed.

2. Add an accent to the first and third beats of each measure.

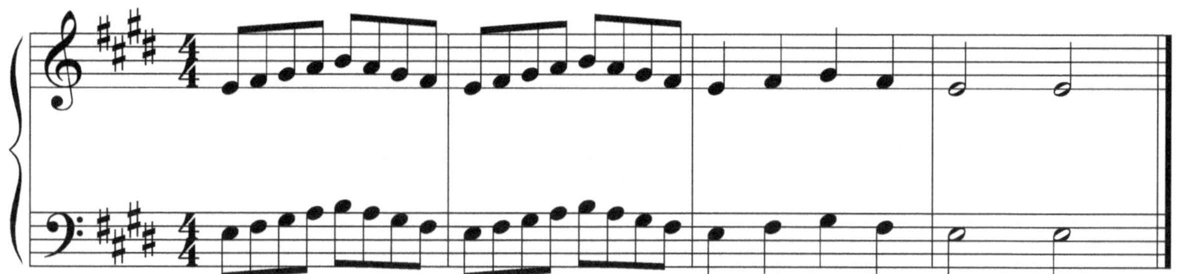

Review

1. Explain the difference between a dot next to a note and a dot over or under a note.

2. What does an accent indicate?

3. List and define three Italian tempo markings.

Lesson Eleven

B Major / G$^\sharp$ Minor

Lesson Eleven: Musical Concepts

Sound Dynamics

In this lesson we will learn four Italian terms for volume of sound. The terms are listed in the chart below along with their common abbreviations and English translations. The volume of sound each term represents is relative to the other terms and does not represent an exact volume.

Abbreviation	Italian	English
f	*forte*	Loud
mf	*mezzo forte*	Medium Loud
mp	*mezzo piano*	Medium Soft
p	*piano*	Soft

Playing *forte* and *piano*

forte

When playing *forte*, do not let the wrist get stiff and in a locked position. The wrist must remain flexible. A stiff or locked wrist leads to a harsh sound.

Playing with a *forte* sound does not mean that the *tempo* is faster. It is the volume of sound that changes and not the speed of the composition.

piano

When playing *piano*, do not let your hand position suffer. A proper hand position must be maintained. Every key must be pressed with a firm touch, yet with less force.

Playing with a *piano* sound does not mean that the *tempo* is slower. It is the volume of sound that changes and not the speed of the composition.

Practice the warm-ups on the next page with the following dynamics:

First time	—	***p***
Second time	—	***mp***
Third time	—	***mf***
Fourth time	—	***f***

B-Major Position, Chord, and Warm-up

If needed, refer to Lesson Four for the exact key to play.

Another way to say "in B-major position" is, "in the key of B Major."

G♯-Minor Position, Chord, and Warm-up

Another way to say in "G♯-minor position" is, "in the key of G♯Minor."

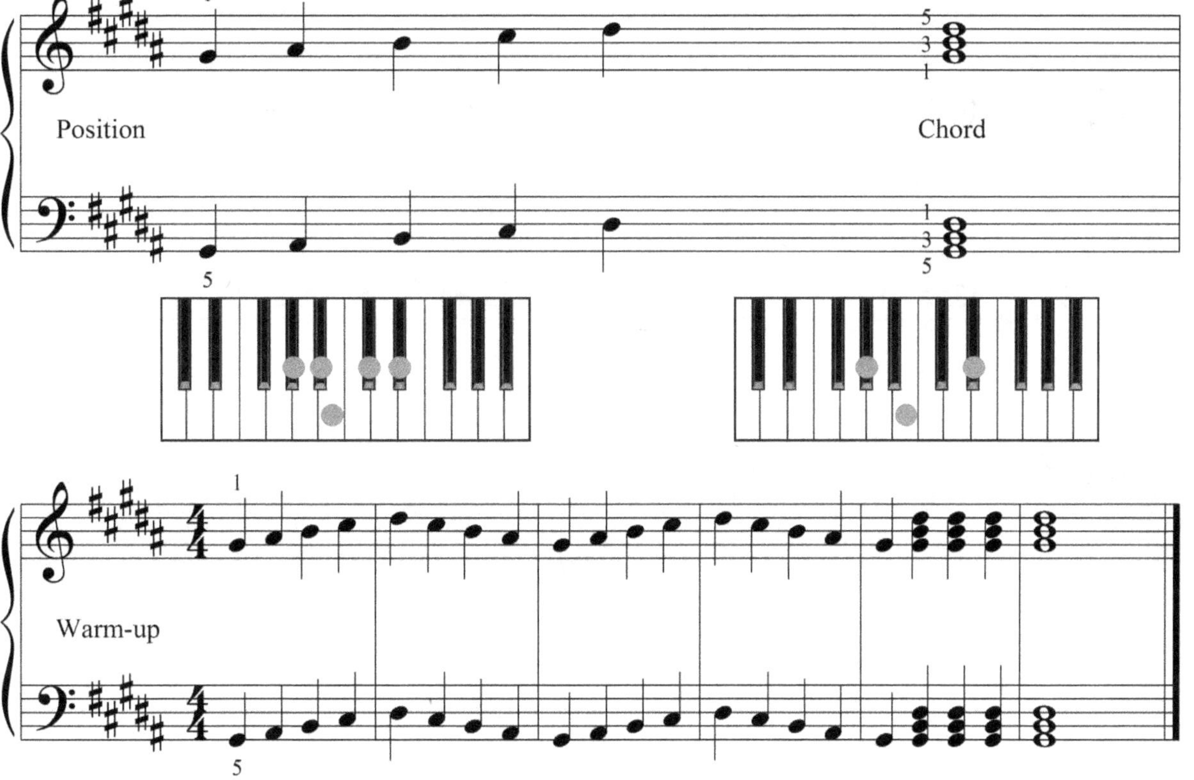

Steps

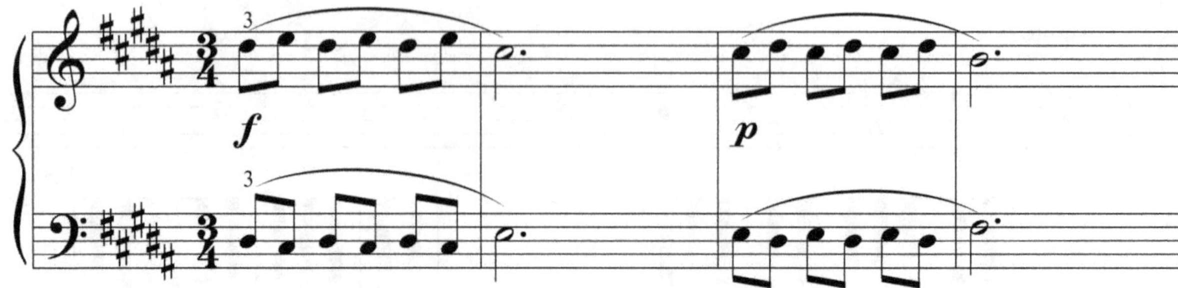

Skips

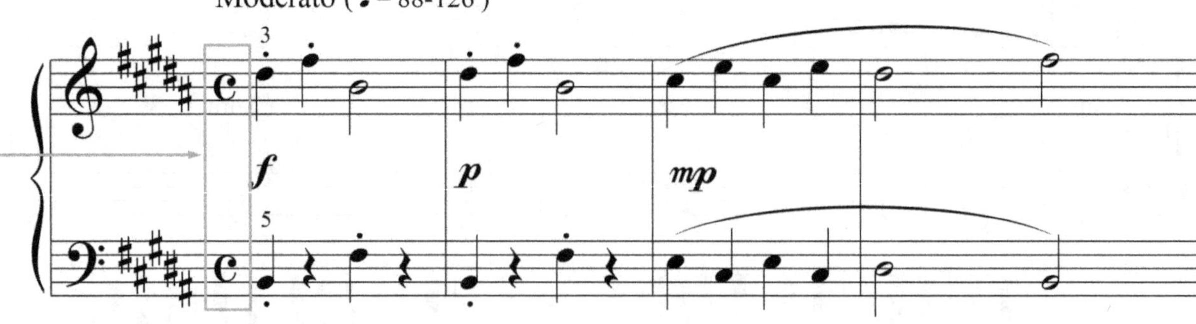

The large "C" in the time signature is an abbreviation for "common time" or 4/4.

My title for this piece:

Andante (♩= 72-88)

5
mf
p
5

1
p
mf
1

p

5
mf
p
p
mf
5

Lesson Eleven: B-Major Technique

Play each exercise applying the *f*, *mf*, *mp*, *p* sound dynamics using a *legato* and *staccato* touch where appropriate.

More Steps

Moderato (♩ = 88-126)

More Skips

Moderato (♩ = 88-126)

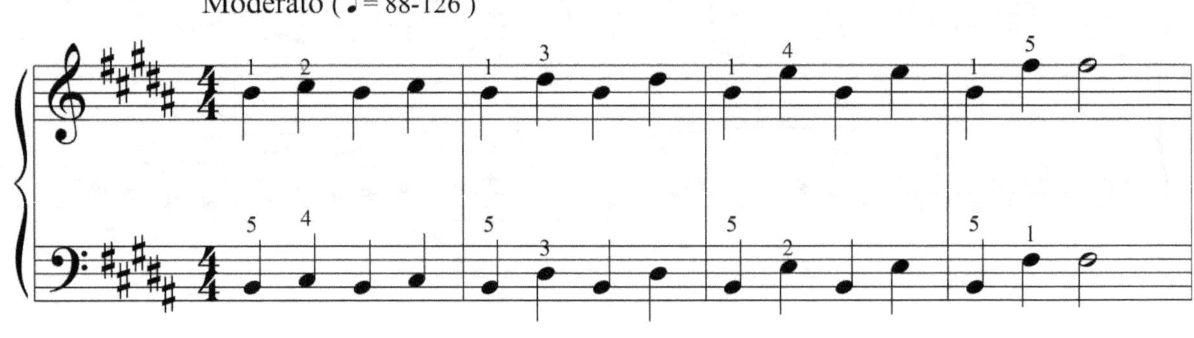

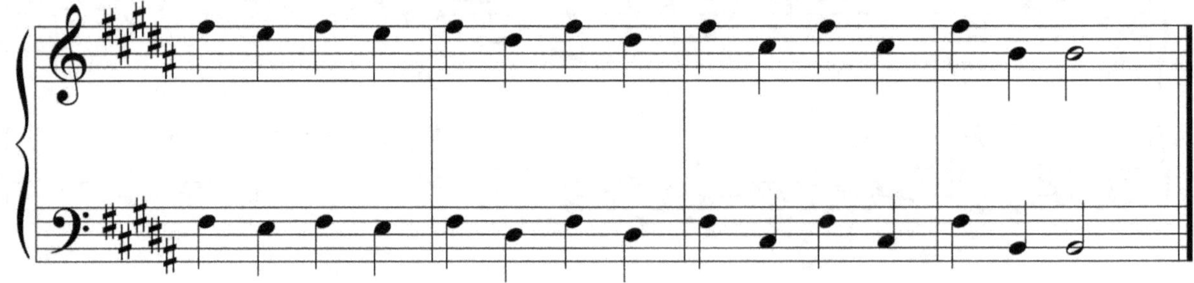

Harmony

Leaps

Steps

Moderato (♩ = 88-126)

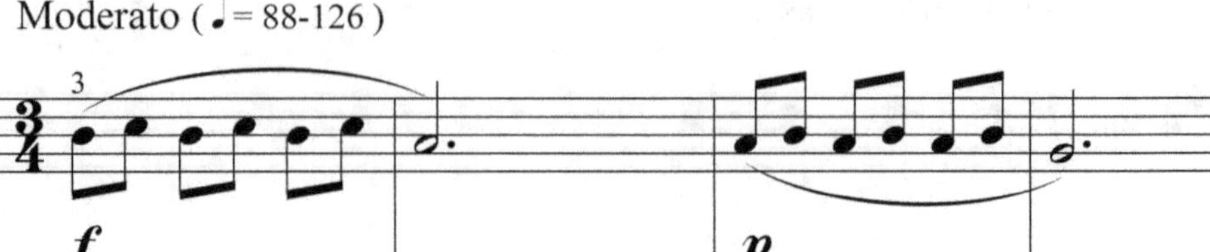

Skips

Moderato (♩ = 88-126)

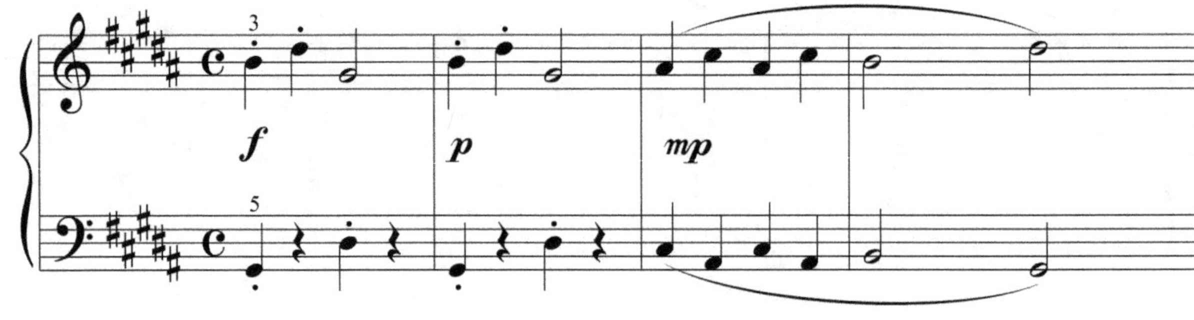

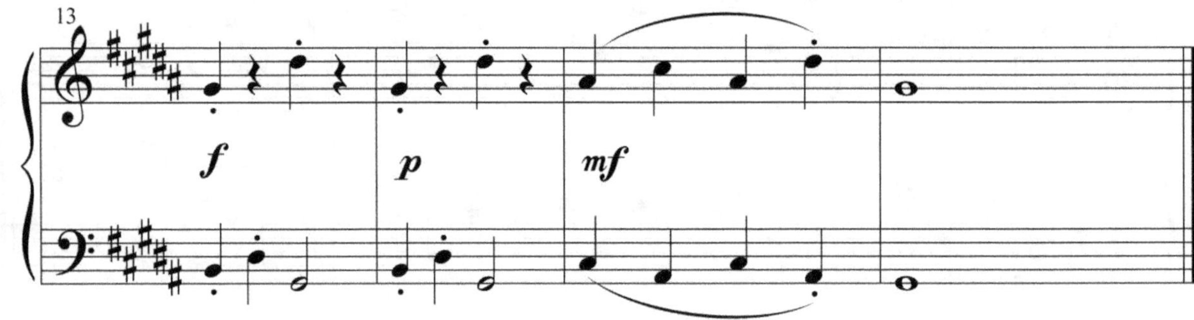

My title for this piece:

Andante (♩= 72-88)

mf

p

5

1

p

mf

p

mf

p

p

mf

Play each exercise applying the *f*, *mf*, *mp*, *p* sound dynamics using a *legato* and *staccato* touch where appropriate.

More Steps

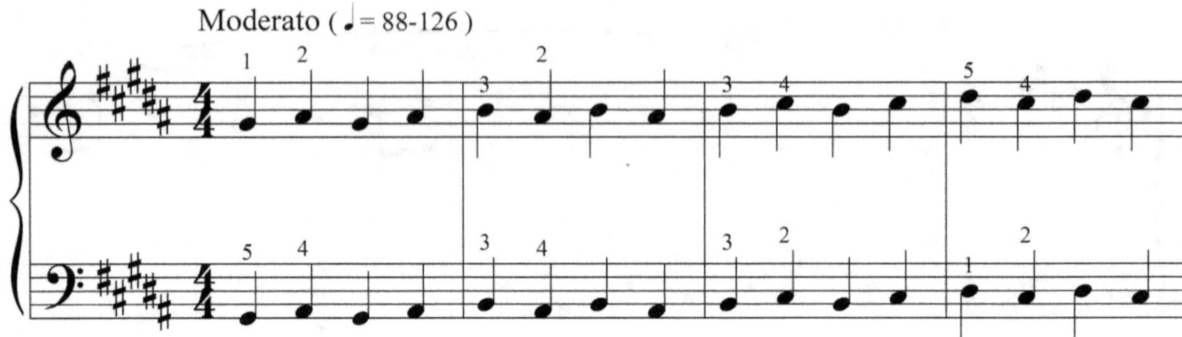

More Skips

Harmony

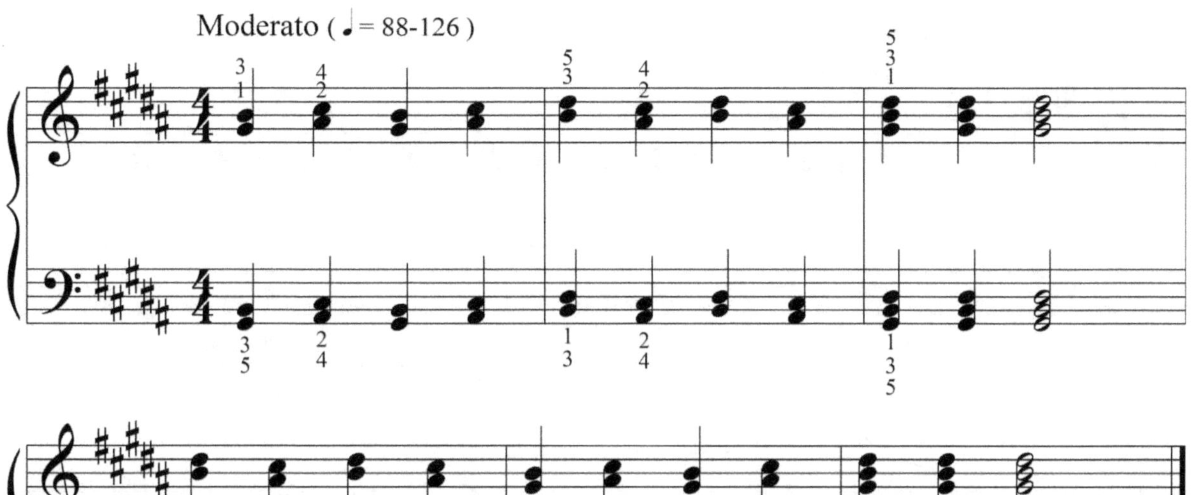

Leaps

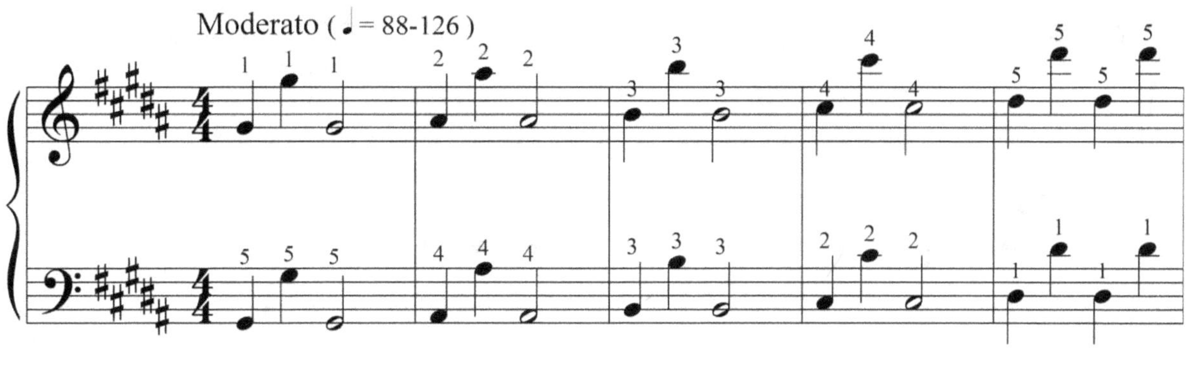

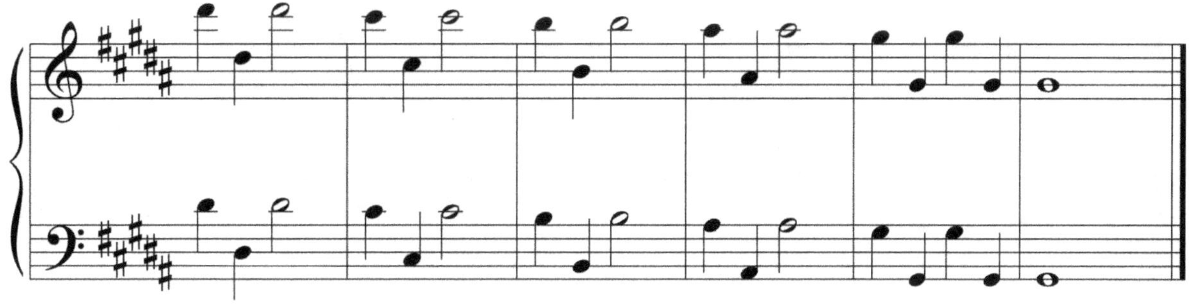

If needed, review pedal instructions on page 90.

*Position Change—the right hand position moves to the B below middle C in measures 1 and 23. The left hand position moves to the G♯ below middle C in measure 15 and to the B below middle C in measure 17.

Recital Piece No. 6

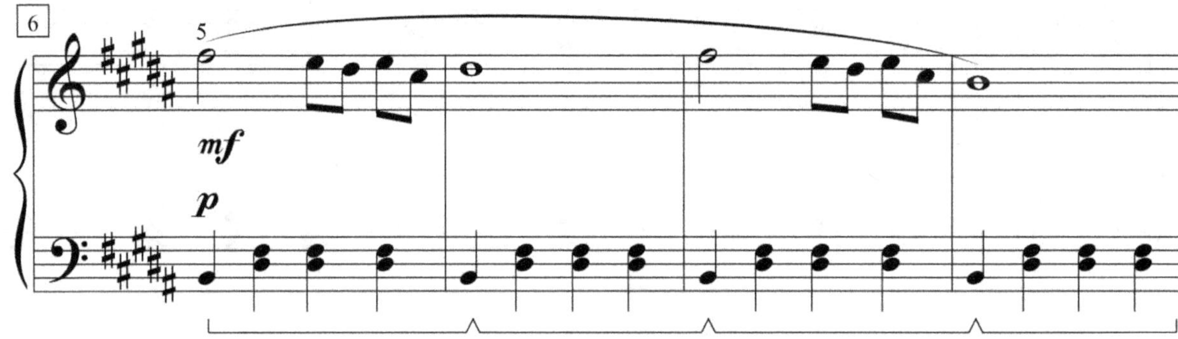

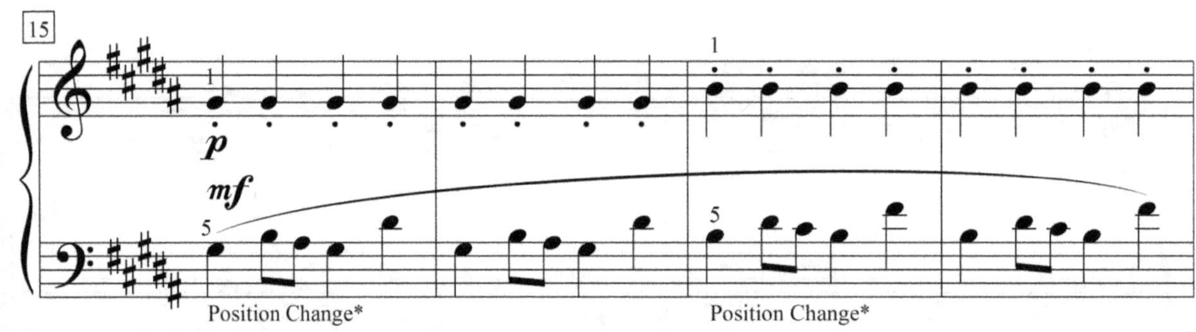

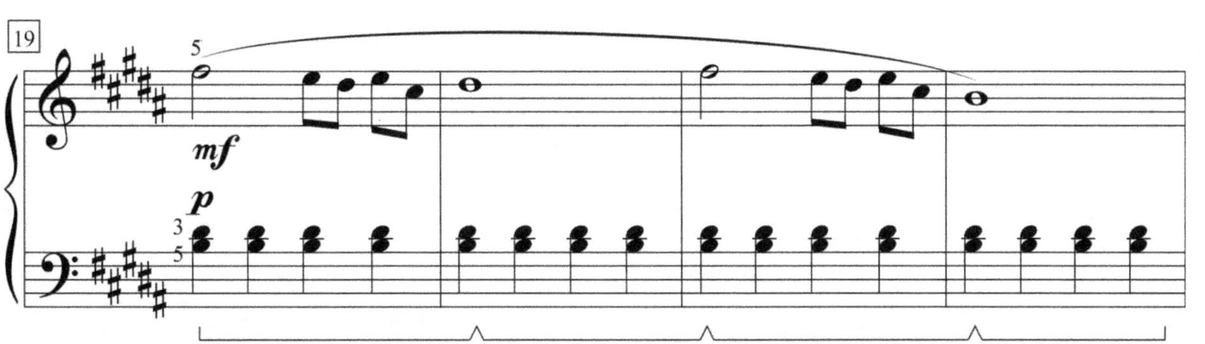
19
5
mf
p
3
5

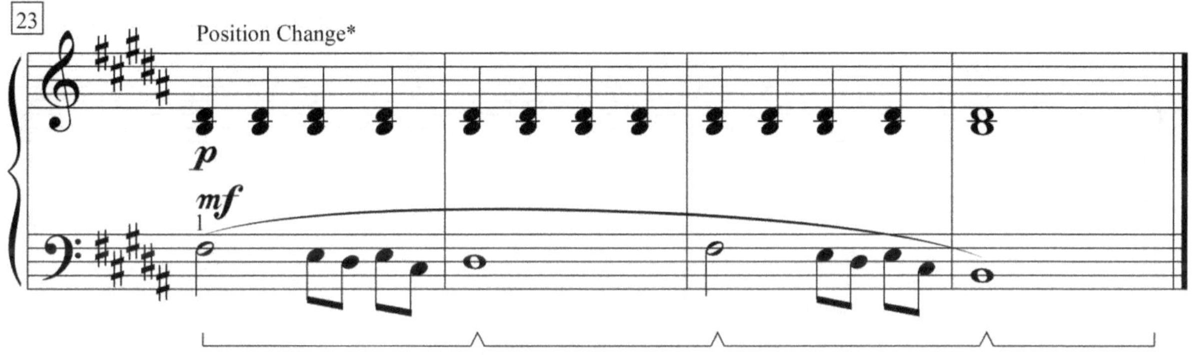
23
Position Change*
p
mf
1

B-Major Position, Chord, and Warm-up

If needed, refer to page 123 to complete the exercise.

1. Draw the notes to the B-major position and chord, and label the keys.

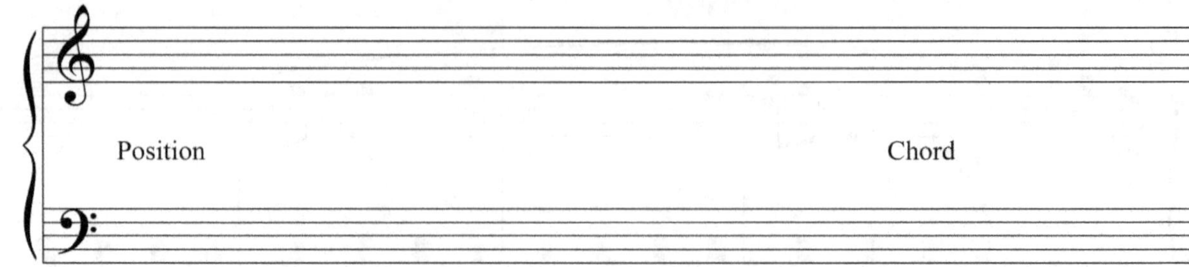

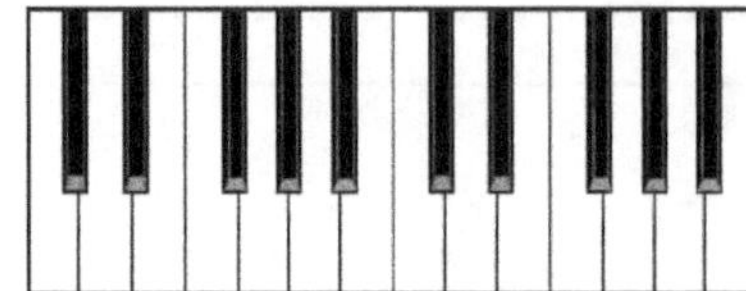

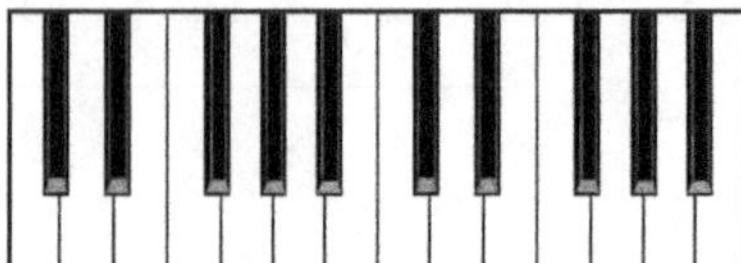

2. Draw the notes to the B-major warm-up.

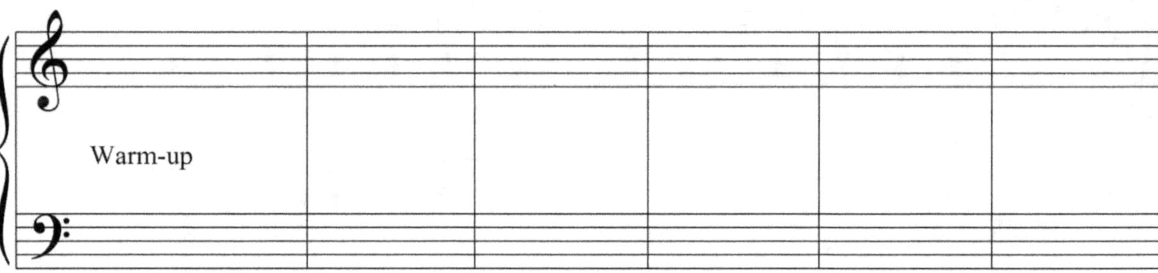

G♯-Minor Position, Chord, and Warm-up

3. Draw the notes to the G♯-minor position and chord, and label the keys.

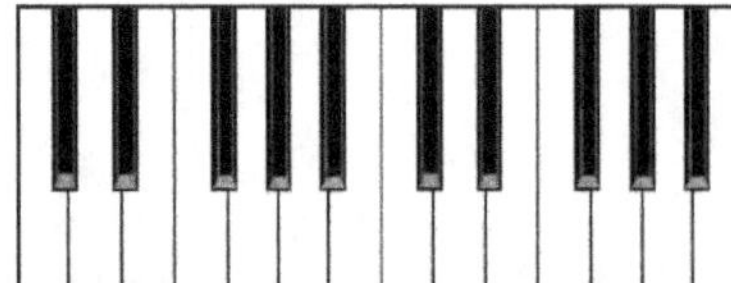

4. Draw the notes to the G♯-minor warm-up.

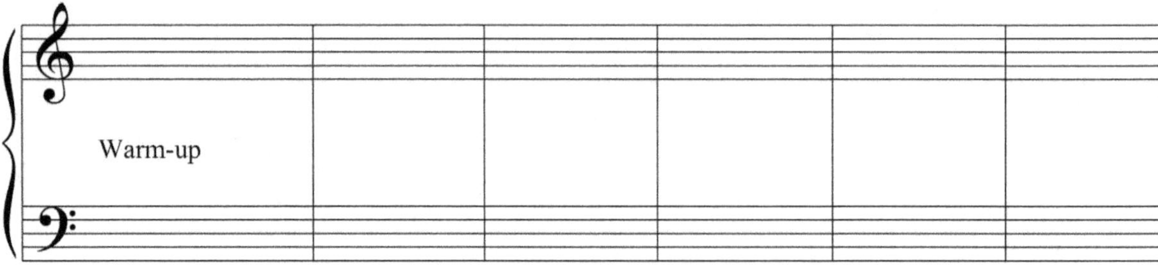

Find the following Italian words:

ALLEGRETTO
ANDANTE
FORTE
MEZZO FORTE
MEZZO PIANO
MODERATO
PIANO
PRESTO

Review

1. Give the Italian term and English equivalent.

Abbreviation	Italian	English
f	________________	________________
mf	________________	________________
mp	________________	________________
p	________________	________________

2. What two things should you remember about playing *forte* and *piano*?

3. What does the term "common time" mean?

Lesson Twelve

F♯ (G♭) Major / D♯ (E♭) Minor

Enharmonic Sounds

The same sound with different names.

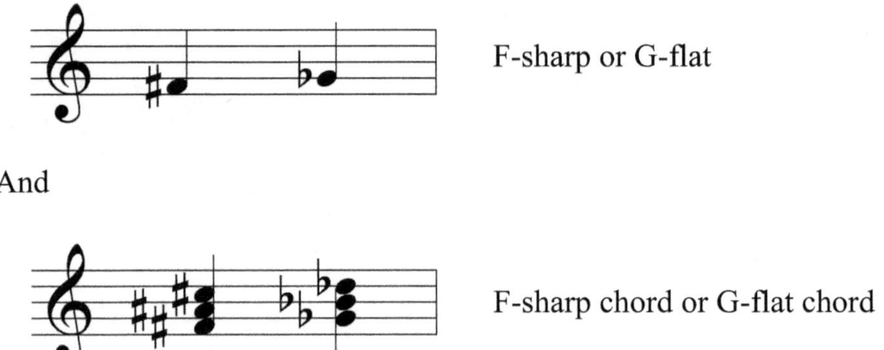

Note: This lesson presents one hand position written in two ways. The F-sharp Major position and its relative minor are found on page 139, while the same position, written in G-flat Major with its relative minor is found on page 141.

Activity

Draw a line from the note on the left side to the matching enharmonic note on the right.

F♯-Major Position, Chord, and Warm-up

If needed, refer to Lesson Four for the exact key to play.

Another way to say "in F♯-major position" is, "in the key of F♯ major."

D♯-Minor Position, Chord, and Warm-up

Another way to say in "D♯-minor position" is, "in the key of D♯ minor."

New Time Signature

So far we have only studied time signatures with a 4 as the lower number.

2	3	4
4	4	4

We now introduce a time signature with an eight as the lower number.

6 indicates that there are six beats in a measure

8 indicates that the eighth note (♪) equals one beat

In this new time signature, you will often find eighth notes in groups of three.

Activity

Draw a measure of repeating eighth notes in 3/4 followed by a measure of repeating eight notes in 4/4.

Draw a measure of repeating eighth notes in 3/8 followed by a measure of repeating eight notes in 6/8.

G♭-Major Position, Chord, and Warm-up

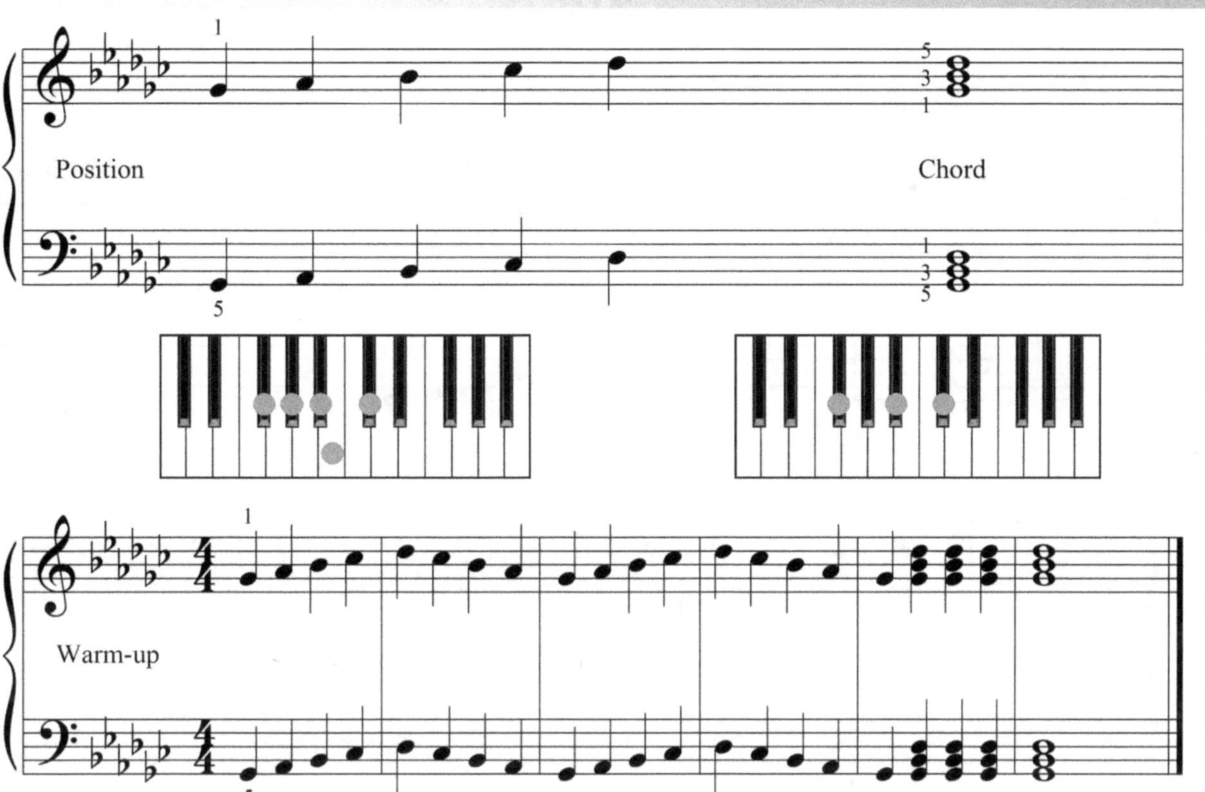

If needed, refer to Lesson Four for the exact key to play.

Another way to say "in G♭-major position" is, "in the key of G♭ major."

E♭-Minor Position, Chord, and Warm-up

Another way to say in "E♭-minor position" is, "in the key of E♭ minor."

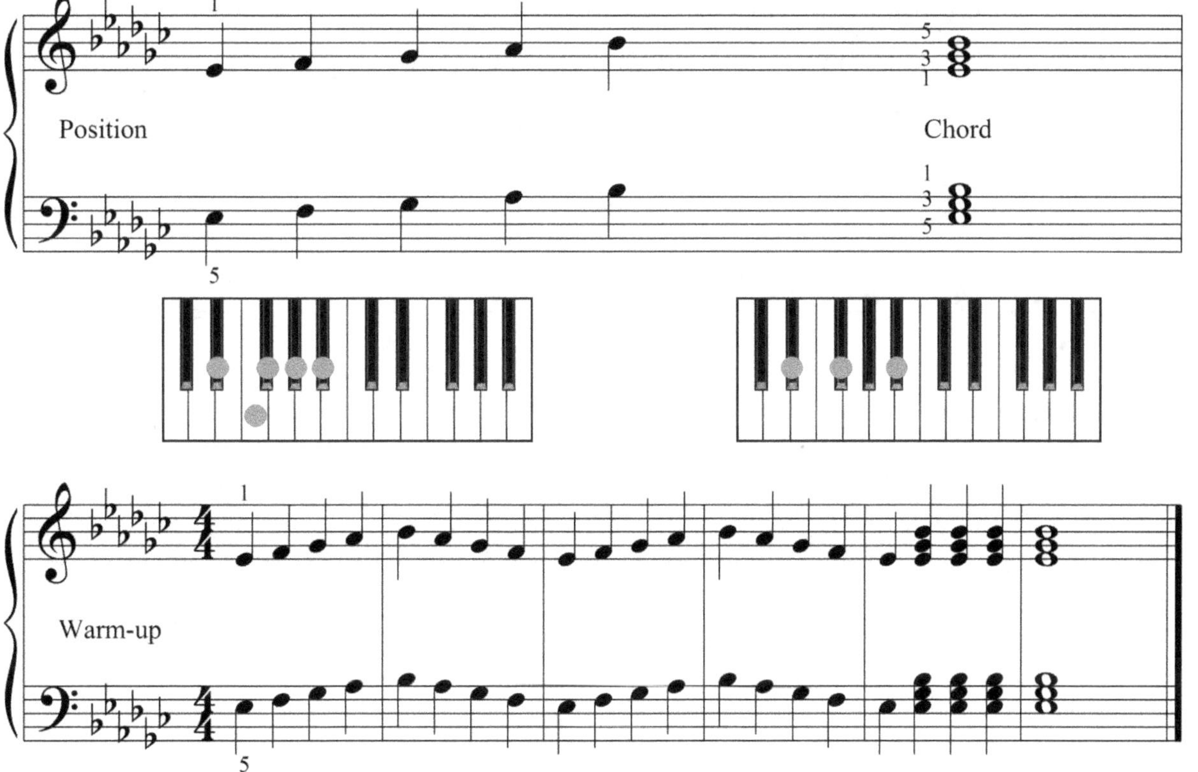

Lesson Twelve: F♯ (G♭)-Major Position

My title for this piece:

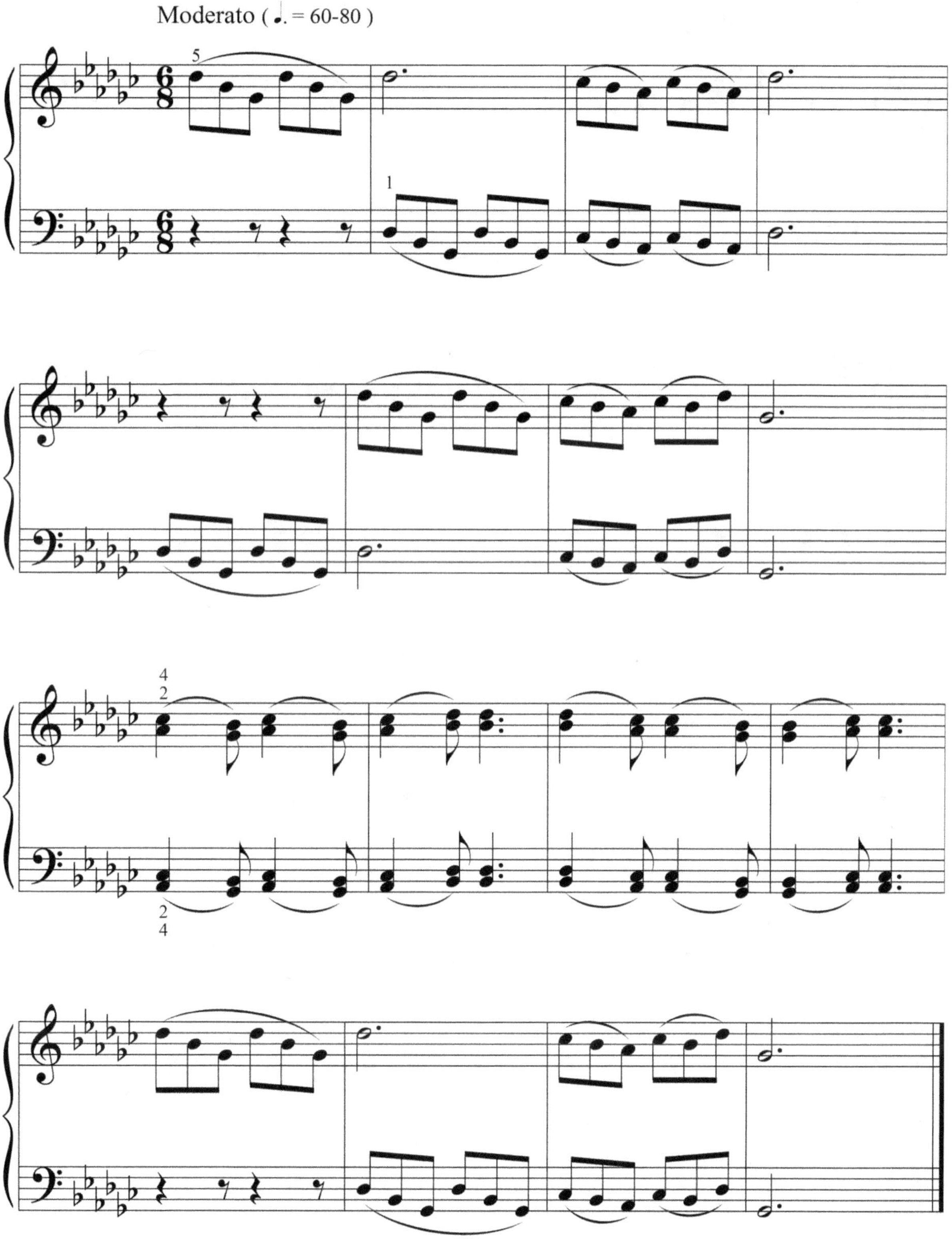

Moderato (♩. = 60-80)

More Steps

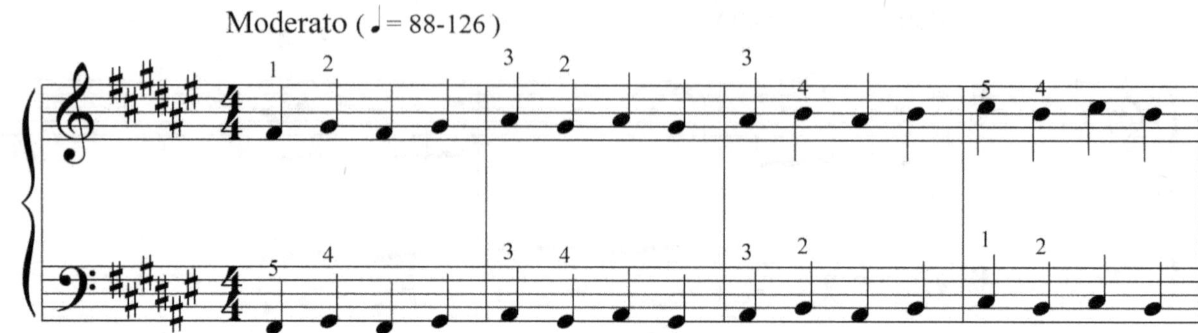

More Skips

Harmony

Leaps

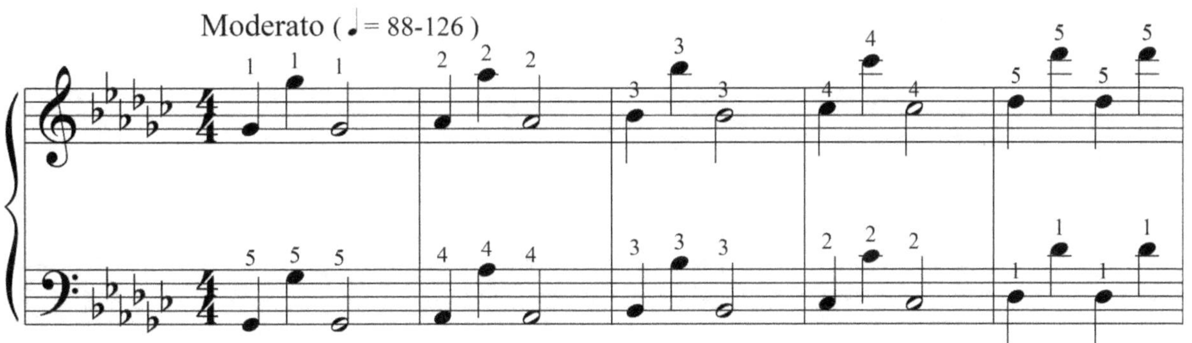

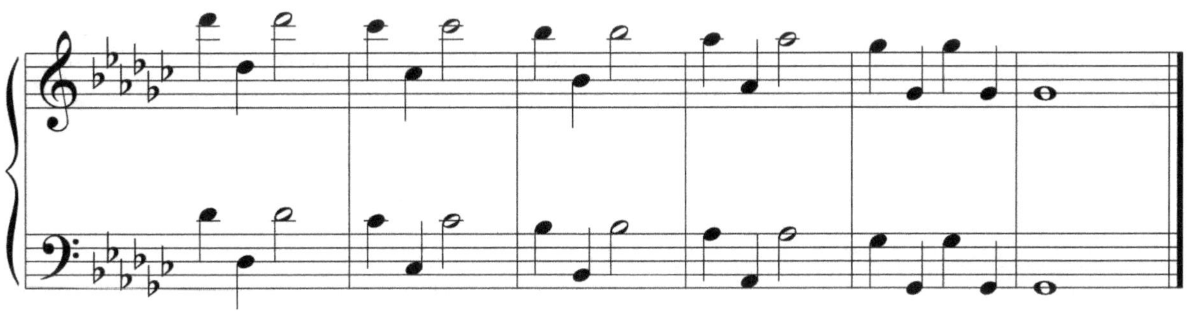

Steps

Skips

Lesson Twelve: D♯ (E♭)-Minor Position

My title for this piece:

Moderato (♩. = 60-80)

More Steps

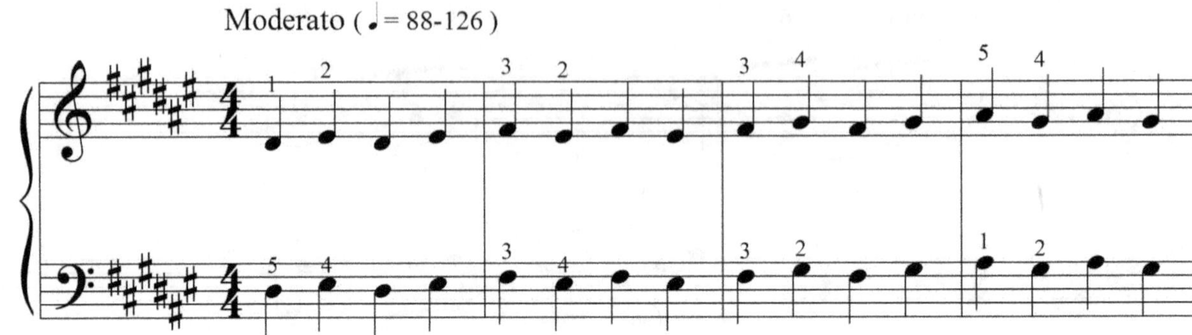

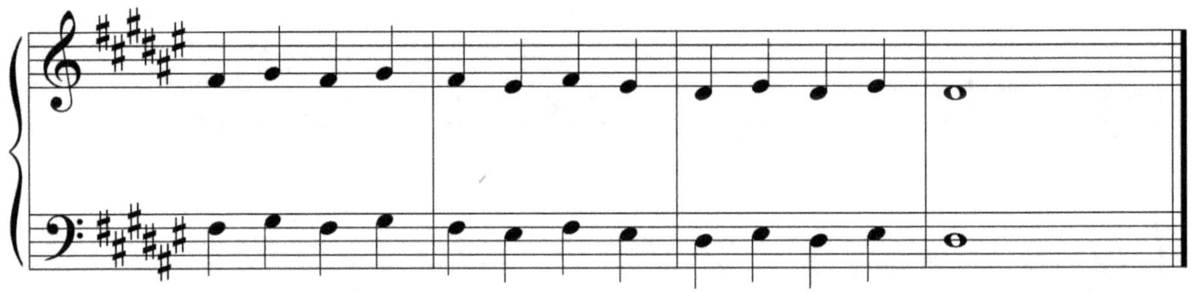

More Skips

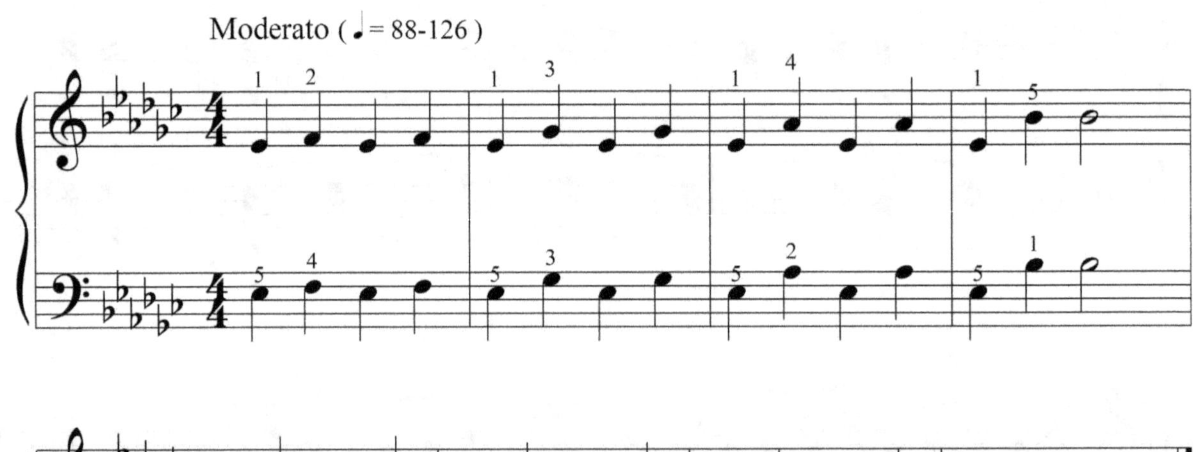

Harmony

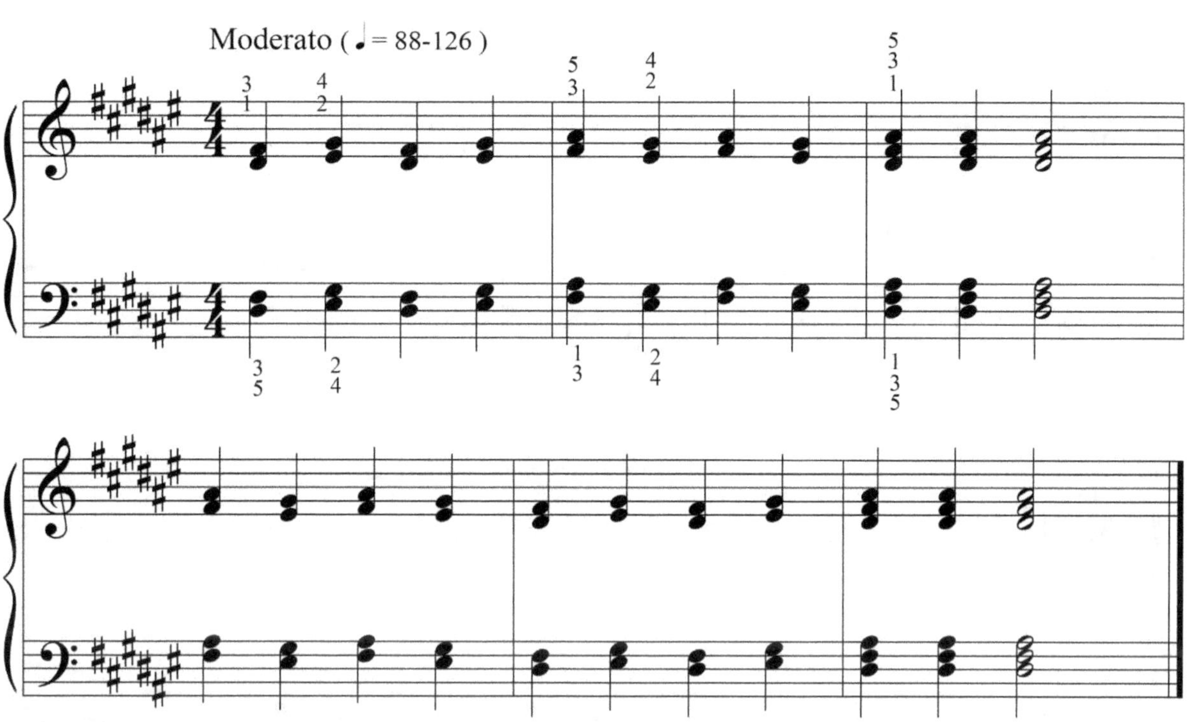

Leaps

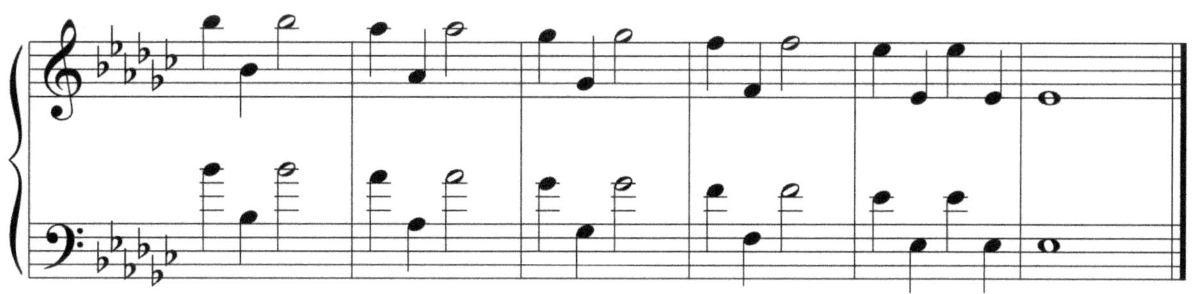

Recital Piece No. 7

*Position Change—the left hand position moves to the G♭ below middle C in measure 13 and 43, and to the G♭ above middle C in measure 45. The right hand position moves to the E♭ below middle C in measure 42 and to second E♭ above middle C in measure 46.

21

mp

25

29

33

mp

mf

41

f

L.H. R.H. L.H. R.H. L.H. R.H. L.H.

Position Change*

Position Change*

F♯- and G♭-Major Position, Chord, and Warm-up

If needed, refer to page 139 to complete the exercise.

1. Draw the notes to the F♯- or G♭-major position and chord, and label the keys.

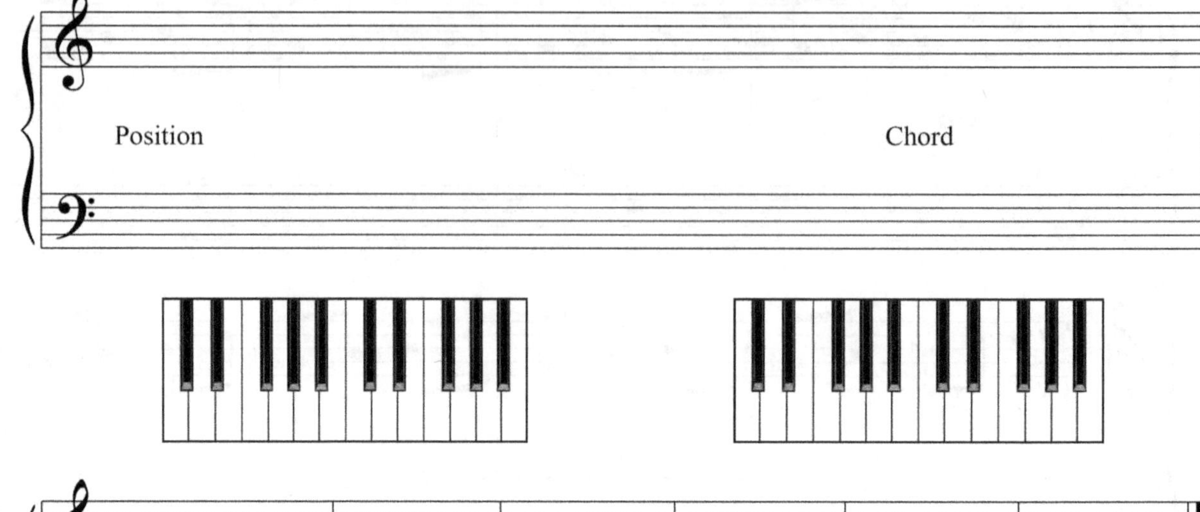

2. Draw the notes to the F♯- or G♭-major warm-up.

Warm-up

D♯- and E♭-Minor Position, Chord, and Warm-up

3. Draw the notes to the D♯- or E♭-minor position and chord, and label the keys.

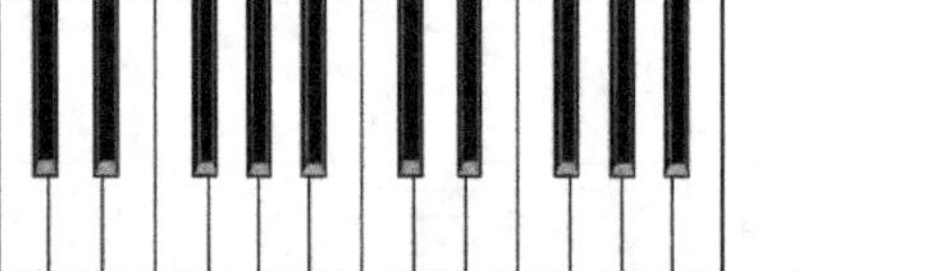

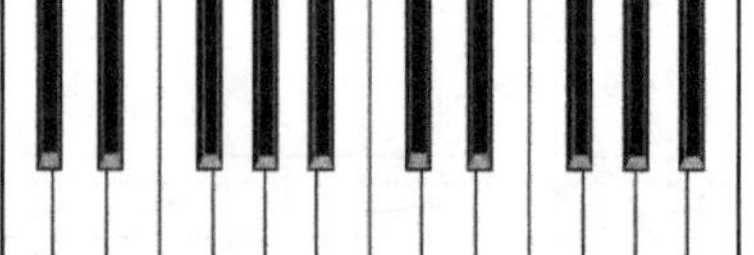

4. Draw the notes to the D♯- or E♭-minor warm-up.

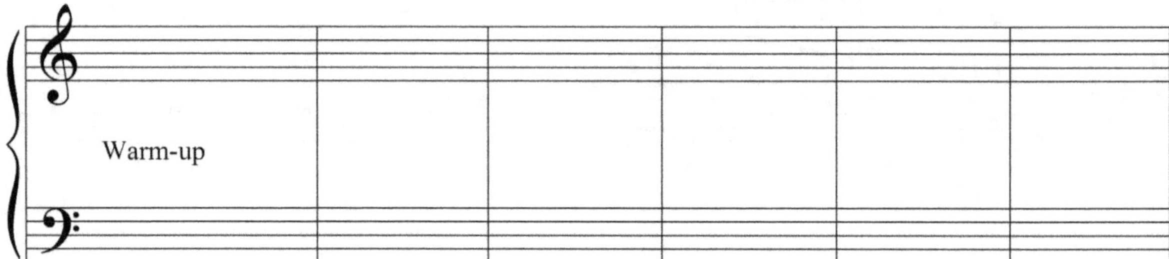

1. Name each of the circled black keys on the keyboard below with a flat (♭) symbol.

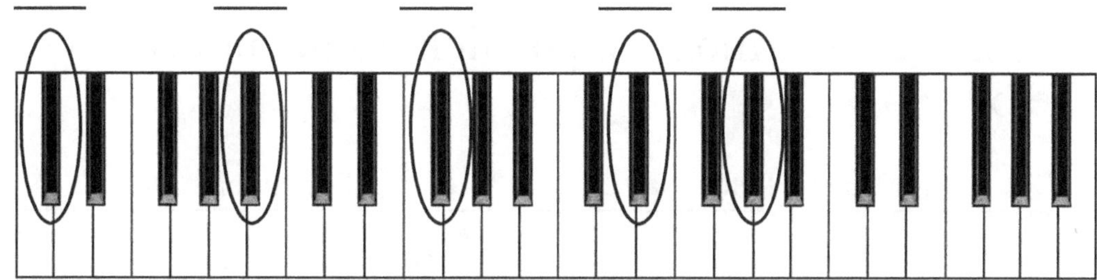

2. Draw two flat symbols (♭) on each line below.
3. Draw two flat symbols (♭) in each space below.

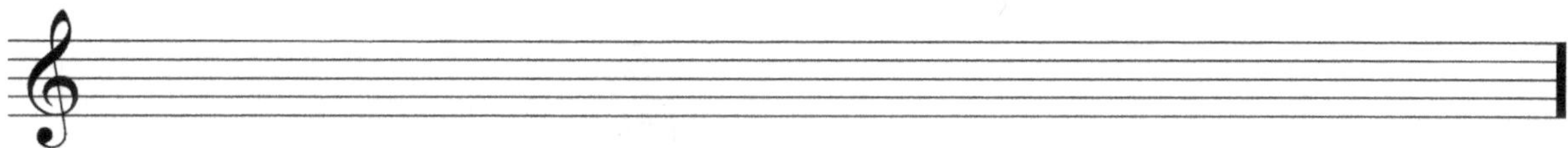

4. Draw two natural symbols (♮) on each line below.
5. Draw two natural symbols (♮) in each space below.

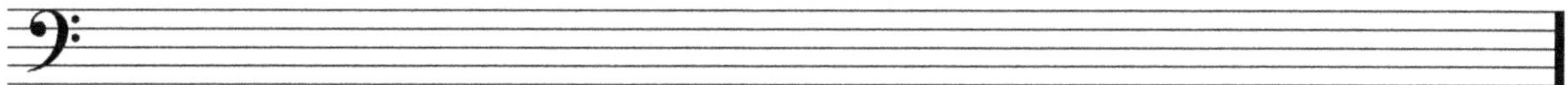

6. Draw the enharmonic equivalent on the staff below.

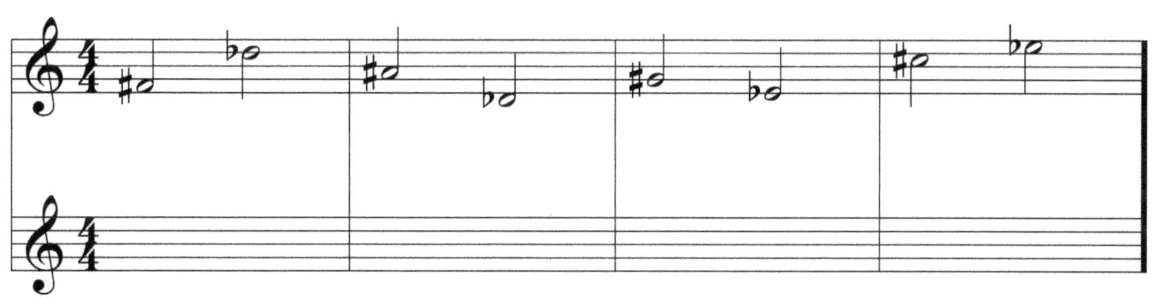

Review

1. Write the enharmonic equivalent to the notes below.

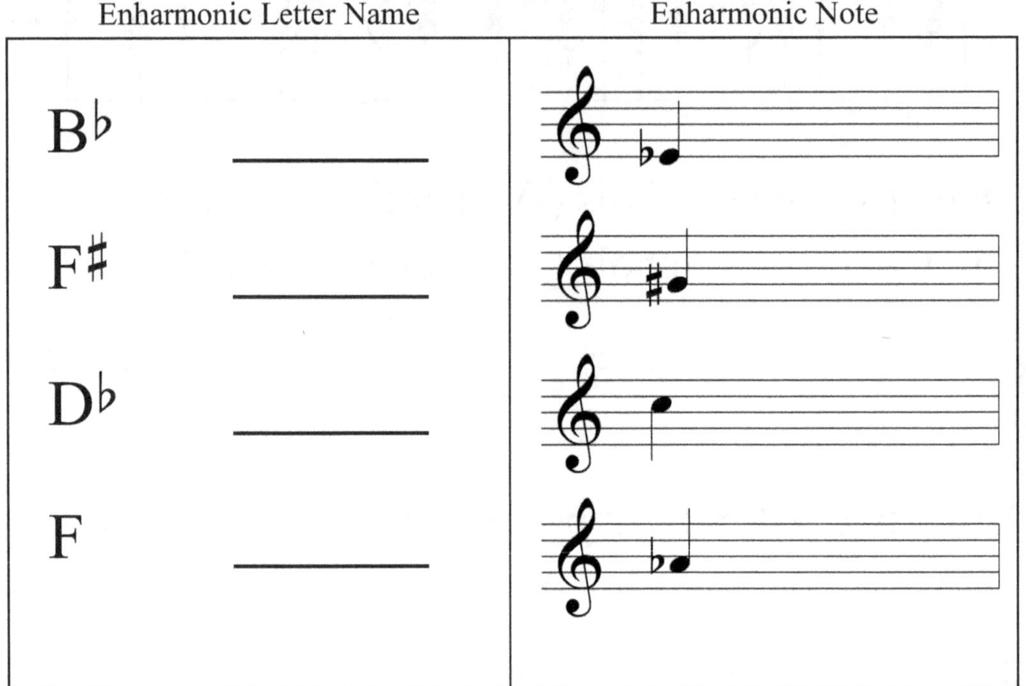

2. Add measure lines to the rhythms below.

$\frac{6}{8}$ ♩ ♪ ♪ ♪ ♪ ♪ ♩ ♩ ♪ ♪ ♪ ♪ ♩ ♪

$\frac{6}{8}$ ♩ ♩ ♩ ♪ ♪ ♪ ♪ ♪ ♪ ♪ ♪ ♪ ♩ ♪ ♩. ♩.

3. Clap the rhythms as you count.

Lesson Thirteen

D♭ Major / B♭ Minor

Repeat Signs

Repeat signs instruct the performer to repeat the music between the signs. When there is no matching repeat sign, you will repeat from the beginning.

OR

Alternate Endings

Often a composer will direct the performer to play a different ending after repeating a passage. This is done with the alternate ending markings.

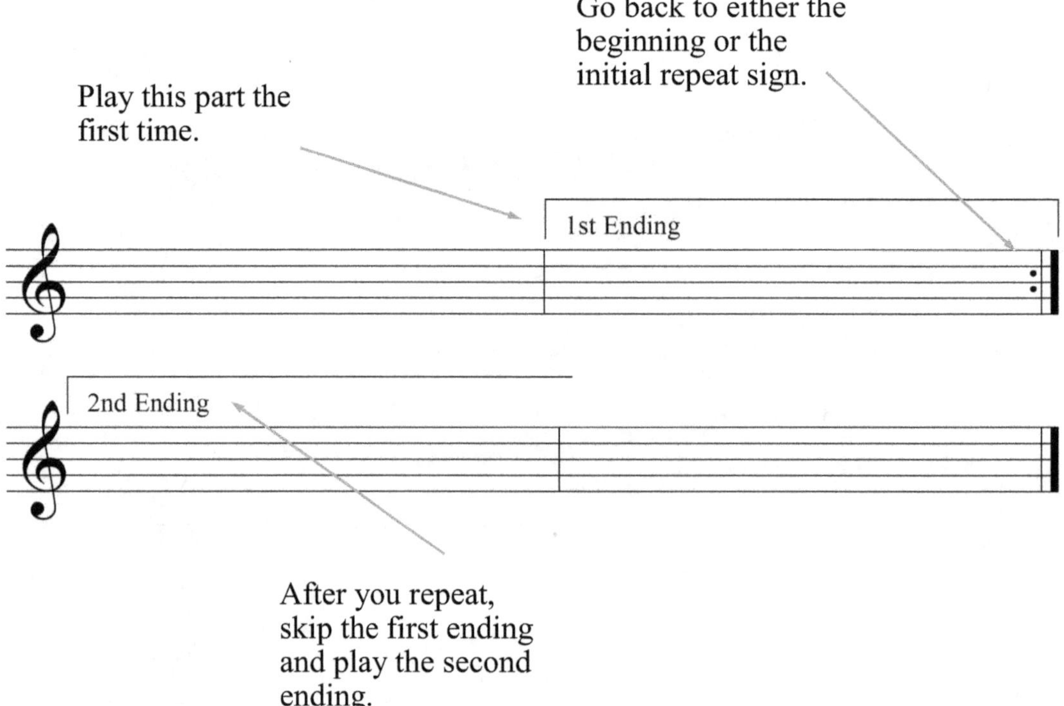

D♭-Major Position, Chord, and Warm-up

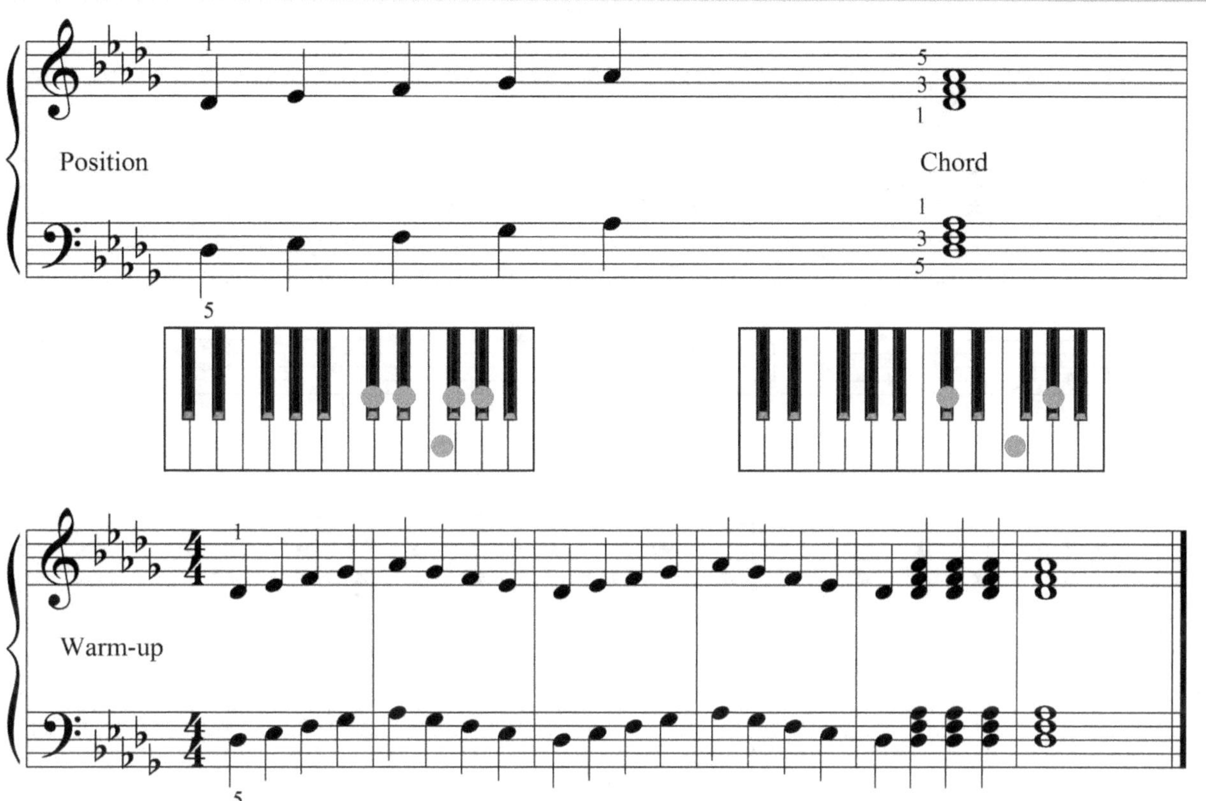

If needed, refer to Lesson Four for the exact key to play.

Another way to say "in D♭-major position" is, "in the key of D♭ major."

B♭-Minor Position, Chord, and Warm-up

Another way to say in "B♭-minor position" is, "in the key of B♭ minor."

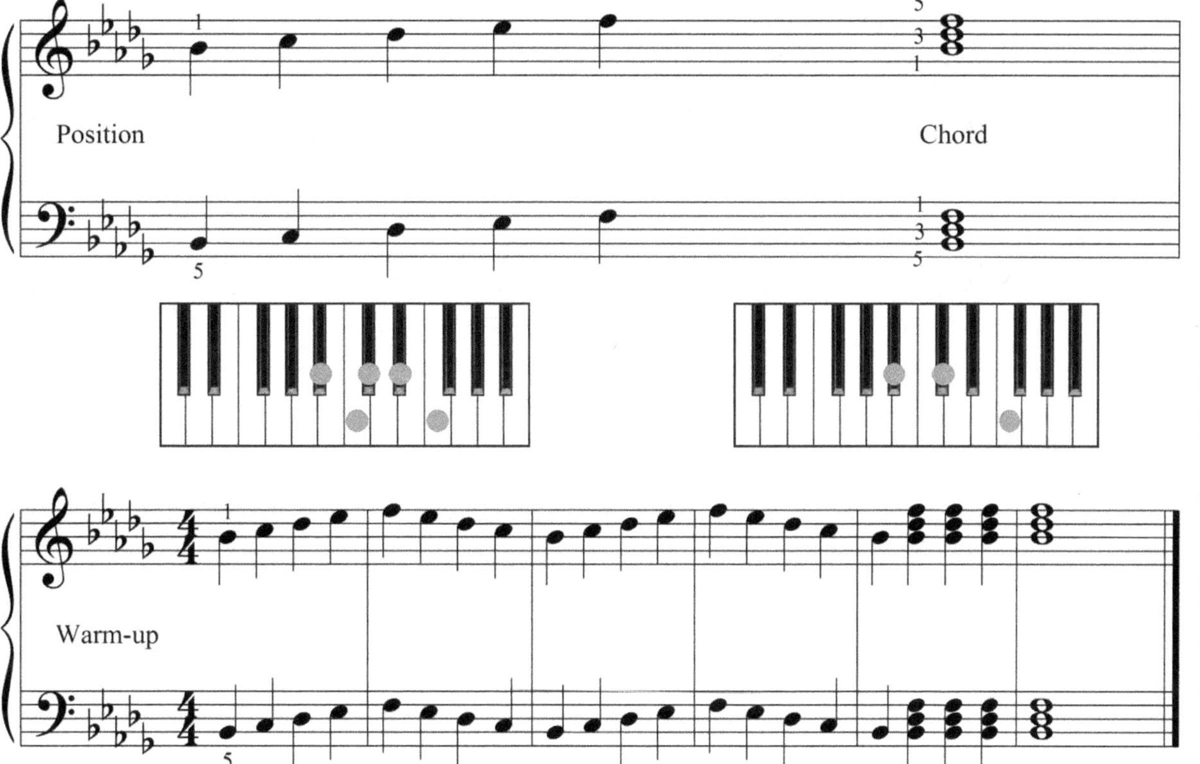

Steps

Moderato (♩= 88-126)

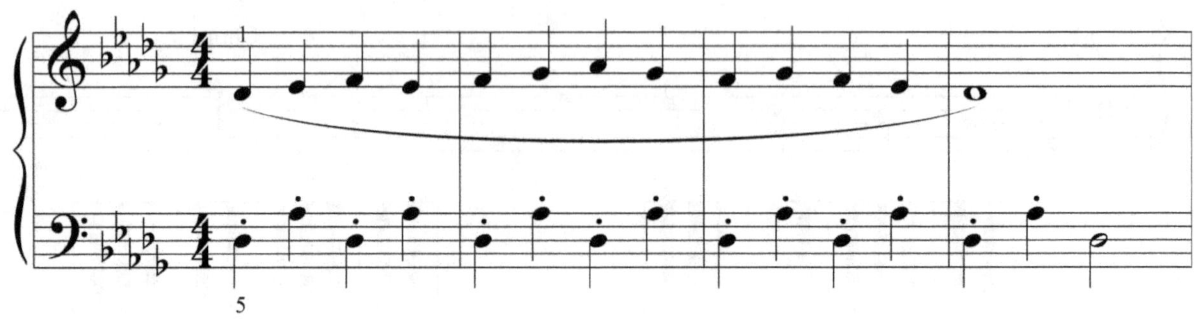

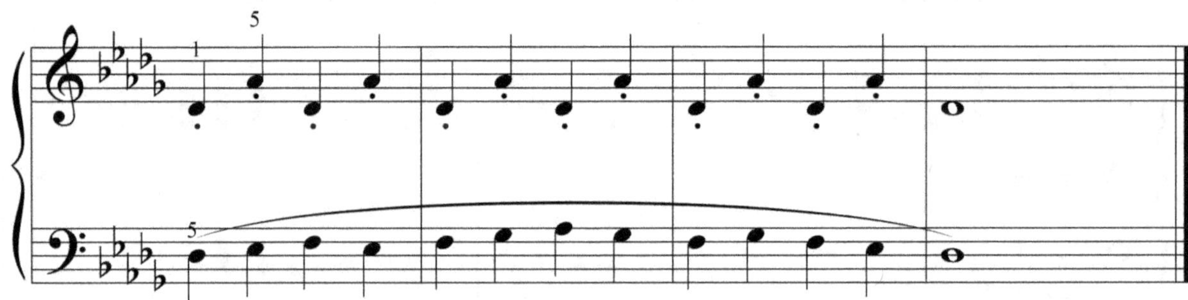

Skips

Moderato (♩= 88-126)

My title for this piece:

Moderato (♩ = 88-126)

f

mf (1st time)

p (2nd time)

f

More Steps

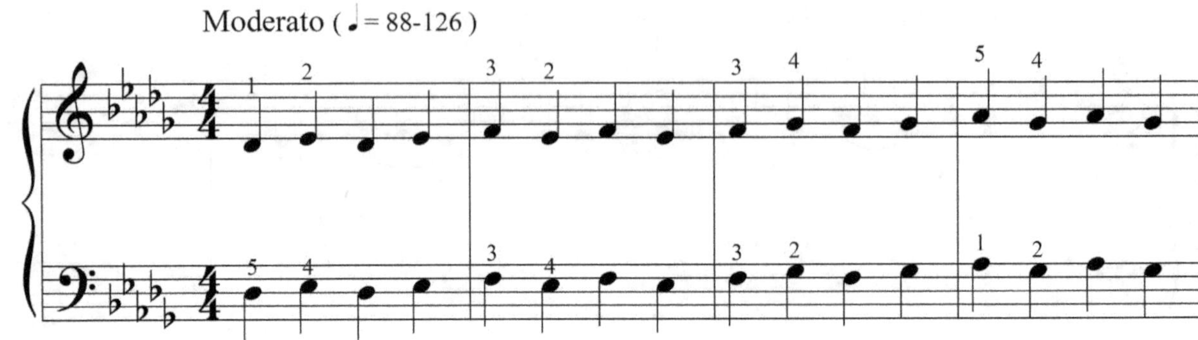

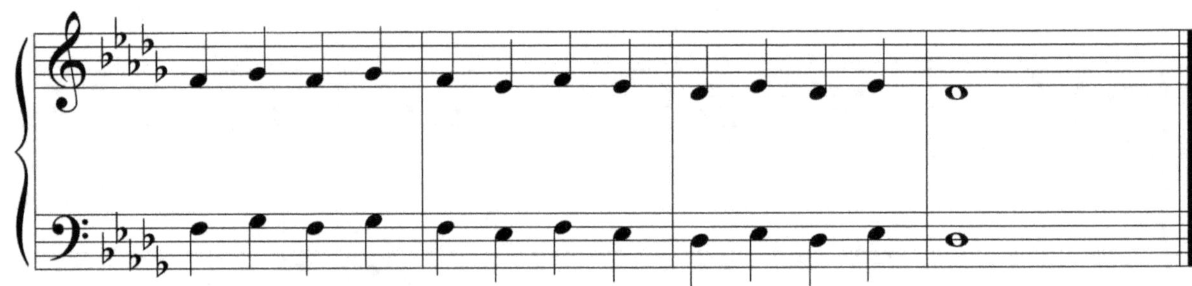

More Skips

Harmony

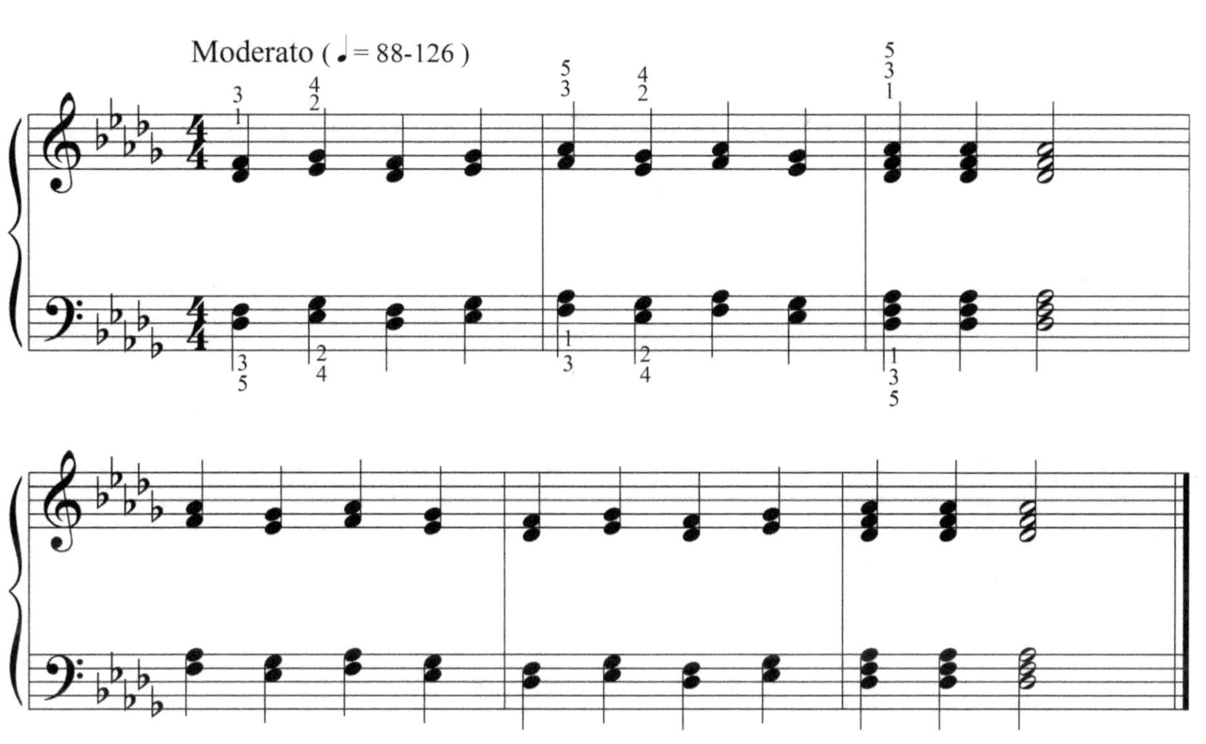

Leaps

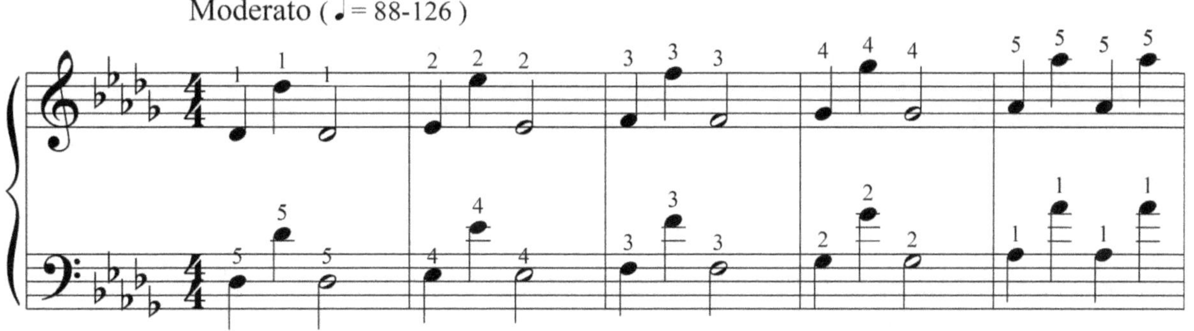

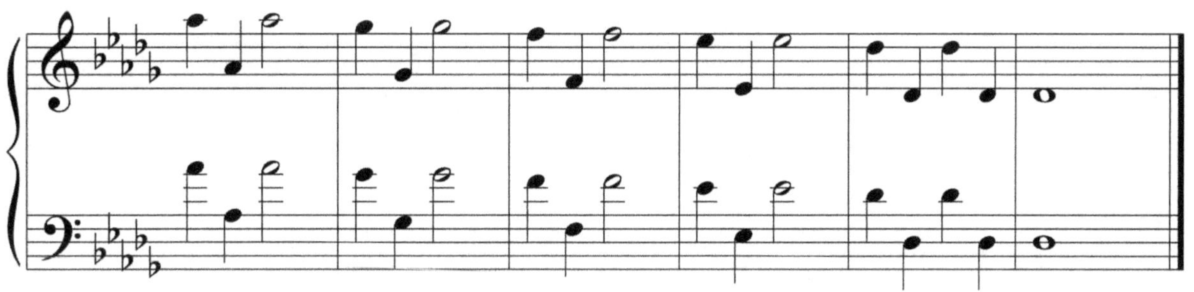

Steps

Moderato (♩ = 88-126)

Skips

Moderato (♩ = 88-126)

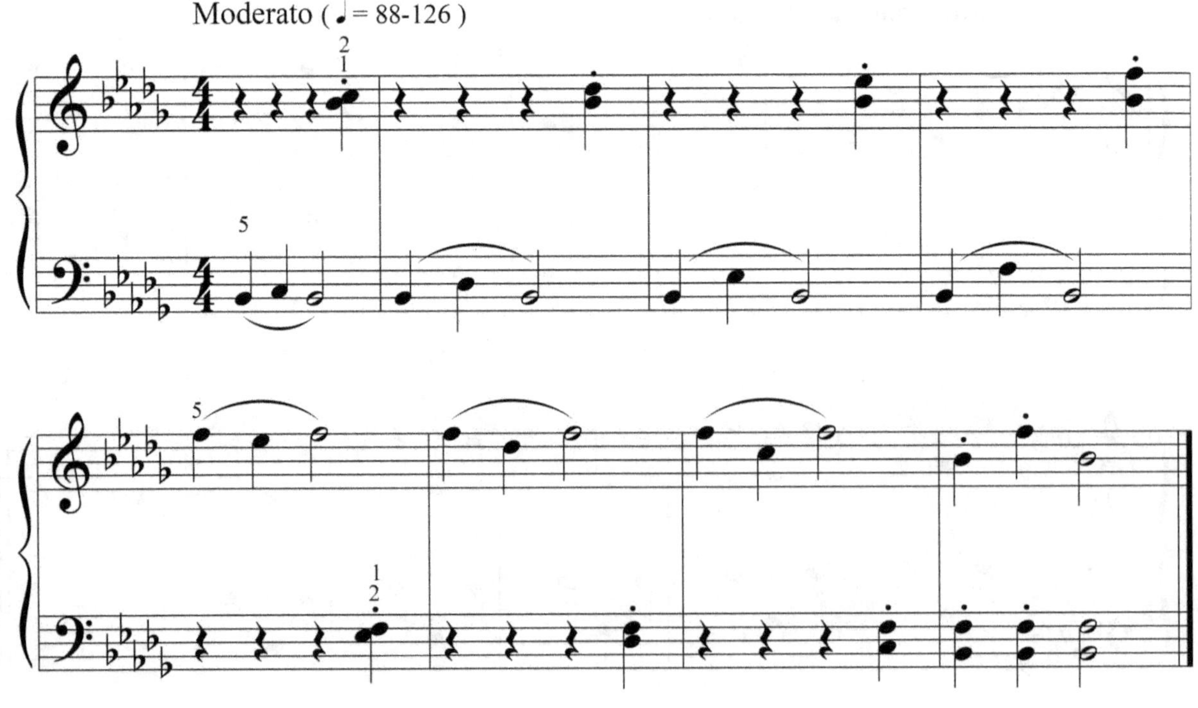

Lesson Thirteen: B♭-Minor Position

My title for this piece:

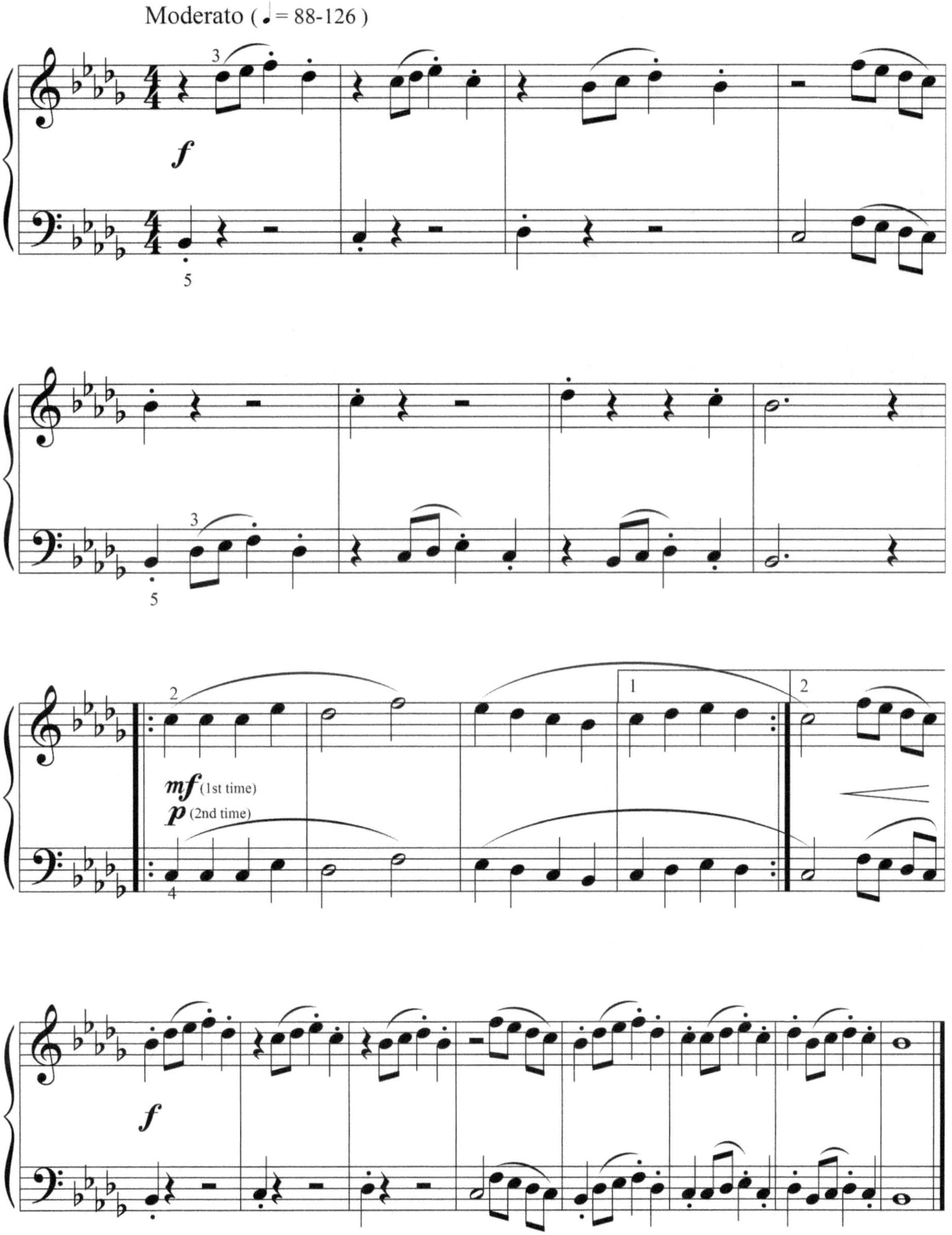
Moderato (♩ = 88-126)
f
mf (1st time)
p (2nd time)
f

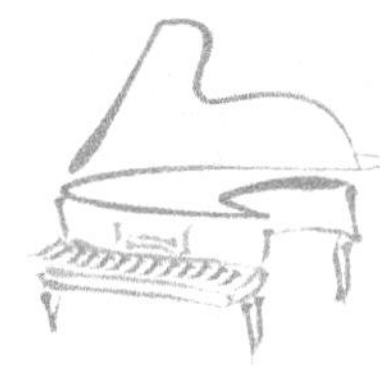

More Steps

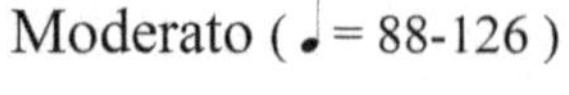

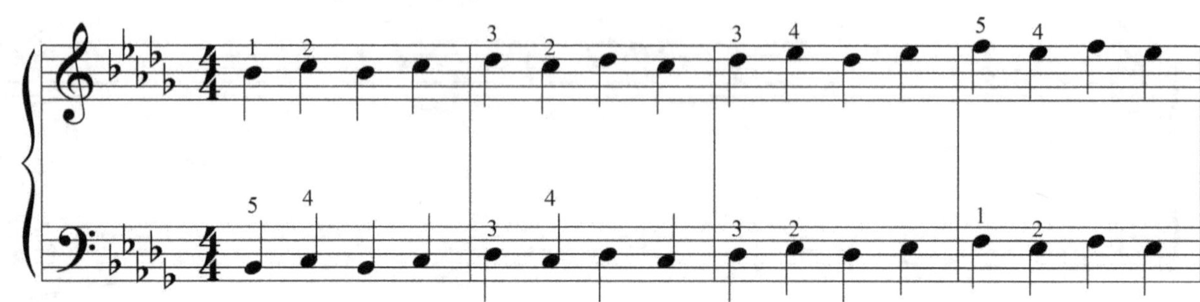

More Skips

Moderato (♩= 88-126)

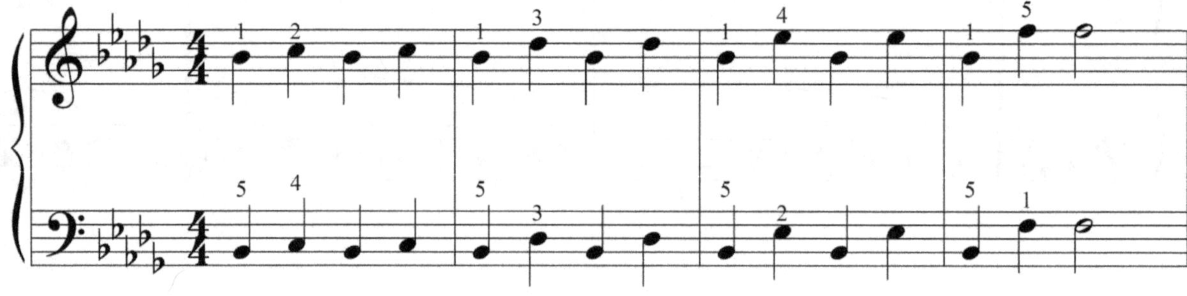

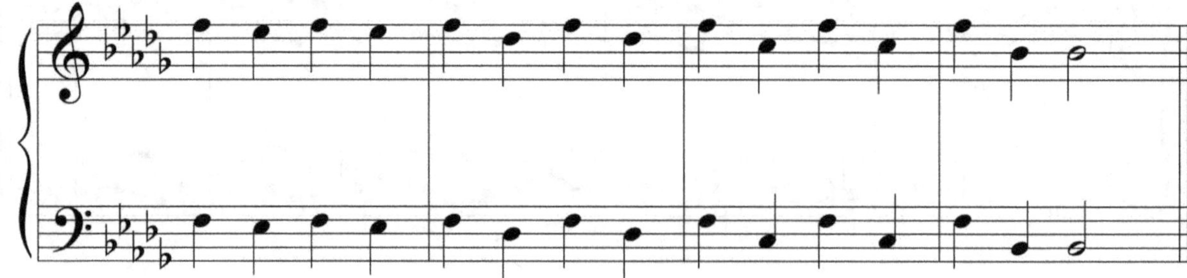

Harmony

Leaps

Recital Piece No. 8

Moderato (♩ = 88)

17

5

mf – *p* (second time)

1

21

mp

mf

25

4

p

mf

29

5

p

mf

33

p

D♭-Major Position, Chord, and Warm-up

If needed, refer to page 157 to complete the exercise.

1. Draw the notes to the D♭-major position and chord, and label the keys.

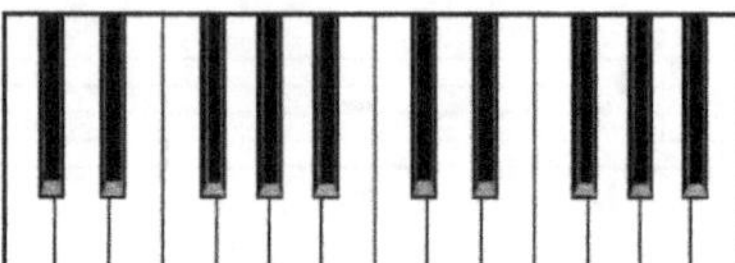

2. Draw the notes to the D♭-major warm-up.

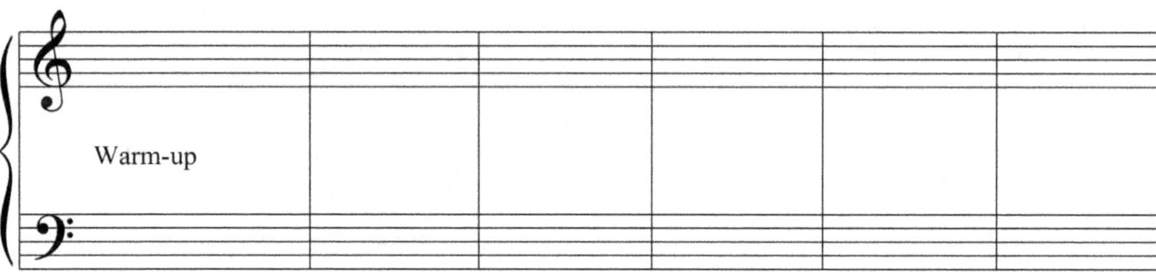

B♭-Minor Position, Chord, and Warm-up

3. Draw the notes to the B♭-minor position and chord, and label the keys.

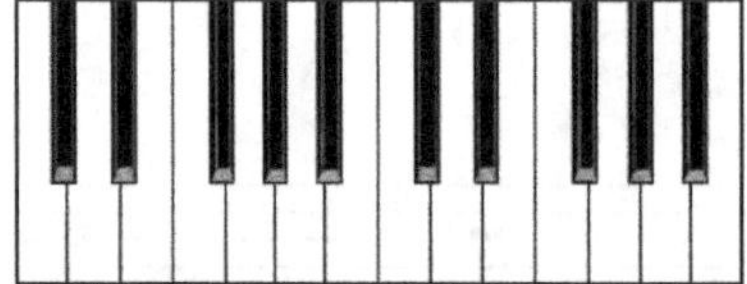

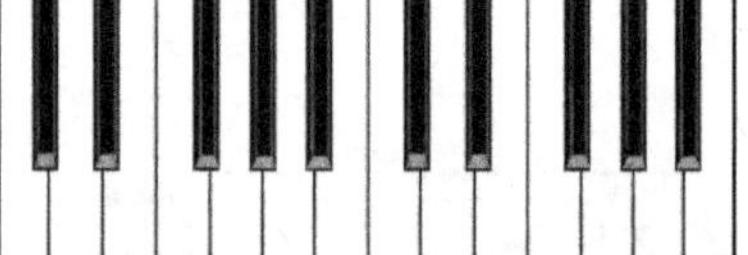

4. Draw the notes to the B♭-minor warm-up.

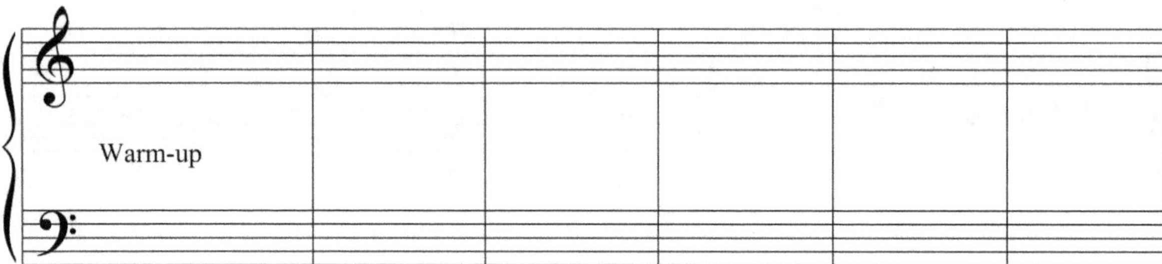

1. Draw the necessary symbols to make measures five and six the first ending and measures seven and eight the second. Then draw the symbols to repeat from measure two.

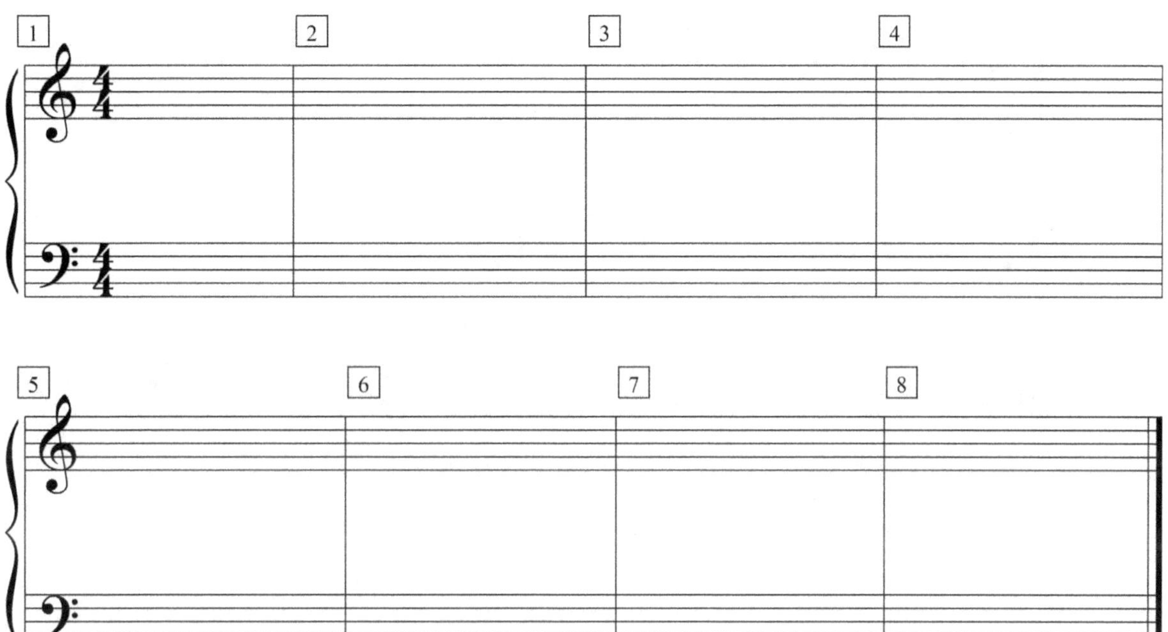

2. Draw the necessary symbols to make measures three and seven first endings and measures four and eight second endings. Each first ending will repeat from the beginning of its staff.

Review

1. How many times will you play measure three? ____

2. How many times will you play measure five? ____

3. How many times will you play measure seven? ____

4. How many times will you play measure eight? ____

Lesson Fourteen

A♭ Major / F Minor

Question: What's the difference between slurs and ties?

Answer: Slurred notes have distinct sounds, while tied notes have the same sound.

Ties

If you have two pieces of string and you tie them together end to end, how many pieces of string will you have?

The answer is one long string.

Musical ties have the same effect on notes. Take two quarter notes, tie them together, and you have one sound the length of two quarter notes.

Ties apply to notes that have the same sound but may or may not have the same rhythmic value.

Sixteenth Notes and Rests

 Sixteenth Note  Sixteenth Rest

One sixteenth note (𝅘𝅥𝅯) is equal to half the value of a eighth note (𝅘𝅥𝅮).

One sixteenth rest (𝄿) is equal to half the value of a eighth rest (𝄾).

One eighth note = two sixteenth notes 𝅘𝅥𝅮 = 𝅘𝅥𝅯𝅘𝅥𝅯 or ♬

One eighth rest = two sixteenth rests 𝄾 = 𝄿𝄿

Assuming a 4/4 time signature, the following chart shows how many sixteenth notes equal the note on the left.

A♭-Major Position, Chord, and Warm-up

If needed, refer to Lesson Four for the exact key to play.

Another way to say "in A♭-major position" is, "in the key of A♭ major."

F-Minor Position, Chord, and Warm-up

Another way to say in "F-minor position" is, "in the key of F minor."

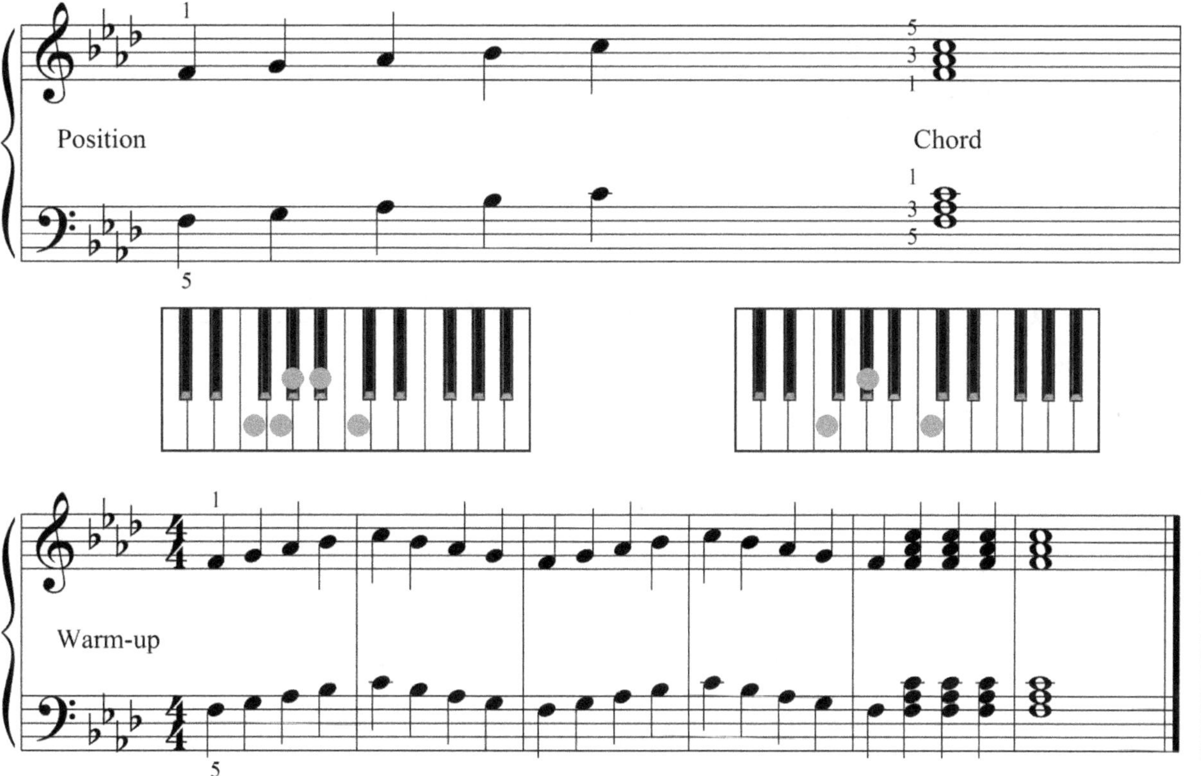

Lesson Fourteen: A♭-Major Position

Steps

Moderato (♩ = 88-126)

Skips

Moderato (♩ = 88-126)

My title for this piece:

Moderato (♩ = 60-80)

More Steps

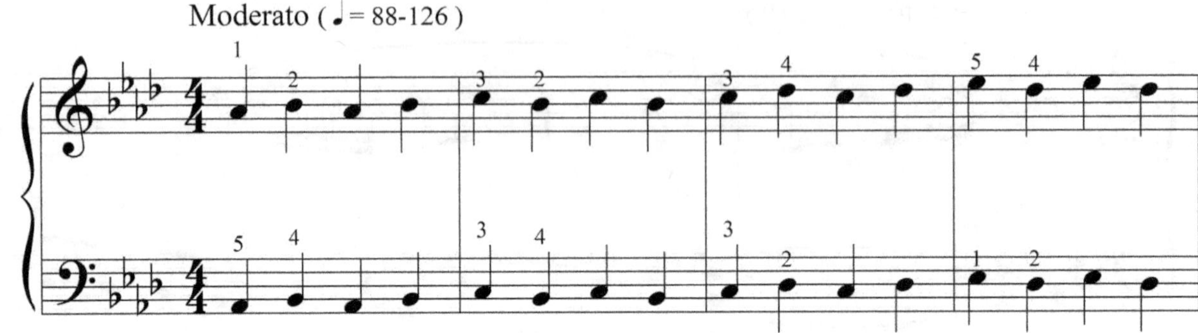

More Skips

Harmony

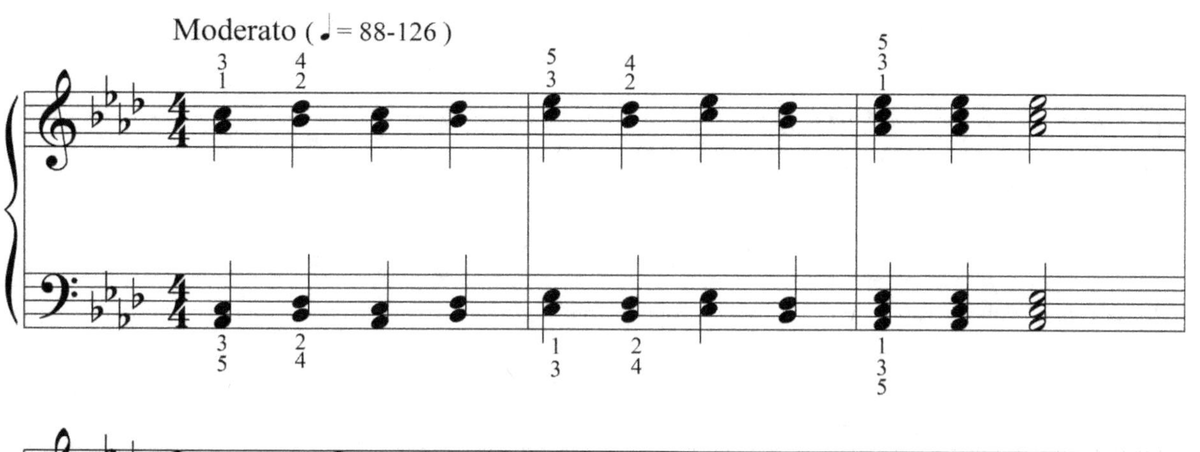

Leaps

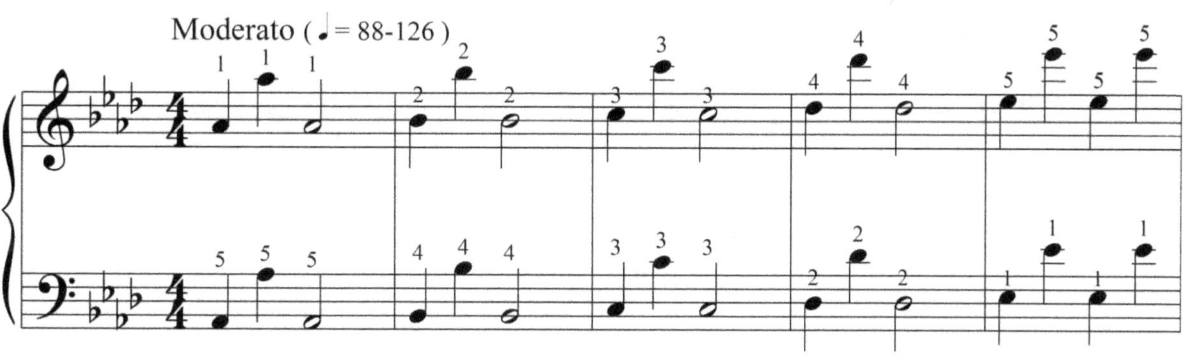

Steps

Moderato (♩ = 88-126)

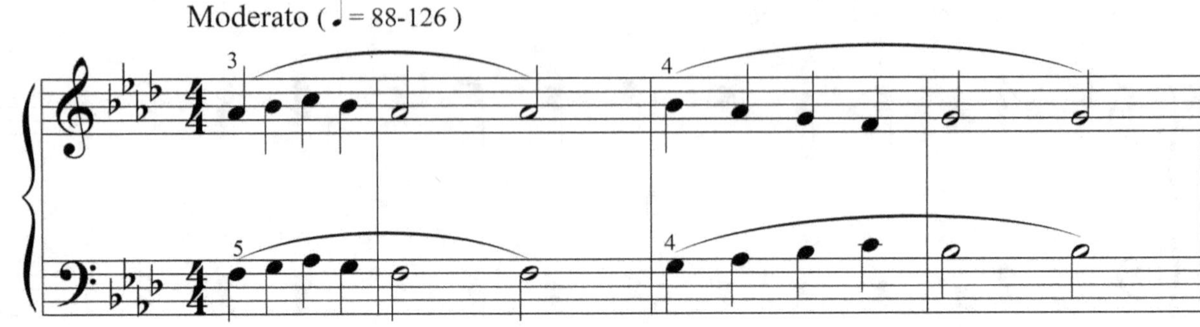

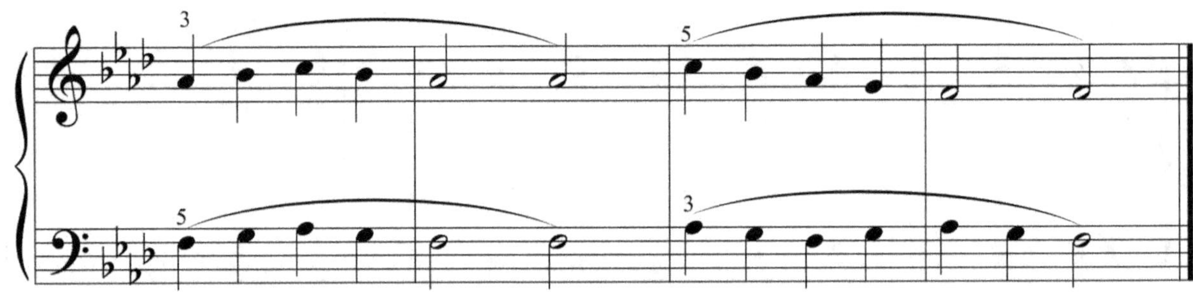

Skips

Moderato (♩ = 88-126)

Lesson Fourteen: F-Minor Position

My title for this piece:

Moderato (♩ = 60-80)

More Steps

Moderato (♩ = 88-126)

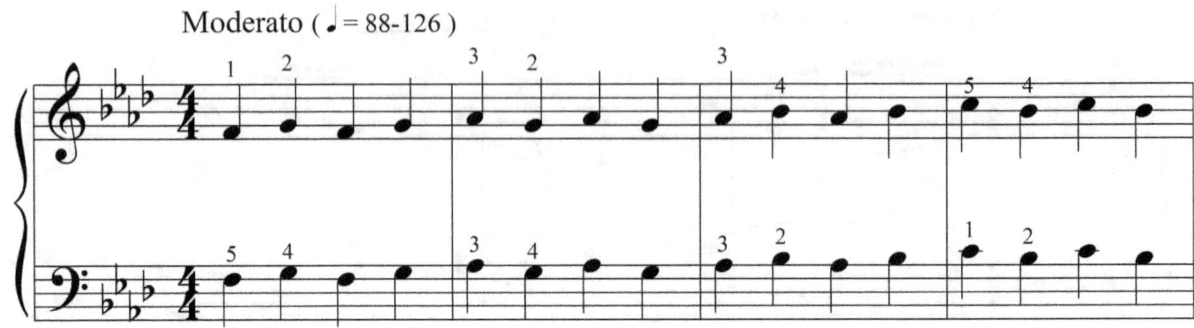

More Skips

Moderato (♩ = 88-126)

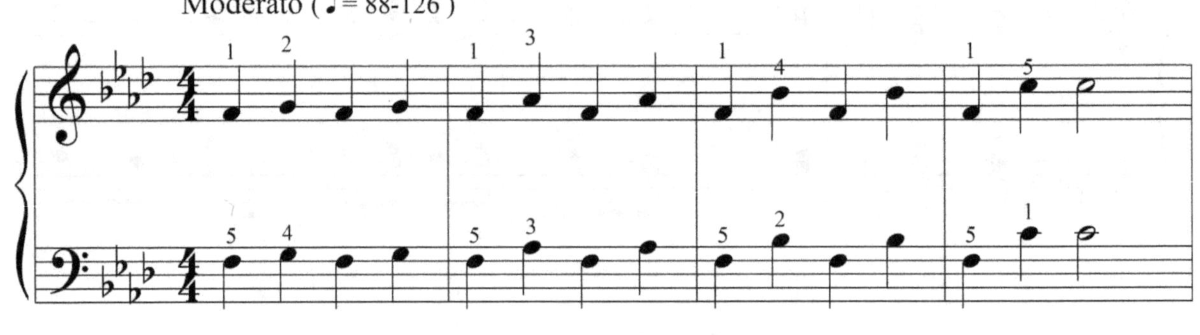

Harmony

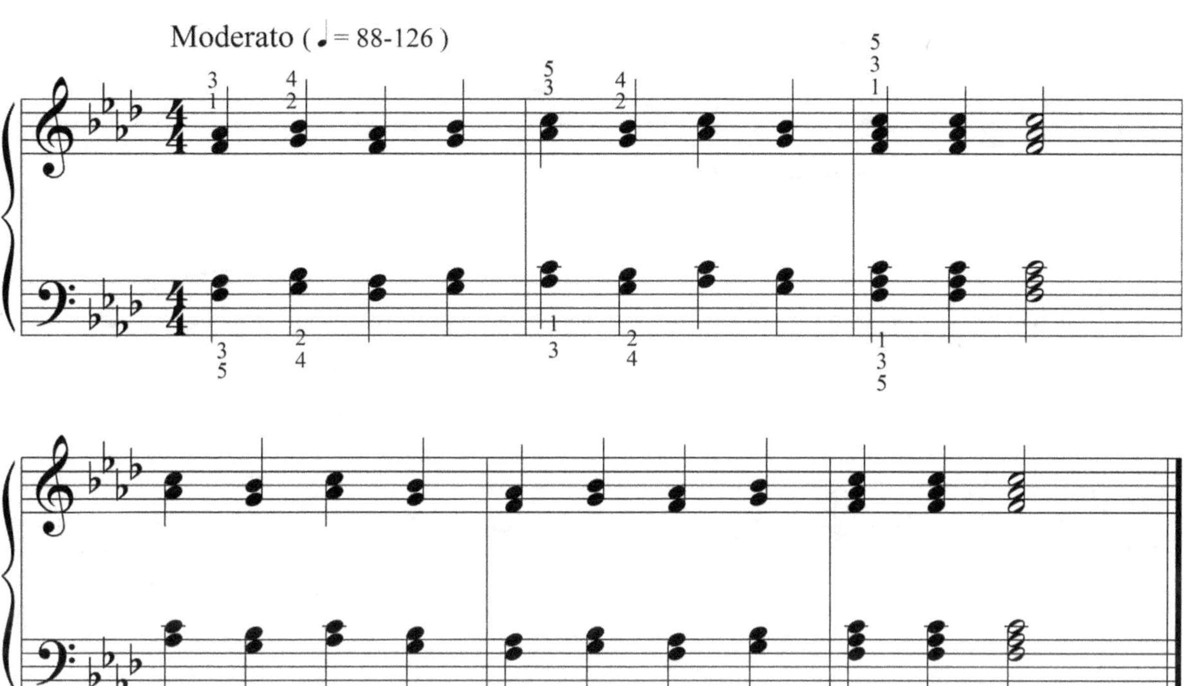

Leaps

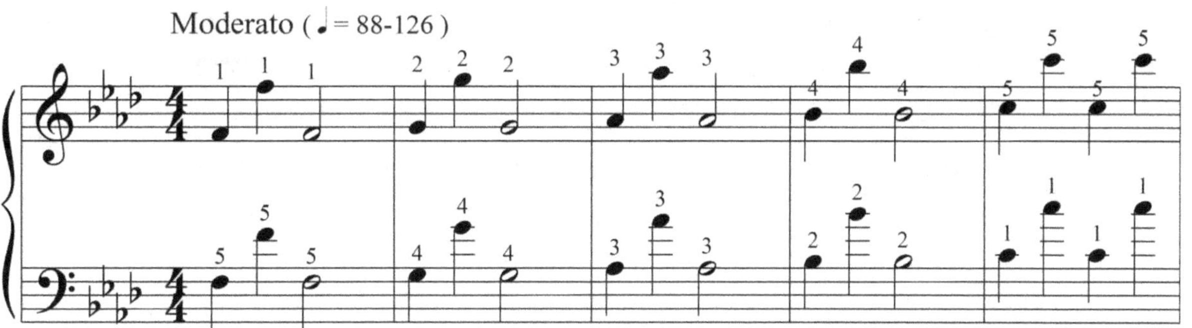

Recital Piece No. 9

13

16

2

2

5

5

mf

1

19

3

1

3

22

3

5

25

2

5

2

f

1

A♭-Major Position, Chord, and Warm-up

If needed, refer to page 173 to complete the exercise.

1. Draw the notes to the A♭-Major position and chord, and label the keys.

2. Draw the notes to the A♭-major warm-up.

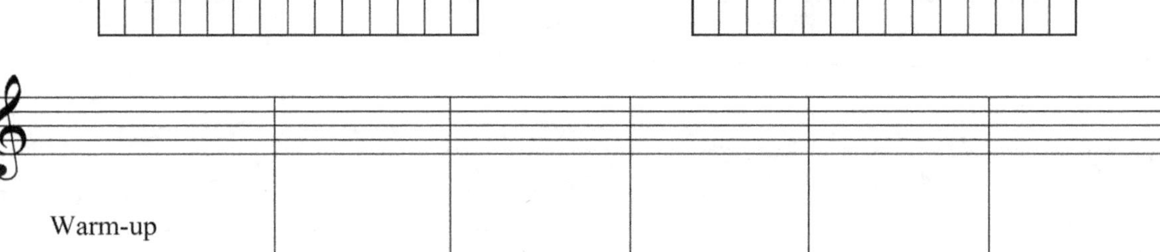

F-Minor Position, Chord, and Warm-up

3. Draw the notes to the F minor position and chord, and label the keys.

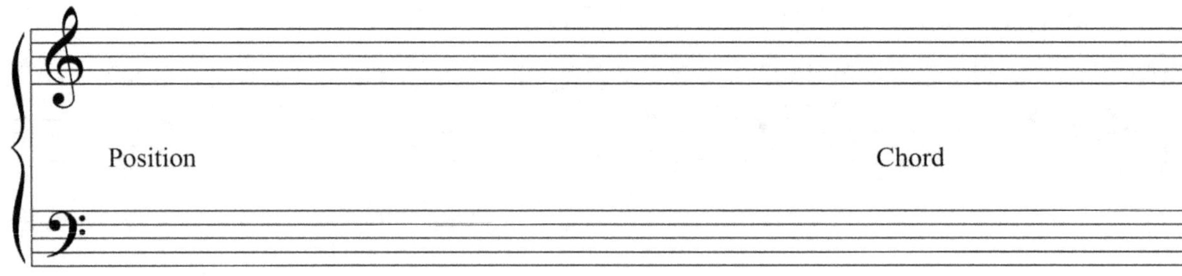

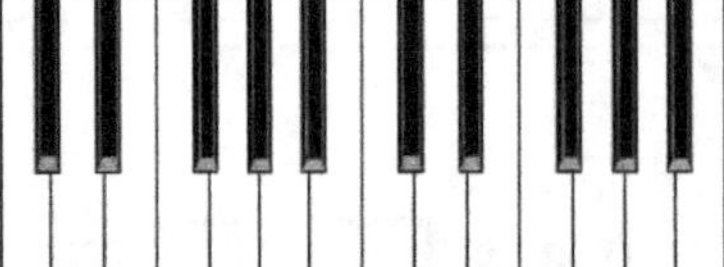

4. Draw the notes to the F minor warm-up.

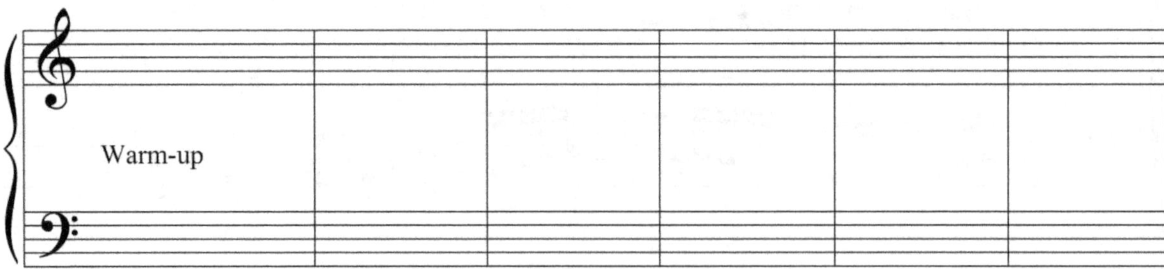

1. On the staff below
   - Draw the key signature for A♭ major
   - Draw three measures in 4/4 time
   - Write four quarter notes in each measure from the A♭-major position—tie the fourth and first beats and slur the second and third beats
   - Use notes from A♭-major position in both clefs

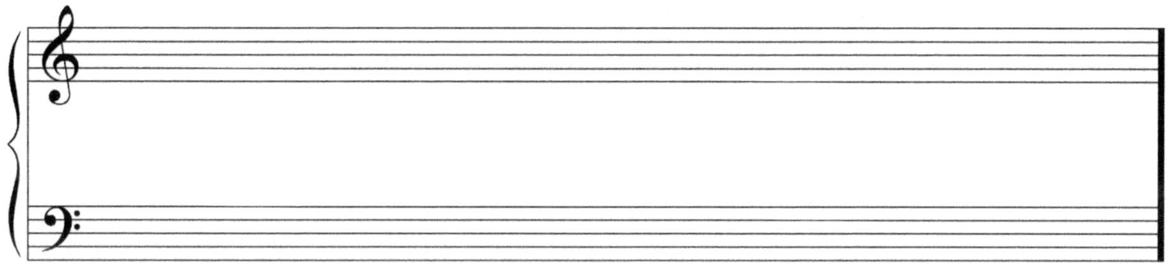

2. Draw as many sixteenth notes as necessary to equal the value of the given note.

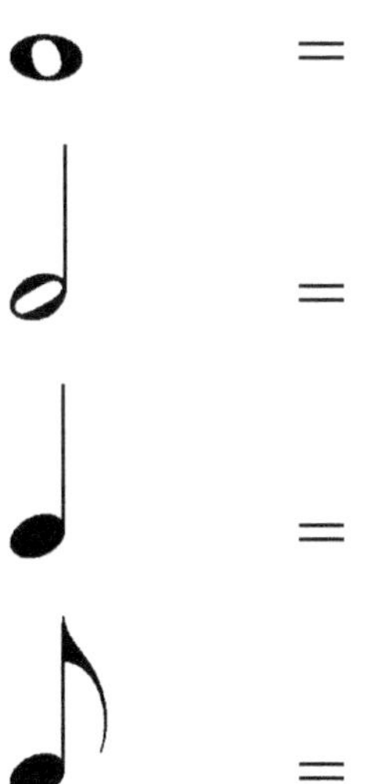

Review

1. Draw a circle around the tied notes and an X through the slurred notes.

2. Assuming a 4/4 time signature, draw the sixteenth notes equal the value of the note on the left.

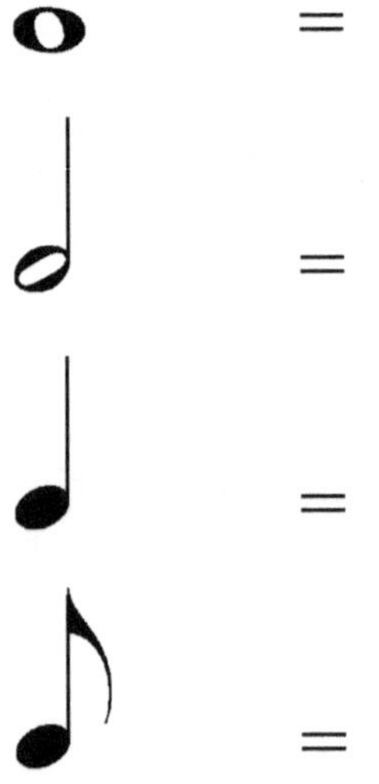

Lesson Fifteen

E♭ Major / C Minor

Intervals

An interval is the measurement of the distance between two notes. It is common to say that two notes are *x interval* apart. Or, that two notes form an *interval of x*. In this lesson, the following intervals are used:

2nds 3rds 4ths 5ths

Melodic Intervals

A melodic interval is the distance between two notes **played in succession**. The examples below are commonly referred to as "melodic 2nd", "melodic 3rd", "melodic 4th", and "melodic 5th".

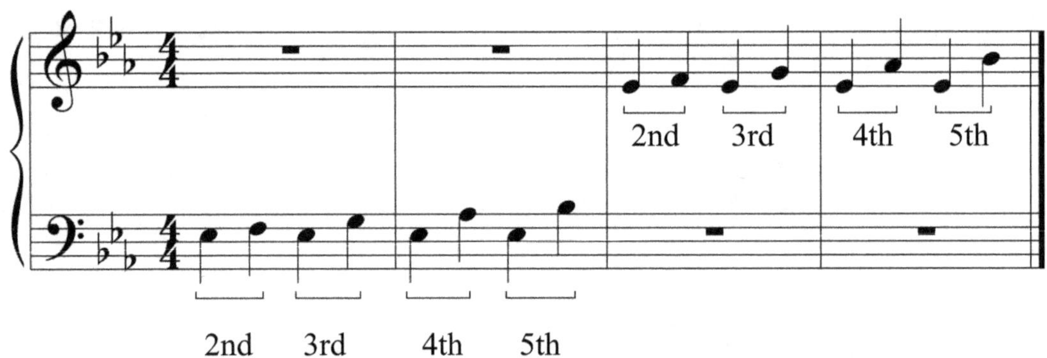

Harmonic Intervals

A harmonic interval is the distance between two notes **played simultaneously**. The examples below are commonly referred to as "harmonic 2nd", "harmonic 3rd", "harmonic 4th", and "harmonic 5th".

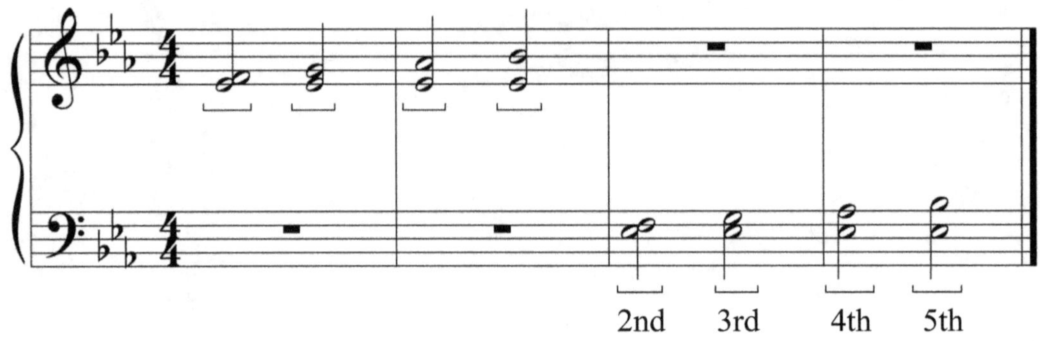

E♭-Major Position, Chord, and Warm-up

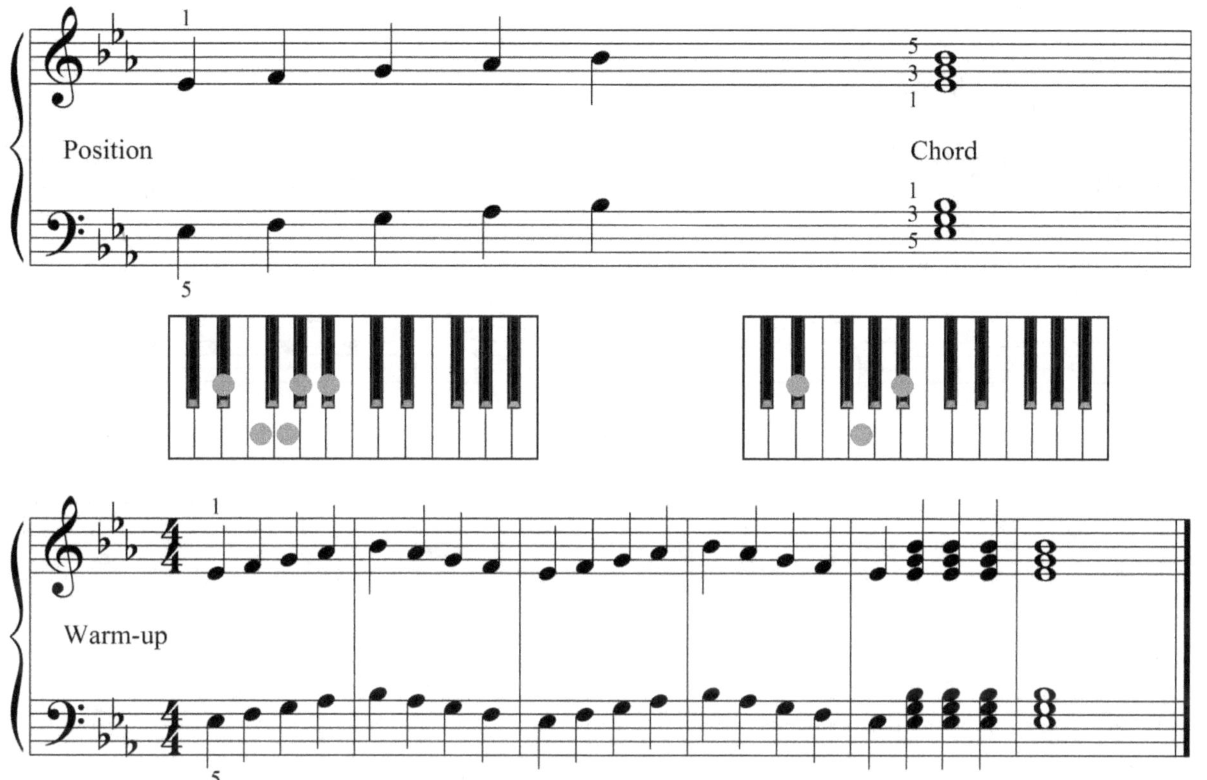

If needed, refer to Lesson Four for the exact key to play.

Another way to say "in E♭-major position" is, "in the key of E♭ major."

C-Minor Position, Chord, and Warm-up

Another way to say in "C-minor position" is, "in the key of C minor."

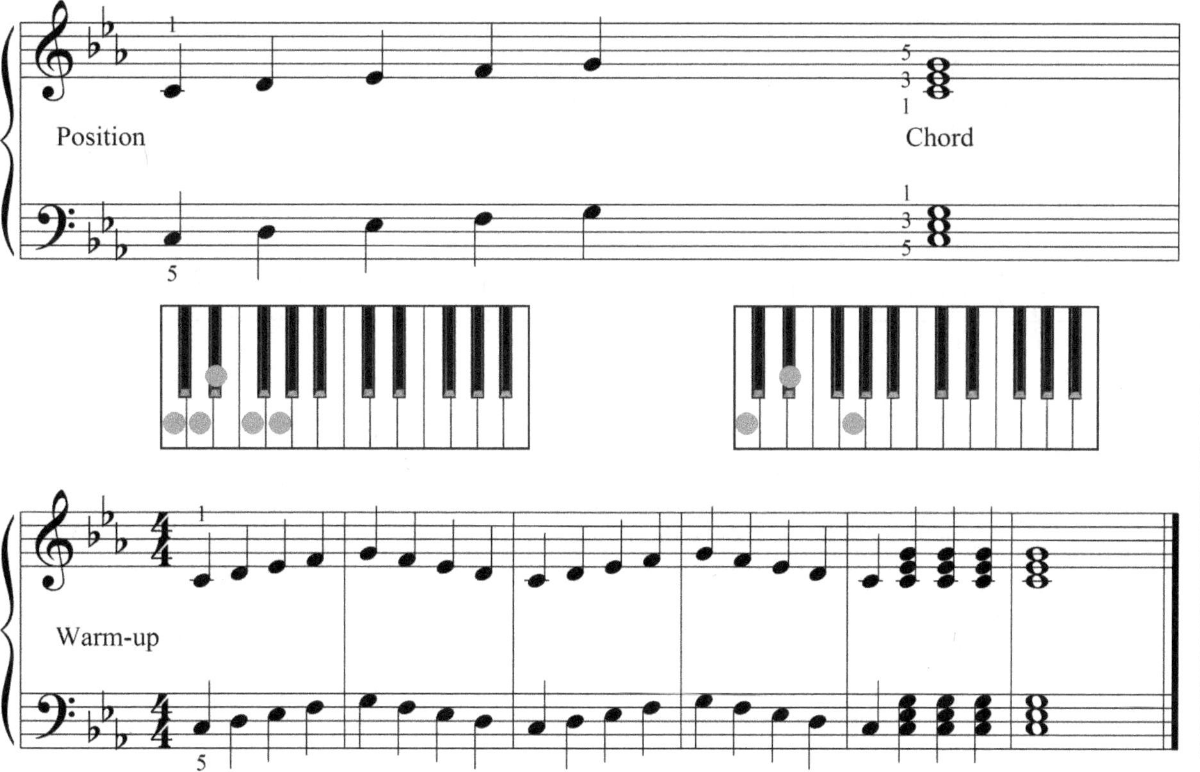

Steps

Moderato (♩ = 88-126)

Skips

Moderato (♩ = 88-126)

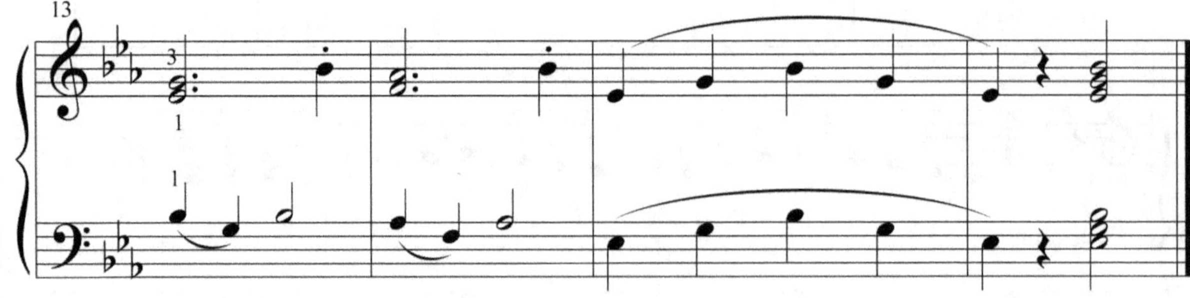

My title for this piece:

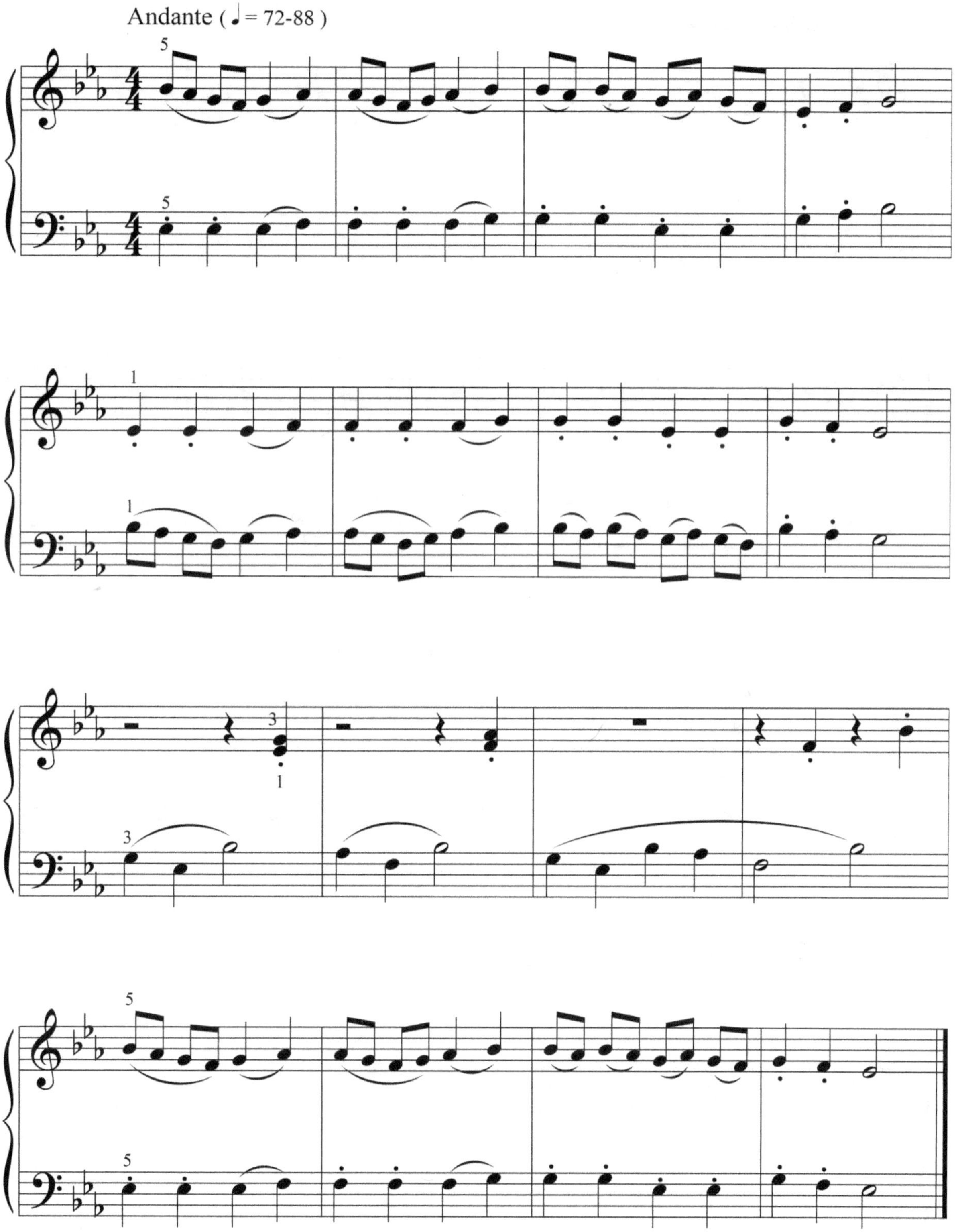

Andante (♩ = 72-88)

More Steps

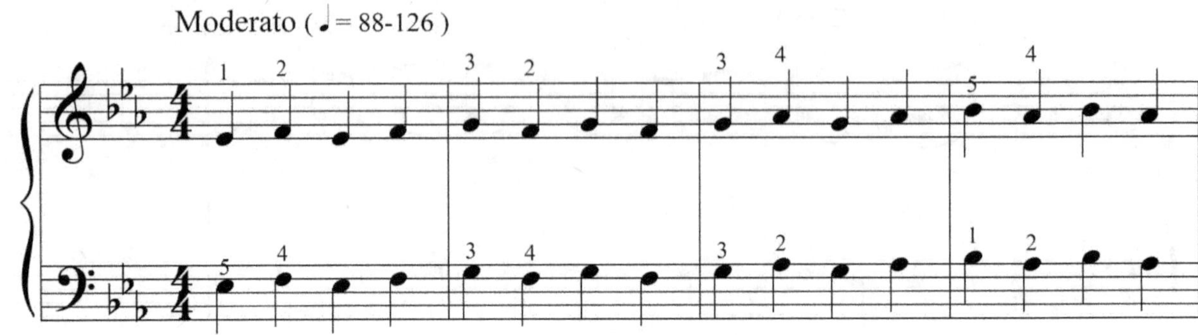

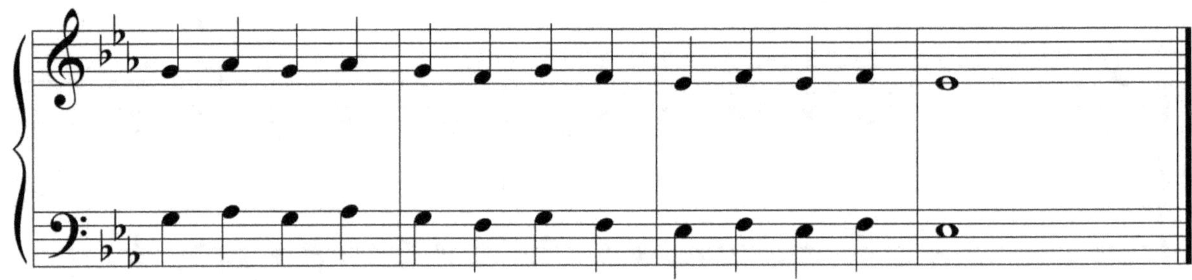

More Skips

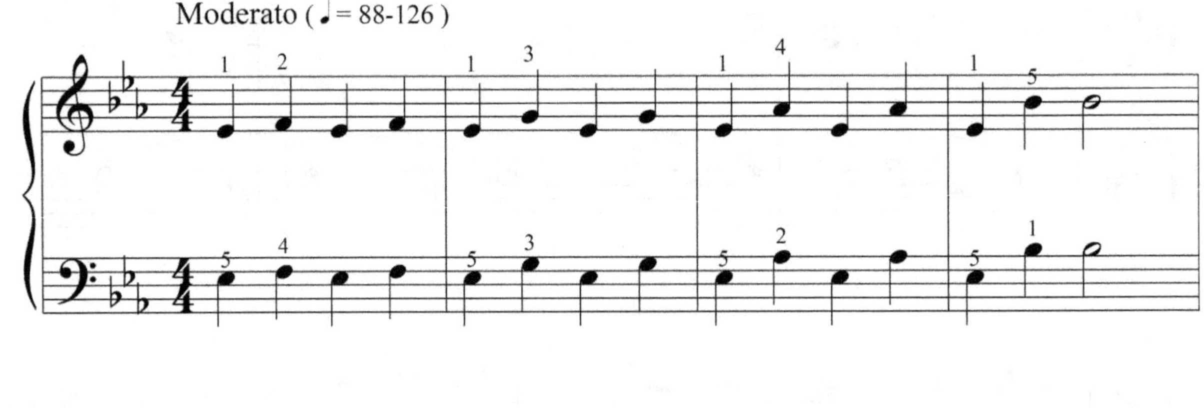

Harmony

Moderato (♩ = 88-126)

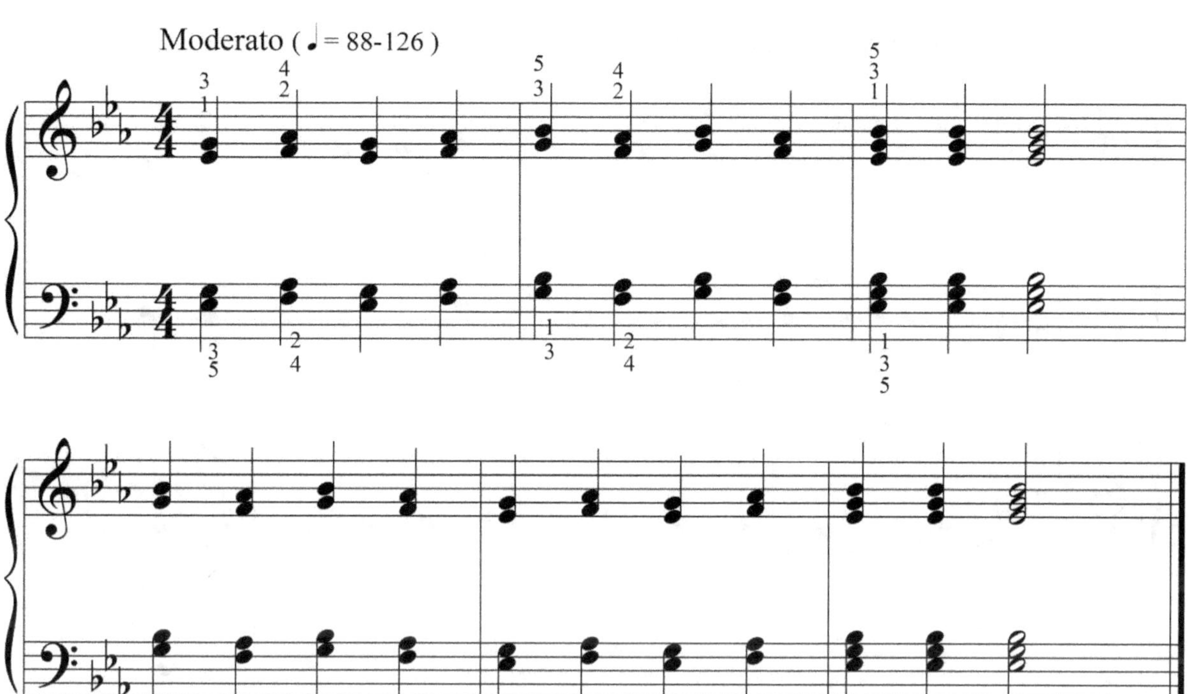

Leaps

Moderato (♩ = 88-126)

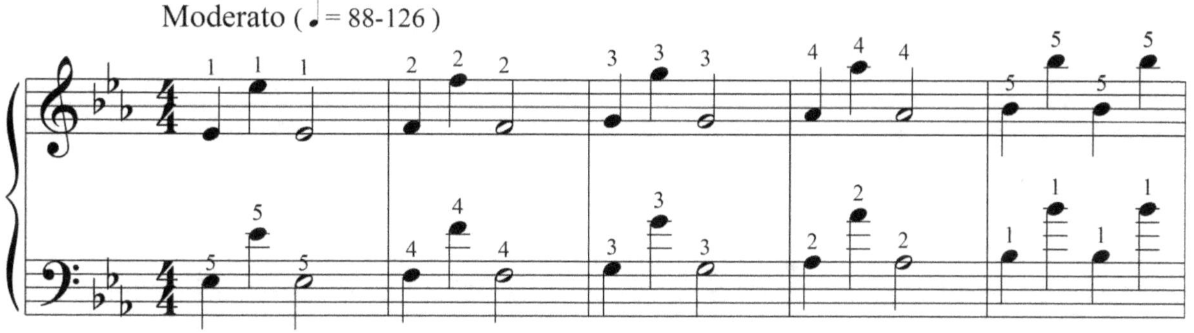

Steps

Moderato (♩ = 88-126)

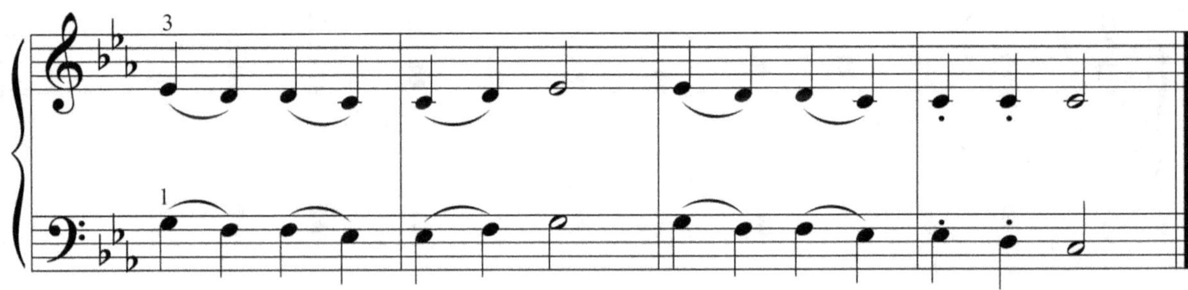

Skips

Moderato (♩ = 88-126)

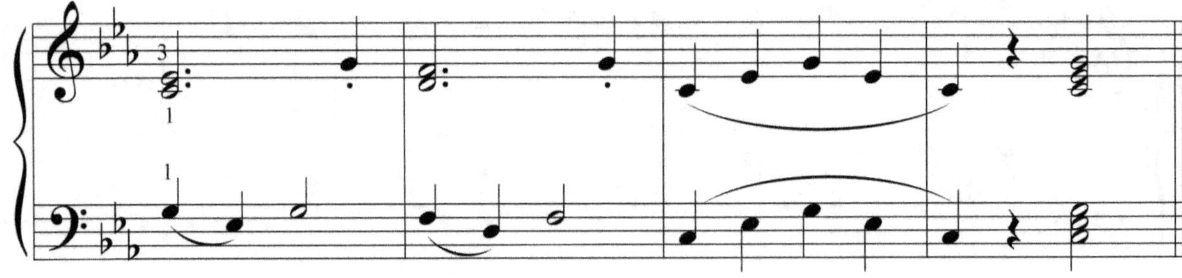

My title for this piece:

Andante (♩ = 72-88)

More Steps

Moderato (♩ = 88-126)

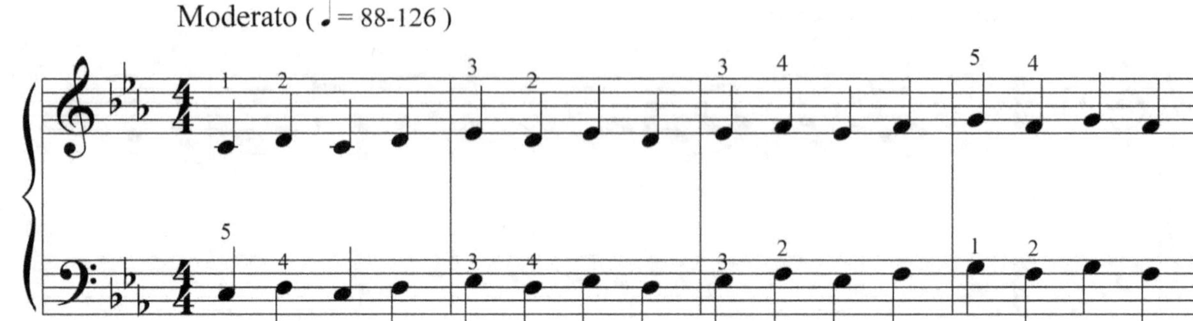

More Skips

Moderato (♩ = 88-126)

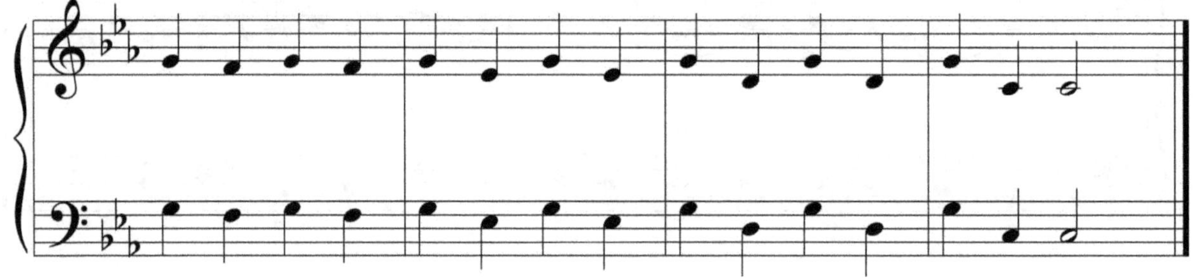

Harmony

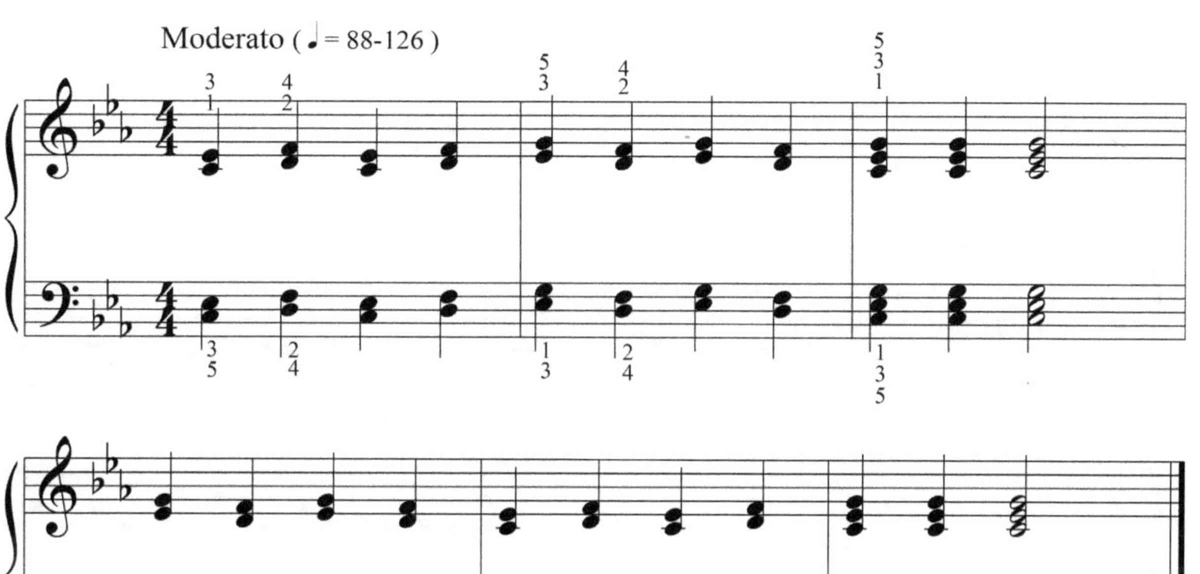

Leaps

Recital Piece No. 10

17

p

22

27

mp

33

39

f

E♭-Major Position, Chord, and Warm-up

If needed, refer to page 189 to complete the exercise.

1. Draw the notes to the E♭-major position and chord, and label the keys.

2. Draw the notes to the E♭-major warm-up.

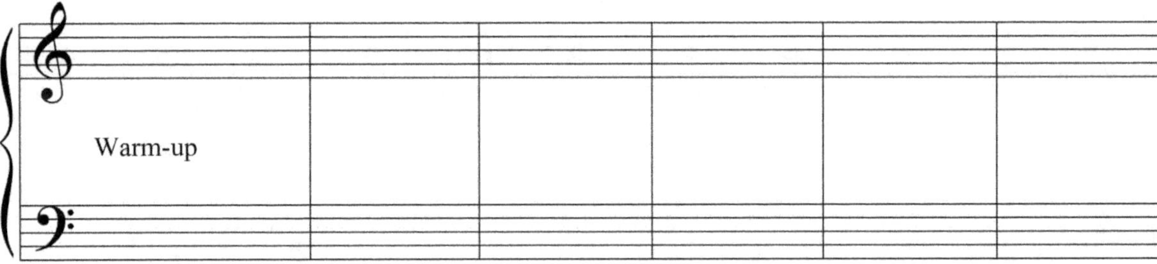

C-Minor Position, Chord, and Warm-up

3. Draw the notes to the C-minor position and chord, and label the keys.

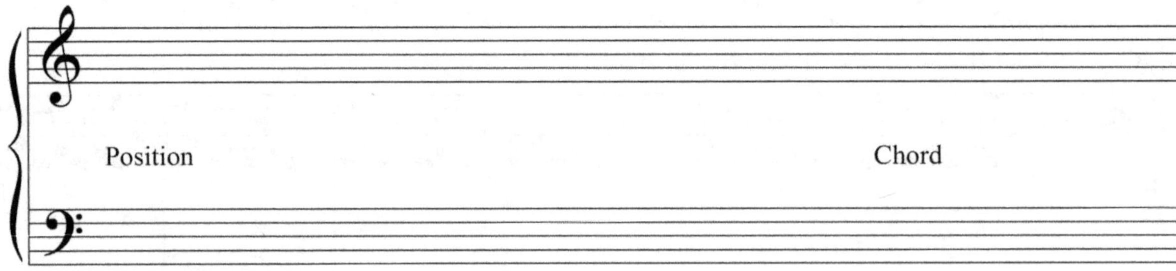

4. Draw the notes to the C-minor warm-up.

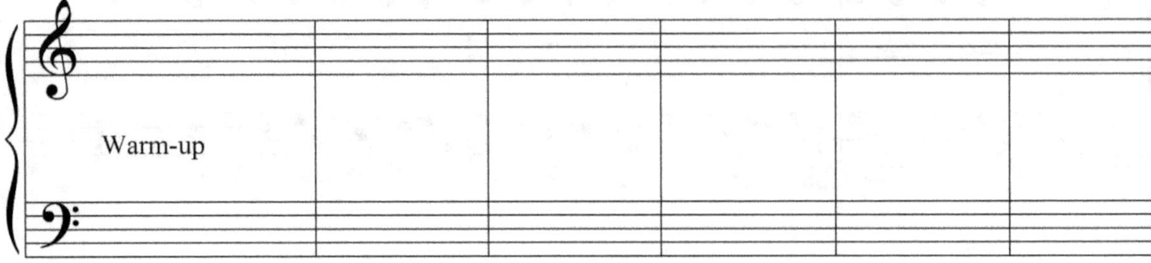

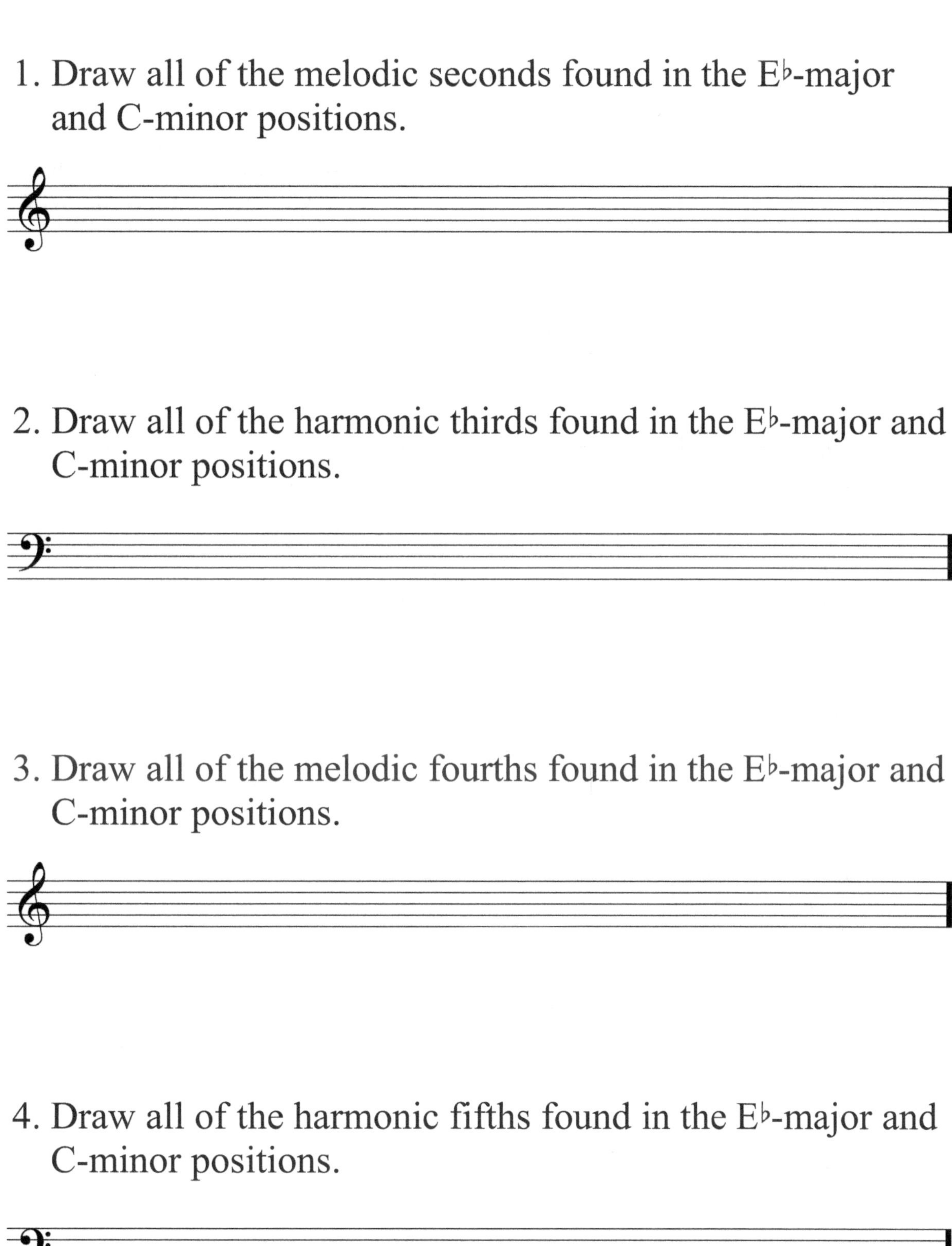

1. Draw all of the melodic seconds found in the E♭-major and C-minor positions.

2. Draw all of the harmonic thirds found in the E♭-major and C-minor positions.

3. Draw all of the melodic fourths found in the E♭-major and C-minor positions.

4. Draw all of the harmonic fifths found in the E♭-major and C-minor positions.

Review

	Name the Interval Size (2nd, 3rd, 4th, or 5th)	Name the Interval Type (Melodic or Harmonic)
1. 	____	____
2. 	____	____
3. 	____	____
4. 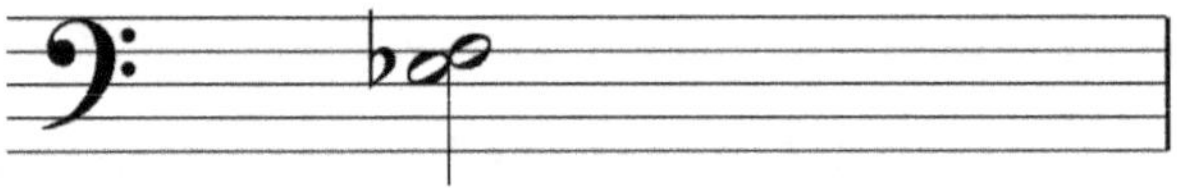	____	____
5. 	____	____
6. 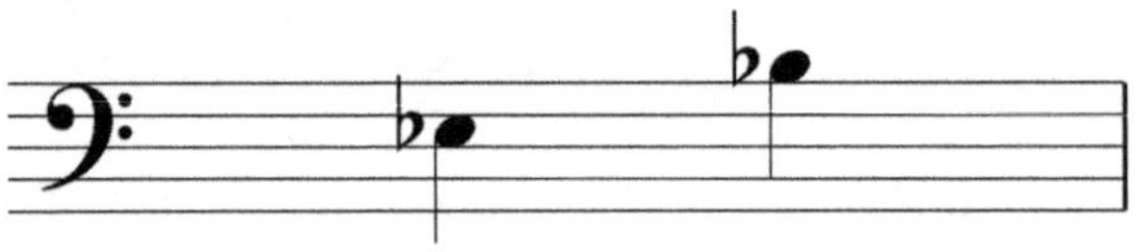	____	____
7. 	____	____
8. 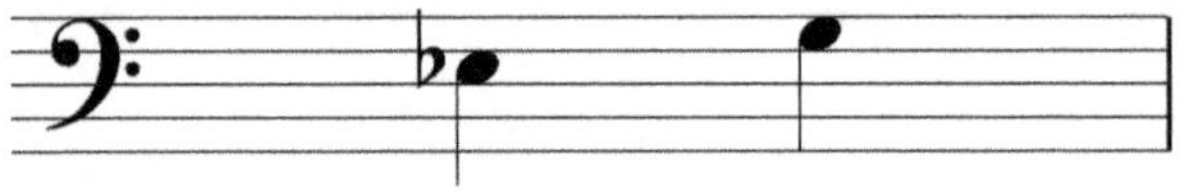	____	____

Lesson Sixteen

B♭ Major / G Minor

Octave Interval

As mentioned in the previous lesson, an interval is the measurement of the distance between two tones. In this lesson we introduce the octave—the distance involving eight tones. For example, the distance from any C to the C immediately above or below involves eight tones. We always refer to this distance as an octave.

Ottava (8va)

Ottava (8va) is an instruction (symbol) indicating that the notes should be played either one octave higher or lower than written depending on whether the instruction is above or below the notes. (Note: Sometimes 8vb is used to indicate that the music should be played an octave lower.) The dotted line that follows the symbol shows how long to apply the instruction.

Play the given notes 1 octave higher.

Play the given notes 1 octave lower.

Fermata

A symbol placed above or below notes indicating that they should be held longer than their usual value. This is commonly accomplished by adding half of the note's value. For example, a half note would be held for the full value of the half note plus the value of a quarter note.

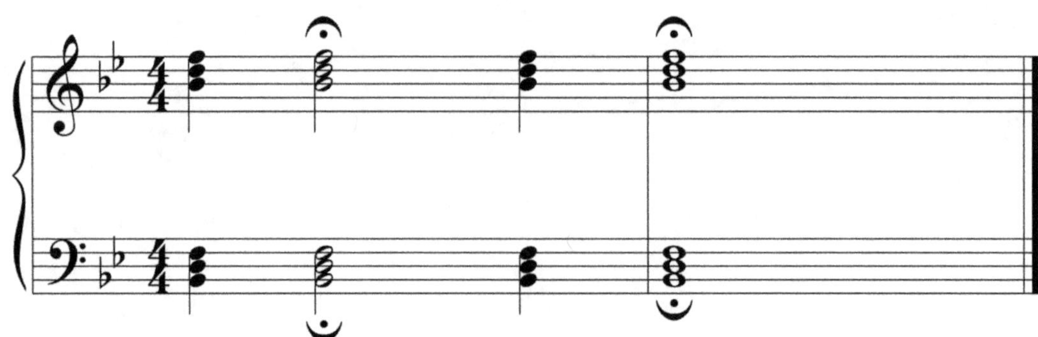

B♭-Major Position, Chord, and Warm-up

If needed, refer to Lesson Four for the exact key to play.

Another way to say "in **B**♭-major position" is, "in the key of B♭ major."

G-Minor Position, Chord, and Warm-up

Another way to say in "G-minor position" is, "in the key of G minor."

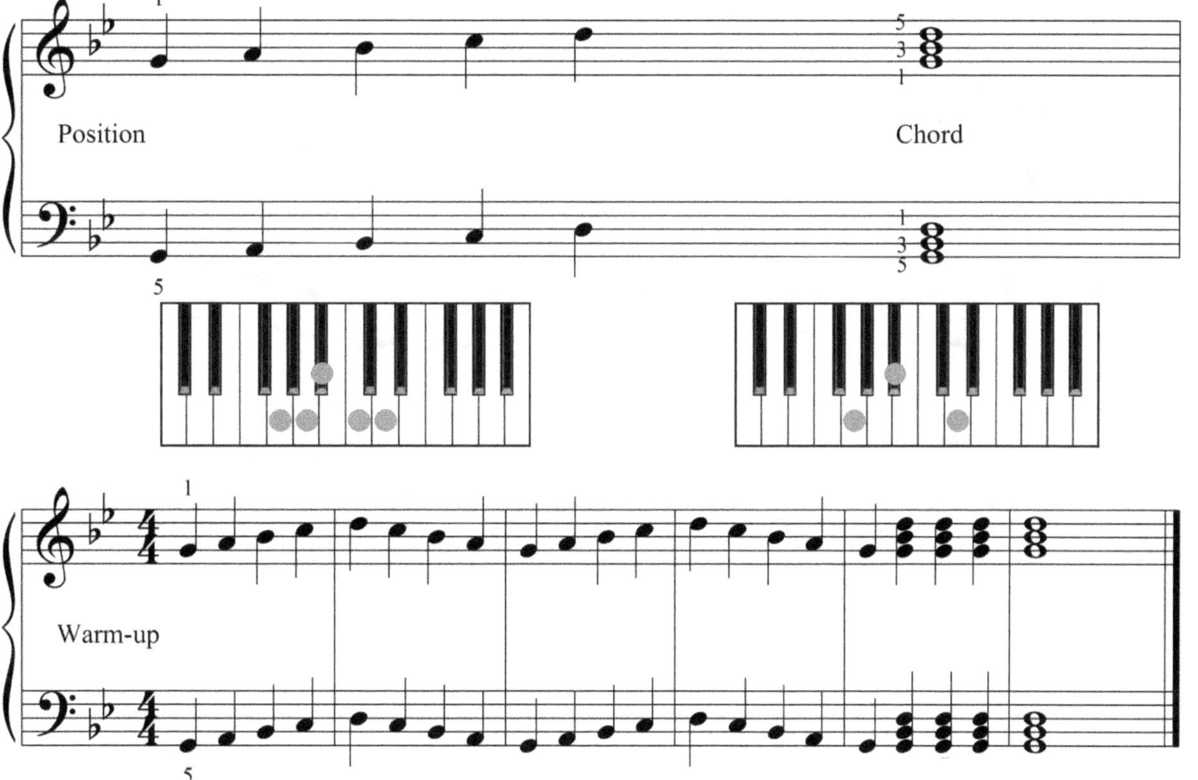

Steps

Moderato (♩ = 88-126)

Skips

Moderato (♩ = 88-126)

My title for this piece:

Andante (♩ = 72-88)

mf

8vb

p

mf

More Steps

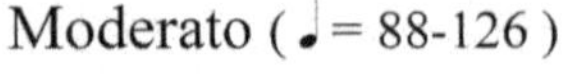

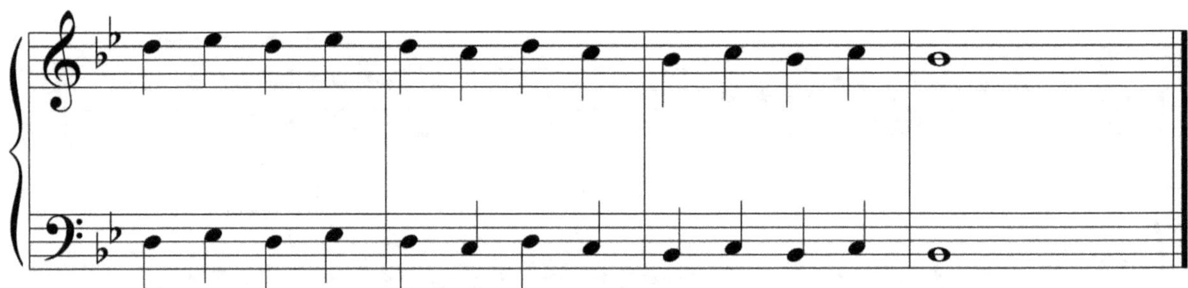

More Skips

Moderato (♩ = 88-126)

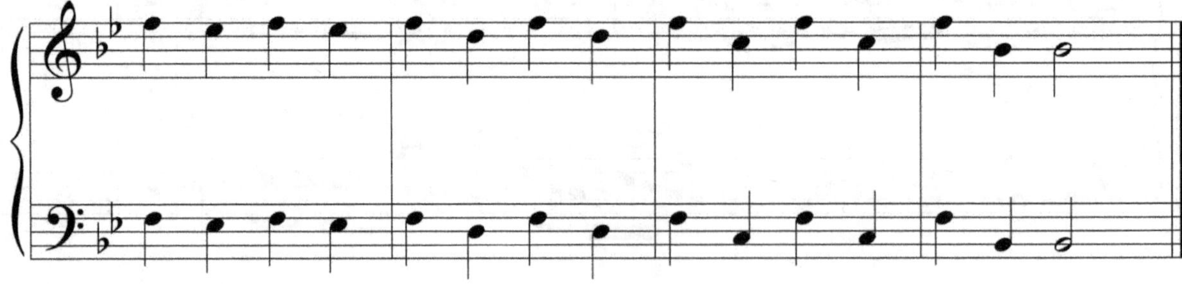

Harmony

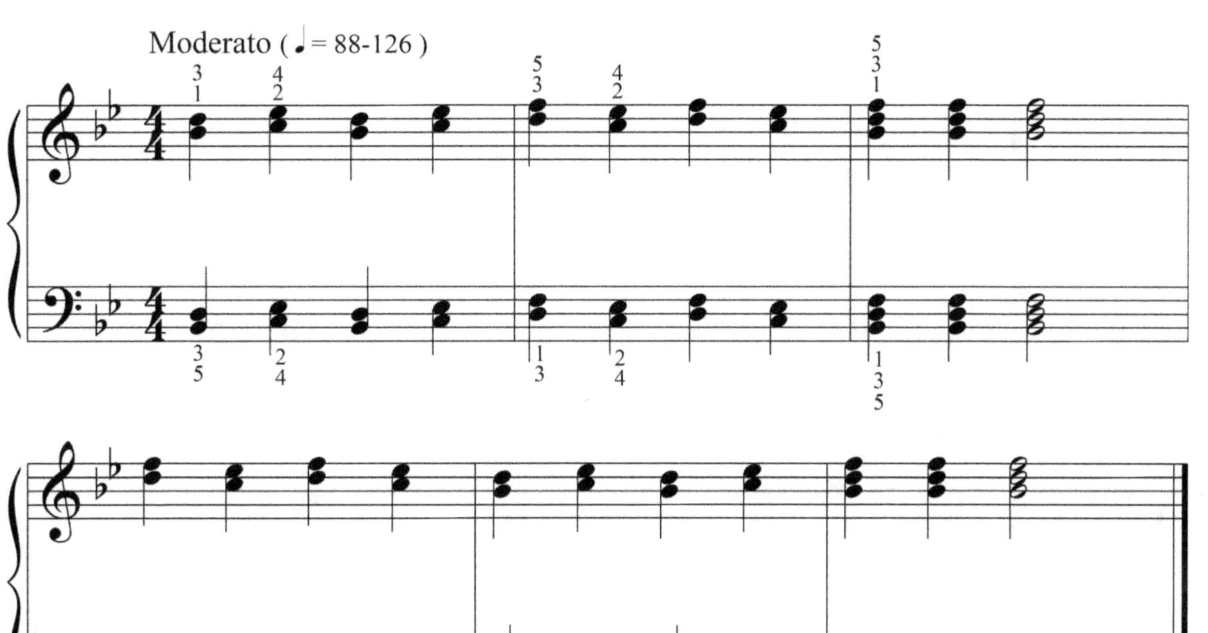

Leaps

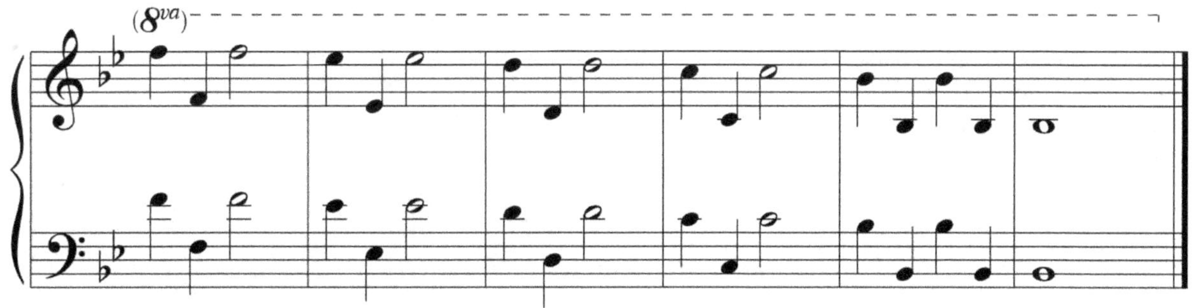

Steps

Skips

My title for this piece:

Andante (♩ = 72-88)

mf

8vb

p

mf

More Steps

Moderato (♩ = 88-126)

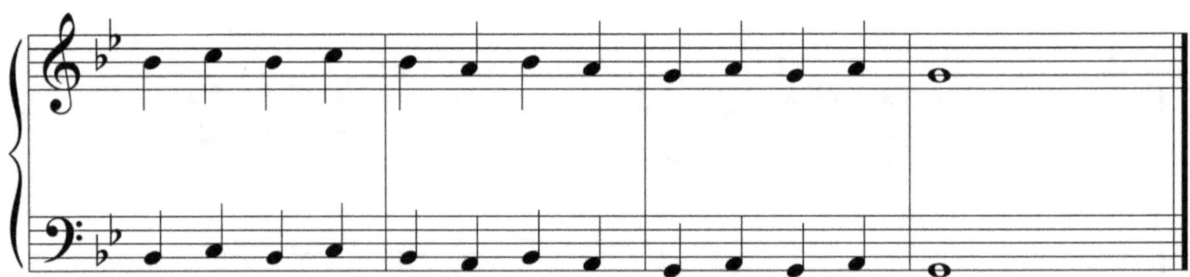

More Skips

Moderato (♩ = 88-126)

Harmony

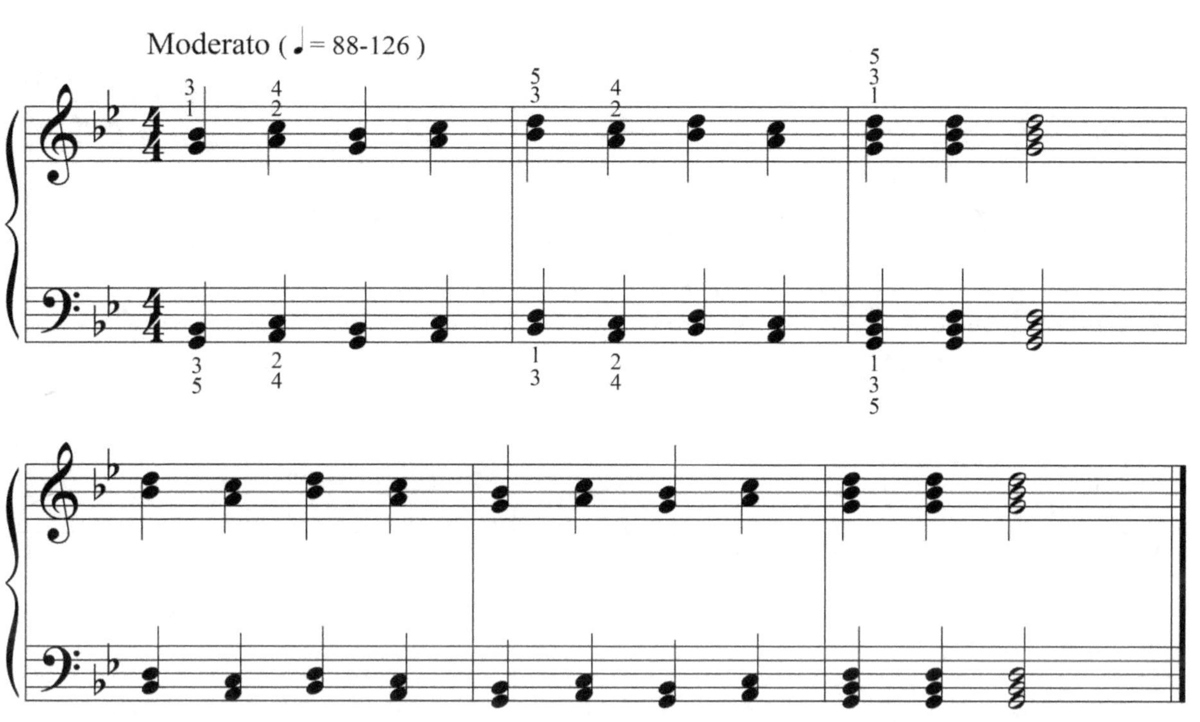

Leaps

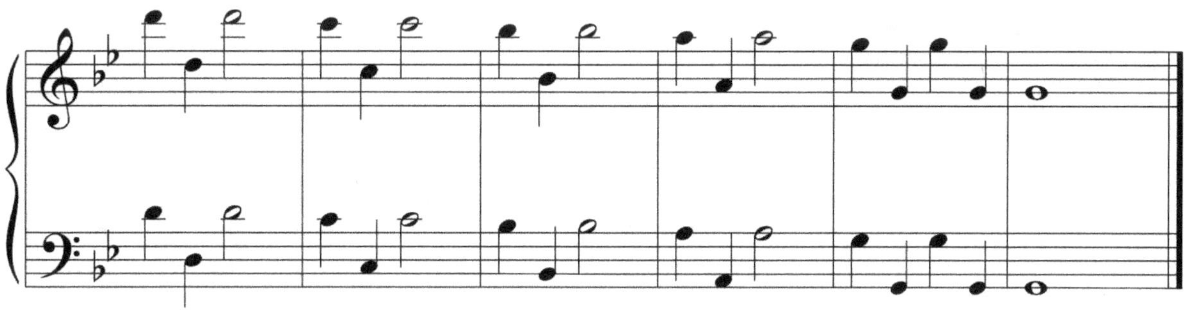

Recital Piece No. 11

17

(8vb)

21

f

25

L.H.

29

R.H.

L.H.

R.H.

L.H.

32

L.H.

R.H.

L.H.

R.H.

L.H.

B♭-Major Position, Chord, and Warm-up

If needed, refer to page 205 to complete the exercise.

1. Draw the notes to the B♭-major position and chord, and label the keys.

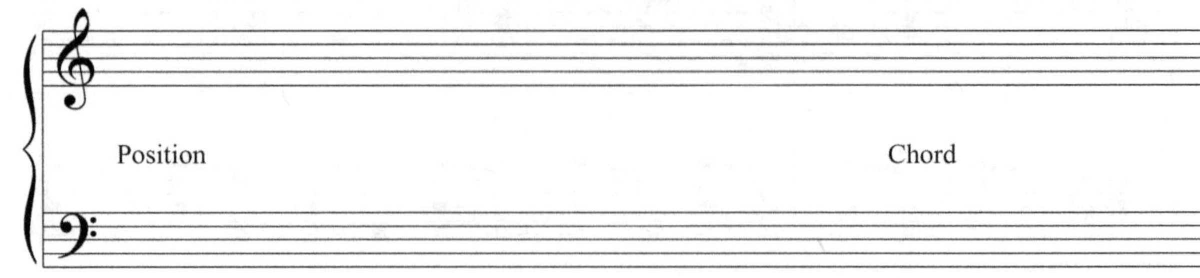

2. Draw the notes to the B♭-major warm-up.

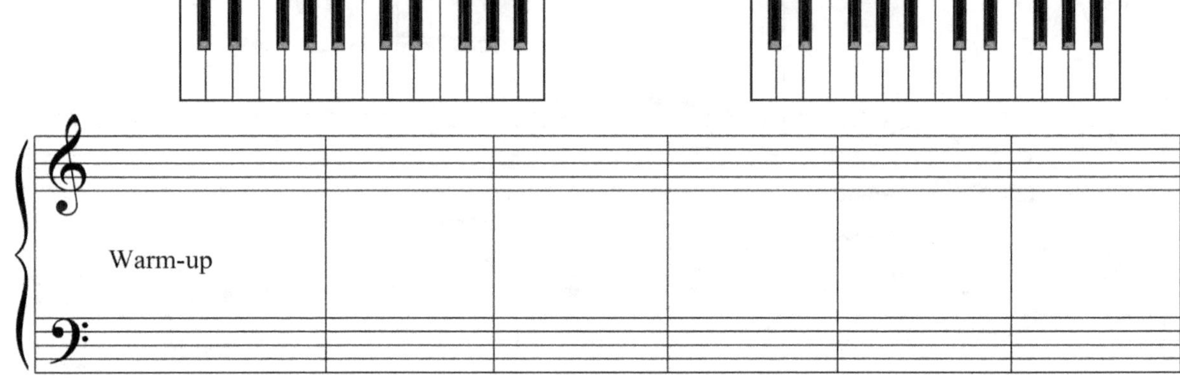

G-Minor Position, Chord, and Warm-up

3. Draw the notes to the G-minor position and chord, and label the keys.

Position

Chord

4. Draw the notes to the G-minor warm-up.

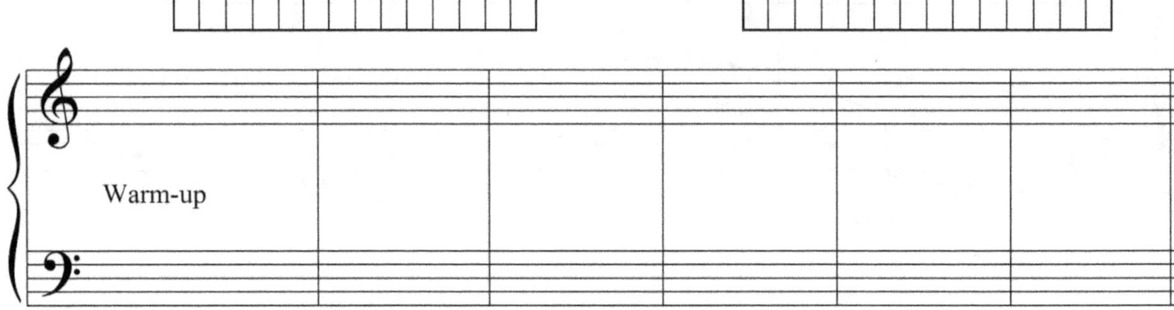

1. Draw the symbol to play the right hand one octave higher and the left hand one octave lower.

2. Draw a *fermata* on the half and whole notes.

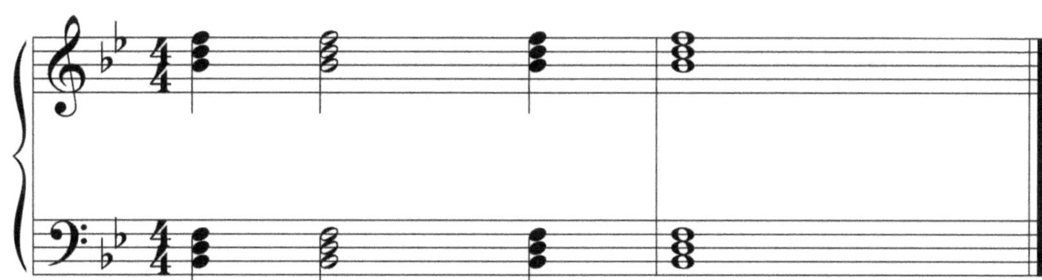

Review

1. Define interval and octave.

2. What note would you play?

3. Draw the *fermata* symbol and define it.

Lesson Seventeen

F Major / D Minor

More Italian Terms

Italian road map:

Da capo - Instruction to go back to the beginning.

Dal segno - Instruction to go back to the sign (𝄋).

Fine - The end after repeating from the beginning or from the sign.

Al coda - A special ending for the piece. After repeating from the beginning or the sign, jump ahead to the section marked:

Coda or 𝄌

Common road map combinations:

Da capo al fine - Instruction to go back to the beginning and stop when you come to the term *fine*.

Or

Da capo al coda - Instruction to go back to the beginning and then skip ahead to the *coda* when you come to the term *al coda*.

Dal segno al fine - Instruction to go back to the sign and stop when you come to the term *fine*.

Or

Dal segno al coda - Instruction to go back to the sign and then skip ahead to the *coda* when you come to the term *al coda*.

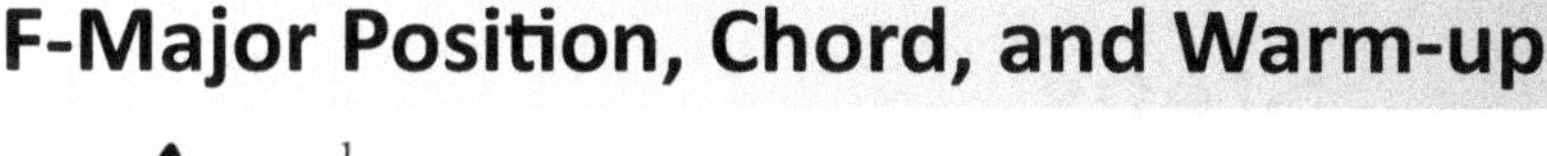

F-Major Position, Chord, and Warm-up

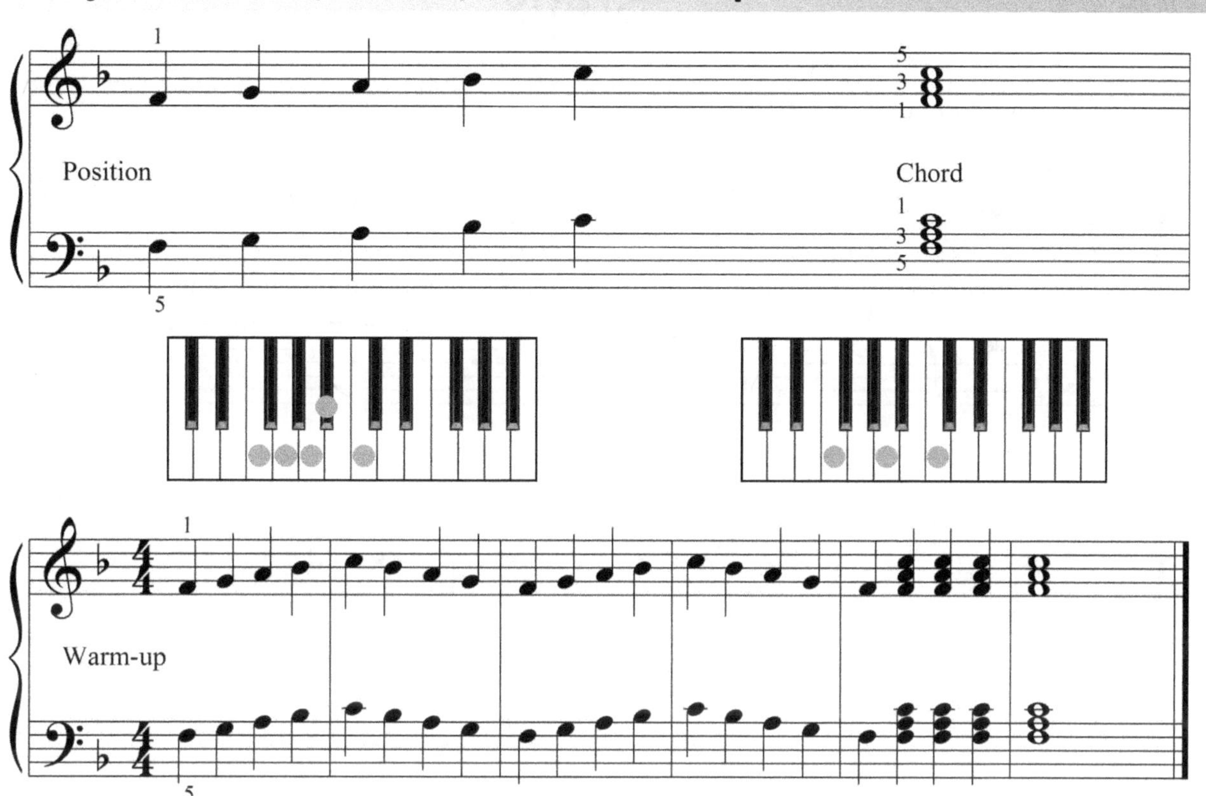

If needed, refer to Lesson Four for the exact key to play.

Another way to say "in F-major position" is, "in the key of F major."

D-Minor Position, Chord, and Warm-up

Another way to say in "D-minor position" is, "in the key of D minor."

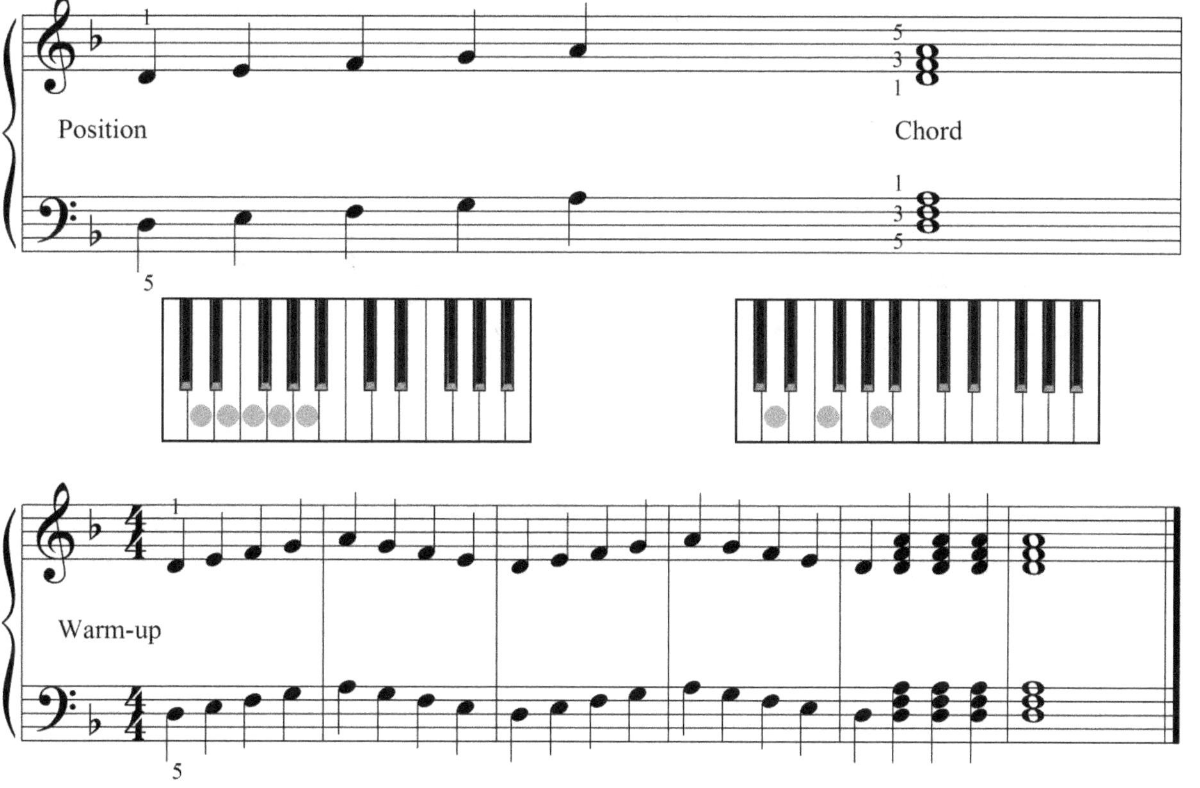

Steps

Moderato (♩ = 88-126)

Skips

Moderato (♩ = 88-126)

My title for this piece:

Allegretto (♩ = 66-88)

More Steps

Moderato (♩ = 88-126)

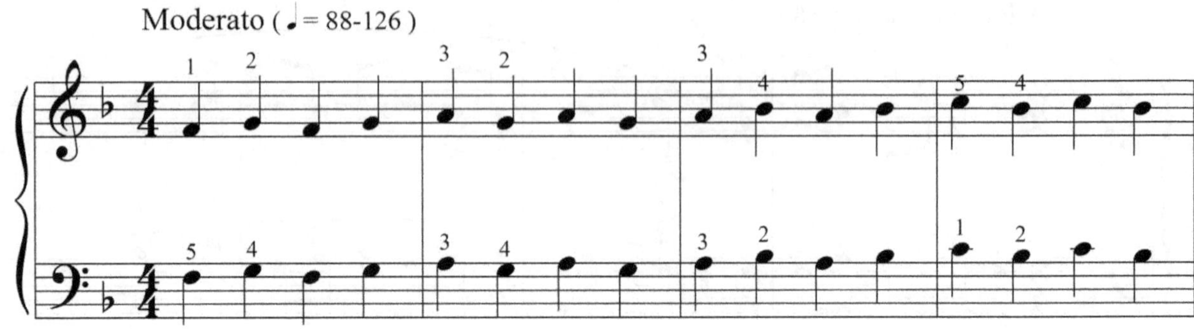

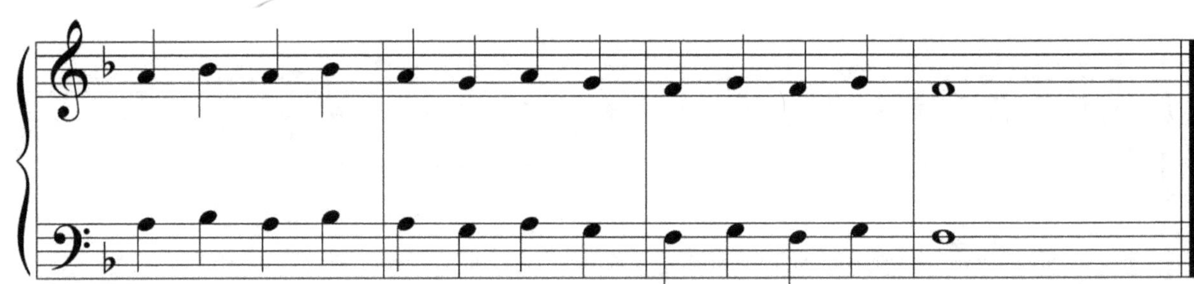

More Skips

Moderato (♩ = 88-126)

Harmony

Moderato (♩ = 88-126)

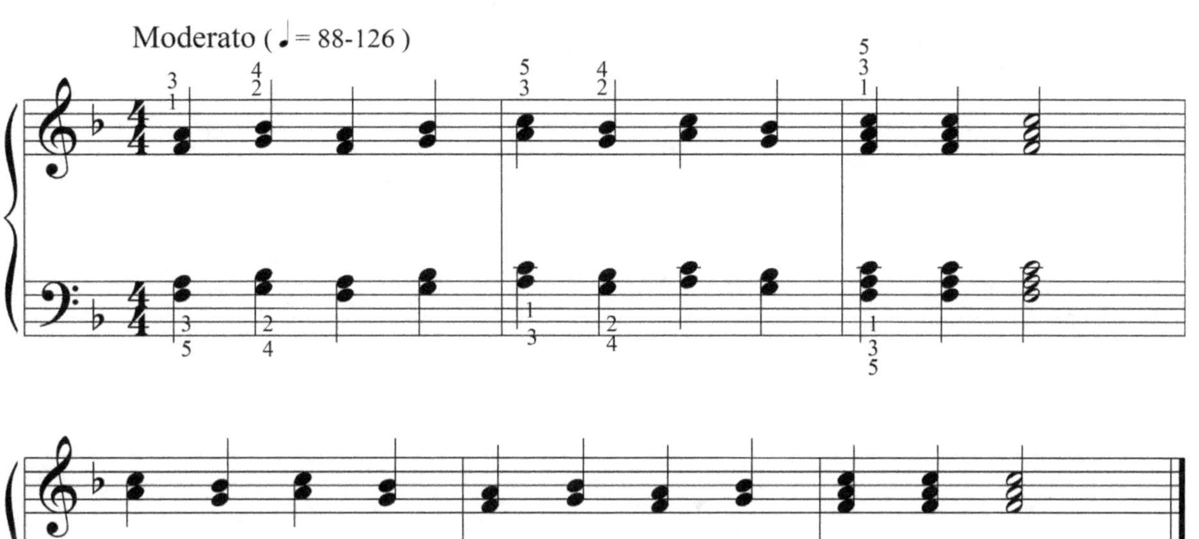

Leaps

Moderato (♩ = 88-126)

Steps

Moderato (♩ = 88-126)

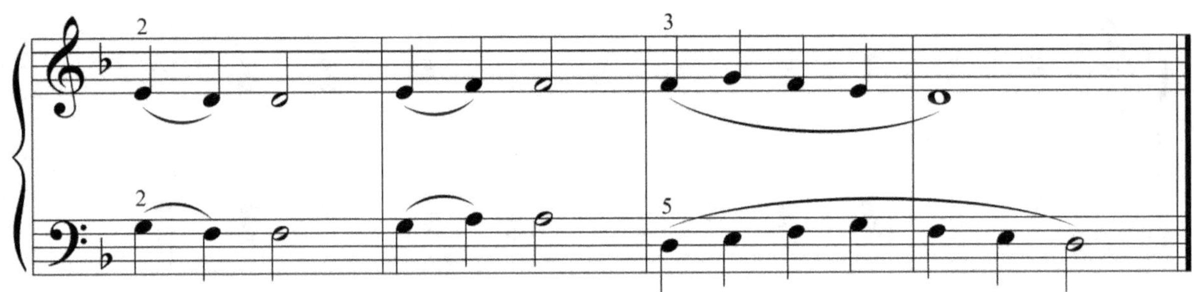

Skips

Moderato (♩ = 88-126)

My title for this piece:

Allegretto (♩ = 66-88)

More Steps

Moderato (♩= 88-126)

More Skips

Moderato (♩= 88-126)

Harmony

Leaps

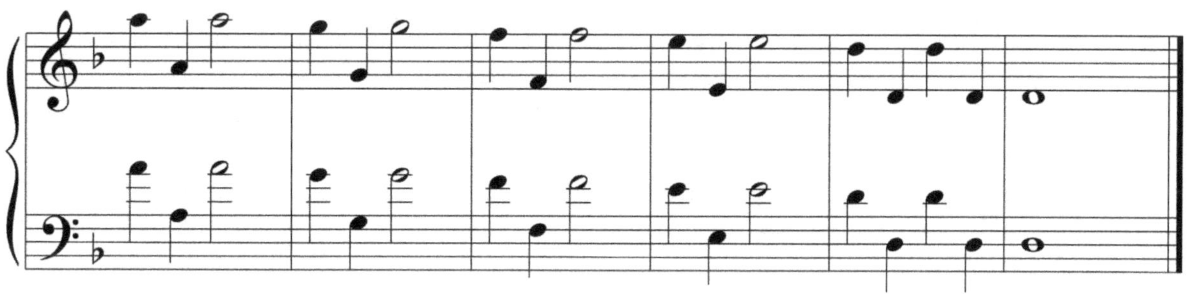

Recital Piece No. 12

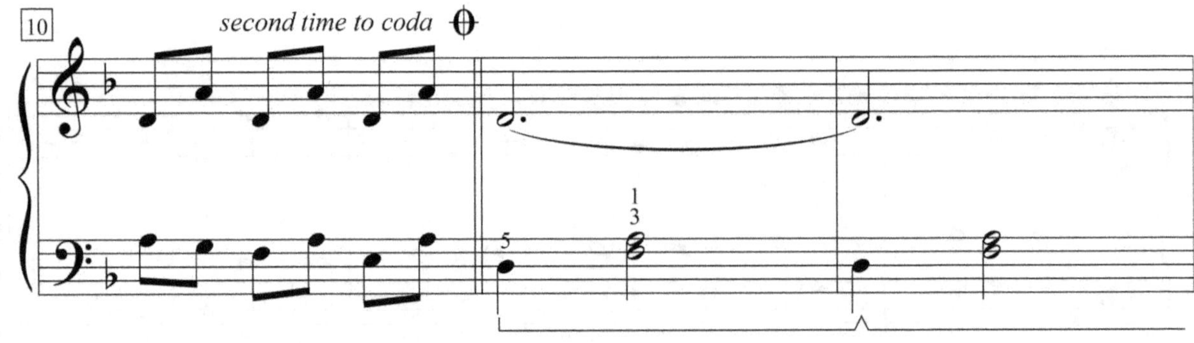

13

p

17

21

D.C. al Coda

27

Coda

8va

L.H.

F-Major Position, Chord, and Warm-up

If needed, refer to page 221 to complete the exercise.

1. Draw the notes to the F-major position and chord, and label the keys.

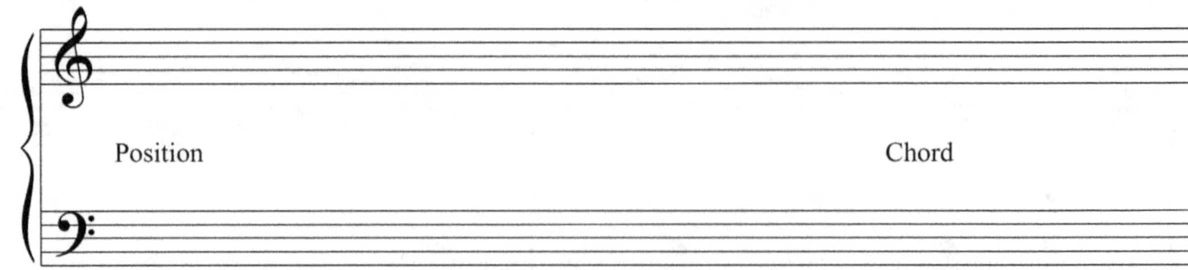

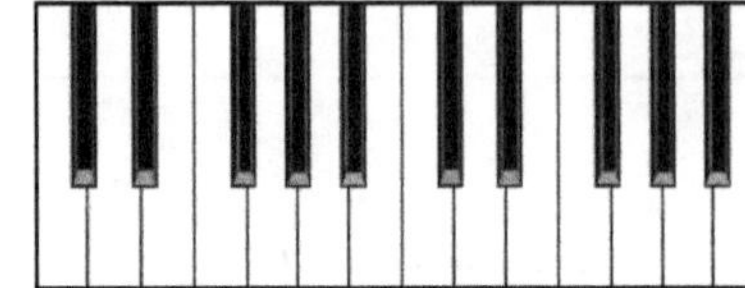

2. Draw the notes to the F-major warm-up.

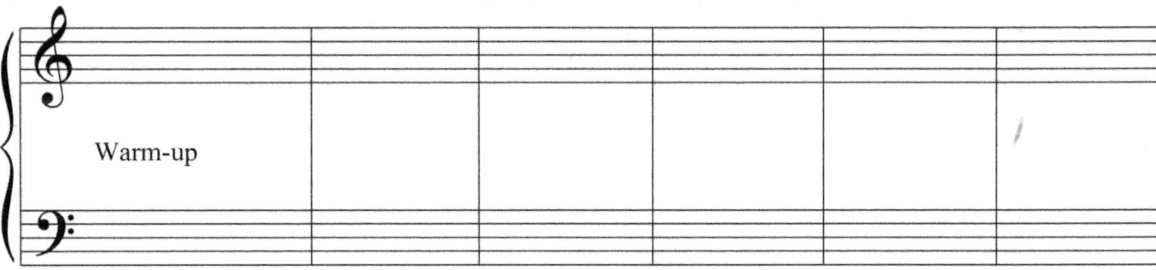

D-Minor Position, Chord, and Warm-up

3. Draw the notes to the D-minor position and chord, and label the keys.

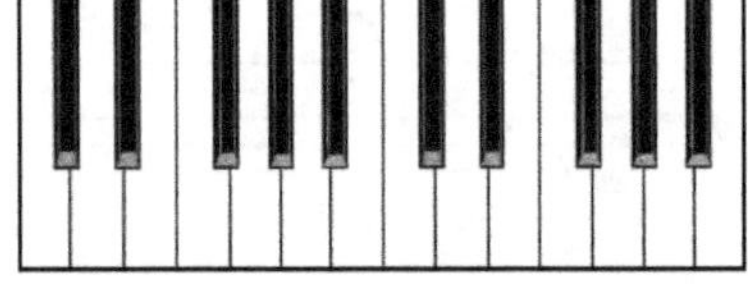

4. Draw the notes to the D-minor warm-up.

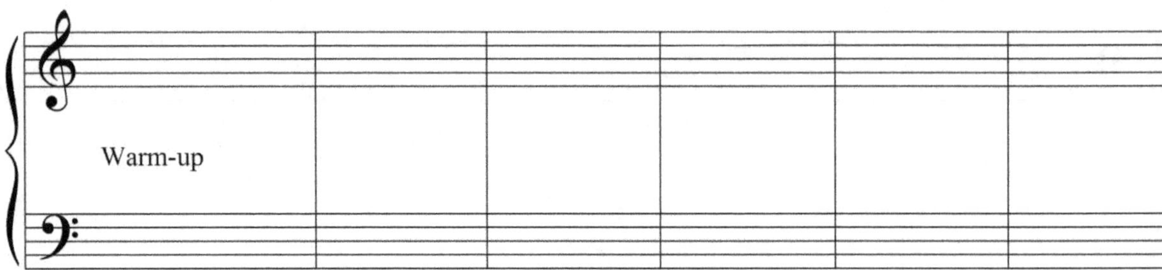

Complete the following crossword puzzle of Italian terms.

Across
1. Instruction to go back to the sign
2. Instruction to jump to a special ending for the piece

Down
1. Instruction to go back to the beginning
2. The end after repeating from the beginning or the sign

2

1

1

2

Review

1. What does *da capo al fine* mean?

2. What does *dal segno al coda* mean?

3. What does *dal segno al fine* mean?

4. What does *da capo al coda* mean?

Congratulations!

This is to certify that

____

Student's Name

has successfully completed Level One of the

Piano Companion Lesson Book

and is now ready for Level Two.

______________________________ ______________

Certifier's Name Date

www.ingramcontent.com/pod-product-compliance
Lightning Source LLC
LaVergne TN
LVHW081402110826
845149LV00010B/1639
9780996121712